D1617571

# Studies in Economic Ethics and Philosophy

Springer
*Berlin*
*Heidelberg*
*New York*
*Barcelona*
*Budapest*
*Hong Kong*
*London*
*Milan*
*Paris*
*Santa Clara*
*Singapore*
*Tokyo*

Studies in Economic Ethics and Philosophy

P. Koslowski (Ed.)
Ethics in Economics, Business, and Economic Policy
(out of print)
192 pages. 1992

P. Koslowski · Y. Shionoya (Eds.)
The Good and the Economical
Ethical Choices in Economics and Management
(out of print)
212 pages. 1993

H. De Geer (Ed.)
Business Ethics in Progress?
124 pages. 1994

P. Koslowski (Ed.)
The Theory of Ethical Economy in the Historical School
345 pages. 1995

A. Argandoña (Ed.)
The Ethical Dimension of Financial Institutions and Markets
264 pages. 1995

G. K. Becker (Ed.)
Ethics in Business and Society.
Chinese and Western Perspectives
232 pages. 1996

P. Koslowski
Ethics of Capitalism and Critique
of Sociobiology
153 pages. 1996

F. Neil Brady (Ed.)

# Ethical Universals in International Business

 Springer

Prof. Dr. F. Neil Brady
Brigham Young University
Marriott School of Management
Institute of Public Management
760 Tanner Building
Provo, Utah 84602
USA

ISBN 3-540-61588-1 Springer-Verlag Berlin Heidelberg New York

Library of Congress Cataloging-in-Publication Data
Ethical universals in international business / F. Neil Brady (ed.).    p.    cm. – (Studies in economic ethics and philosophy) "In March of 1995 the Third annual SEEP (Studies in economic ethics and philosophy) Conference was held at Brigham Young University in Provo, Utah" – Pref.
    Includes bibliographical references.
    ISBN 3-540-61588-1 (alk. paper)
1. International business enterprises – Moral and ethical aspects – Congresses. 2. Business ethics – Congresses. 3. Social responsibility of business – Congresses. I. Brady, F. Neil. II. SEEP-Conference on Economic Ethics and Philosophy (3rd: 1995: Brigham Young University) III. Series. HD62.4.E86 1996 174'.4–dc20 96-38660 CIP

© Springer-Verlag Berlin · Heidelberg 1996
Printed in Germany

The use of general descriptive names, registered names, trademarks, etc. in this publication does not imply, even in the absence of a specific statement, that such names are exempt from the relevant protective laws and regulations and therefore free for general use.

SPIN 10546032      42/2202-5  4  3  2  1  0 – Printed on acid-free paper

# Preface

In March of 1995 the Third Annual SEEP (Studies in Economic Ethics and Philosophy) Conference was held at Brigham Young University in Provo, Utah. Normally sponsored by the Forschungsinstitut fur Philosophie Hannover and held in Marienrode, Germany, this conference seeeks to draw scholars from around the world to discuss topics of common interest.

I thank Dr. Professor Peter Koslowski, Editor-in-Chief of the series for helpful guidance at every step. I thank the Marriot School of Management and the Center for the Study of Values in Organizations at Brigham Young University for considerable financial support for this conference. The faculty and staff of the Institute of Public Management were particularly helpful in providing assistance during the conference. And I thank Ms. Chyleen Arbon for her tireless help in preparing this manuscript for publication.

# Contents

# CONTENTS

# CONTENTS

## Chapter 9

## Chapter 10

## Chapter 11

# Introduction:
# A Typology of Ethical Theories

### NEIL BRADY

> "Man's world is manifold, and his attitudes are manifold. What is manifold is often frightening because it is not neat and simple. Men prefer to forget how many possibilities are open to them. (Walter Kaufman, "I and You: A Prologue", Prologue to Martin Buber's *I and Thou*, New York: Charles Scribner's Sons, 1970. p. 9)

As an academic discipline with a curricular presence, the field of business ethics is only about fifteen or twenty years old at least in the United States. Given the youth of this field, there still exists much diversity of thought and little agreement regarding the most fundamental concepts and theories. Although most would agree that Kantian deontology and utilitarian ethics would be hard to ignore, other approaches such as Aristotle's teleology or contemporary theories of caring receive varying attention, depending on the training and interests of those involved. So, aside from Kant and Mill, the field of business ethics has had considerable difficulty consolidating professional opinion regarding essential theoretical contributions.

1

With the increasing interest shown in international business, this confusion is highlighted. It is as though the community of scholars suffers from a kind of interpersonal subjectivism which mimics the cultural relativism that is often taken for granted in international business affairs. Is agreement not possible? Can we identify no orientations to ethics in international business that offer hope for universal application?

On March 30-April 1, 1995 a conference was held at Brigham Young University in Provo, Utah to discuss the possibility of ethical universals in international business. Twelve scholars from around the world were invited to present papers and discuss the ethical issues associated with international business activity. The revised papers from that conference are included in this volume. They represent a variety of perspectives from scholars in various fields, including economics, philosophy, business ethics, religion, and political philosophy.

In introducing their papers, I thought it might be helpful to develop and explicate a schema of theoretical possibilities in ethics. Such a schema provides a kind of "ethical geography" to give a sense of place to the various papers, and helps to characterize the basic orientation of each paper.

The usefulness of this schema might go well beyond serving the functional needs of this preface, however, and three possibilities stand out. First, it takes us one step beyond mere eclecticism in business ethics: we don't need to be "hunters and gatherers" in this field; we can be more like "farmers of ethical theory." We can harvest the theoretical fruits row by row by trying to think in a more disciplined, systematic way about theoretical possibilities in the field. Second, this schema raises the question of consistency across schematic cells, suggesting that conflict and dilemma in ethics is a product of the necessary multi-faceted nature of ethics. Finally, it helps us to adjust our thinking regarding the relative worth of a variety of ethical positions.

## I. A Schema for Ethical Theory

There are two very important distinctions in the history of ethical theory. One is the ancient distinction between universals and particulars, and the other is the more recent distinction between deontology and teleology in ethics. Below, I make use of these distinctions to build a simple matrix of possibilities for ethical theory. But first, the distinctions. . . .

# A TYPOLOGY OF ETHICAL THEORIES

## 1. Universals and Particulars in Ethics

Typically, ethicists have sought universals in ethics--some kind of invariant that would prescribe behavior for all human beings. Such invariants might take the form of norms, principles, policies, or goals that would cut across both cultures and across time. An example might be "No one should ever break a promise." Universals confer unity and stability upon ethics. Without some kind of invariant, ethics runs the risk of degenerating into individual subjectivism or cultural relativism.

What frustrates this search is ethical reality: Human living is so rich with concrete detail that the capacity of formal abstractions to deal with such particulars is sorely tested by the limitless variation in human experience. There just seem to be exceptions to every rule. But particulars are more than just obstacles to the construction of ethical universals; they are the concrete stuff of ethical life. They make life interesting. And without close attention paid to particulars, ethical theory quickly reduces to dogma and ideology.

Both universals and particulars are important for business ethics. As William James once wrote, "There is very little difference between one man and another, but what differences there are are very important" (1919, pp. 256-6). Iris Murdock has written the same thing: "...So far as goodness is for use in politics and in the marketplace it must combine its increasing intuitions of unity with an increasing grasp of complexity and detail" (1970, p. 96). Similarly, ethical theories can focus either on the similarities among persons or their differences, but it is unusual for a theory to do both. So, the distinction between universals and particulars provides the first useful distinction for mapping out the possibilities in ethical theory.

## 2. Deontology and Teleology--and Caring

During the last two hundred years, no other distinction has been so important for ethical theory than the distinction between deontology and teleology. Most developments in ethics have placed themselves in one or the other of these two camps, and philosophers have repeatedly called attention to this modern tension in ethical theory.

A teleological ethic is an ethic of purpose. It looks beyond any given act itself to assess the contribution of the act toward the achieving one's purposes. Human beings have purposes or ends. To some extent, we may share such purposes, or we may each have purposes of our own in accordance with our individual capacities

3

or potentials. To a teleologist, an act that promotes these purposes is moral; one that impedes them is immoral.

Modern teleologists like John Stuart Mill have tried to identify the highest human purposes and assign levels of moral acceptability to other purposes. In an increasingly liberal world, however, this became increasingly difficult. Therefore, in this century teleology has evolved into a kind of "democratic teleology" known as "utilitarianism." According to utilitarian ethics, we simply try to select those alternatives for action that promise to provide the greatest overall happiness for persons according to each person's idea of happiness. In short, it seeks maximization of personal preferences, or utility maximization.

By contrast, a deontological ethic is an ethic of duty. It does not look beyond the act itself to weight it against a purpose or aim; it simply regards the act itself as its duty, regardless of the consequences. In the case of religious duties, God or some other authority specifies human duty. National policy, state and local statutes, and community norms are also examples of duties based on authorities of various types. Some deontologists have thought that human reason alone is sufficient to determine what actions one should and should not do. In this case, we go beyond local and state authority as the source of prescription, and the result is universal ethical principles. An example might be "Thou shalt not kill." Of course, exceptions are easy to produce, and such a principle would need further specification; but its general thrust is to apply to all human beings, regardless of citizenship.

If a schema were constructed at this point, using the above two philosophical distinctions alone, it would have a sound footing. Both distinctions are fundamental in the history of ethical theory. However, although the distinction between universals and particulars seems conceptually complementary and comprehensive, the distinction between deontological and teleological ethics does not seem to carry the same promise. There might be something that both are leaving out that still needs to be taken into consideration.

Some modern writers have suggested that both deontological and teleological ethics are flawed in the same way, namely through excessive emphasis on individualism and detachment. Michael Stocker writes, for example,

> "To embody in one's motives the values of current ethical theories is to treat people externally and to preclude love, friendship, affection, fellow feeling, and community--both with others and with oneself. To get these great goods while holding those current ethical theories requires a schizophrenia between reason and motive" (1976, p. 461).

So, if the schema constructed here is to be as inclusive as possible, and if it is to avoid overlooking any important theoretical contributions, it must include theories that are based on psychological attachment, on social relations, and on the caring attitudes associated with such relations. Such theories spring not from a sense of duty, nor from a hope or purpose, but simply from an interpersonal connectedness--an ethic of caring (Noddings, 1984).

What bothers me about adding a third category to the deontological-teleological distinction is that one side of our schema begins to look more eclectic and less systematic: Deontological-Teleological-Caring is not a traditional trichotomy, and it stands vulnerable to all kinds of complaints regarding "category mistakes," and so on. Nevertheless, at the risk of appearing merely experimental, but with the hope of being more inclusive, I adopt this ugly little trichotomy for use in constructing the promised schema.

This trichotomy is not completely without merit, however. In her book, *The Moral Prism* (Macmillan, 1979), Dorothy Emmet identifies three fundamental types of ethical theories, none of which can be ignored without introducing major flaws into the comprehensive view of human morality. She adds axiology to the traditional deontology-teleology dichotomy. According to her, axiological theories represent human feeling, sentiment, and approval. Christopher Hodgkinson takes a similar position in his *Towards a Philosophy of Administration* (St. Martin's Press, 1978). He classifies all ethical theories into transrational, rational, and subrational theories, which roughly correspond to the three categories I develop here.

From another perspective, the traditional Christian trichotomy of "faith, hope, and charity" comes very close to capturing the same content but in a more elegant way. Of course, the faith, hope, and charity referred to in the *New Testament* are of a specific and restrictive type, but I want to use this trichotomy in its least restrictive mode and without implying any specifically Christian content. For a person who holds to a teleological ethic, for example, I believe the same can comfortably be referred to as an "Ethic of Hope." One's aim or purpose can be also articulated as one's hope. Similarly, an ethic of caring can be described as an Ethic of Charity. Again, this designation should be taken in its most inclusive form, referring to any kind of care or caring relation. Finally, a deontological ethic may be thought of as an "Ethic of Faith." This reconstruction may be a little less intuitive than the other two, but it is a fairly tight fit: One must have faith in the authority or source of moral obligation, whatever it may be. Ethical duty implies faith in something; it does not simply exist independent of human acceptance. For example, even Kantian deontology demands an acceptance of Reason as authoritative for one's life; one need not trust Reason, however, any more than a religious authority, a legislative council, or a family patriarch. So, duty arises from a trust in the source of the duty--an Ethic of Faith.

The linkage of "deontological-teleological-caring" to "faith-hope-charity" may be a little experimental, but it does have some advantages. First, for a Christian, it supplies at least a superficial sense of unity that the "teleology-deontology-caring" trichotomy may not provide, and it challenges one to explore the interconnections of these three types of ethical theory to see whether the unity is just superficial or whether there is more substance to it. Second, the addition of a third category to the traditional teleology-deontology debate should at least invite a more comprehensive look at ethical theory; furthermore, it invites us to look at the relationships among these theories in less adversarial and more cooperative ways. Third, it enables us to compensate for some historical features of the development of deontological and teleological theories. Many current scholars agree that deontological and teleological theories have come to us with a marked but unnecessary emphasis on individualism and objective detachment. Adding the third category of caring allows us to treat the other two categories as historical views, not just theoretical possibilities.

Having said all of this, it is now possible to construct the schema and examine its contents.

### 3. A Matrix of Ethical Theories

Using the distinction between "universals and particulars" as one side of the matrix, and using "deontology, teleology, and caring" as the other side, we can construct a 2x3 matrix of possibilities for ethical theory.

|  | Deontology (Faith) | Teleology (Hope) | Caring (Charity) |
|---|---|---|---|
| Universals | 1. Universal Duty (Ethic of Universal Principles) | 3. Universal Teleology (Character Ethic) | 5. Universal Care (Ethic of Love for Humanity) |
| Particulars | 2. Particular Duties (Situation Ethic) | 4. Particular Teleology (Ethic of Self-Actualization) | 6. Particular Care (Ethic of Personal Relationships) |

As it is difficult to capture the full content of a category simply by naming it, I offer brief descriptions of each cell of the schema below.

# A TYPOLOGY OF ETHICAL THEORIES

## a) Ethic of Universal Principles

This "voice" and the next make different assumptions about the nature of situations. An ethic of universal principles assumes that situations human beings encounter are similar enough that rules or principles can be adopted that become ethical guides and deserve our allegiance. Consequently, it is reasonable to act according to principle. Thus, we all have similar obligations: no killing, no stealing, no harming, etc. So, we adopt principles in our lives as objects of commitment. When a person tries to do what's right against strong pressures to do otherwise, even though it might be a little thing, we often explain ourselves by saying "It's a matter of principle," meaning "despite pressures to the contrary, I can ascertain what is right and do it."

Immanuel Kant is clearly the classic representative of this point of view. He argued that human beings are creatures of Reason, meaning that we are ultimately free to act according to principle and contrary to personal preference, appetite, public opinion, or demands of the situation. This philosophy has come to be important in our age for such matters as civil rights, justice, fairness and equality as citizens and employees.

## b) Situation Ethics

This "voice" assumes that the nature of situations is uniqueness, preventing us from abstracting reliable principles. Instead, principles and rules are blinders which impede our efforts to be reasonable. People who adopt this approach are impressed with the concrete richness and variety of situations. How could any rule apply universally given the variety of possible situations one could encounter? So, situation ethicists don't think much of rules; rather, one is expected to use good judgment, be intuitive. The case approach to ethics is one application of this point of view; indeed, the practice of both law and medicine illustrate professional judgments that are largely situationally determined.

The modern "father" of situation ethics is Joseph Fletcher, but a host of existential philosophers could be included here, as well.

## c) Character Ethics

This "voice" and the next focus on the nature of the self for ethical guidance. Character ethicists tend to appeal to "human nature" as the source of their knowledge. According to this view, human beings can flourish only by pursuing certain virtues, such as knowledge, fortitude, forgiveness, humility, and so on. These are virtues that apply to all human lives. To fail to pursue such virtues is to fail to achieve full humanity in one's life. The difference between this view and an ethic of universal principles lies in the direction of one's vision: Character ethicists are forward-looking. Their ethic is an ethic of goals, purposes, ends, consequences.

7

The ethicist of principle looks backward. Principles are usually passed on in tradition. In any case, we have to have them before we can act on them; the character ethicist is hoping to achieve the goal toward which one's actions are directed.

Aristotle is the great "character ethicist." This point of view has also been developed well by Catholic theologians, such as Germain Grisez and John Finnis. The Protestant Ethic of the last century, and even contemporary business gurus like Stephen Covey, are character ethicists.

### d) Ethics of Self-Actualization

By contrast with the character ethicist, this voice is more impressed with particular purposes or ends than with general human character traits. What impresses the person who holds this point of view are the differences in people. Stereotypes don't work. We are all different. And one would not expect another person to accept one's own goals and aspirations; they are personal. The uniqueness of the individual is important. One must be true to oneself. One's responsibility is to determine what one is to become and then strive to achieve that. Lives lived apart from their true selves are sad and frustrating. The single most important ethical determinant is not the situation, not others, but the self: What is the nature of this unique self and how is that important for how a situation is handled? Remember: there is no "one best way" to get something done. That is because each person's self is so different. For one person, a compassionate approach might be best, while for another a more intellectual approach might work best, etc.

One important modern representative of this view is Abraham Mazlow, whose discussions of self actualization have permeated texts on organization behavior. Various ways of describing personality types and managerial types are made possible only by assuming people are highly constrained by their personal natures. To go one step further and argue that they ought to nourish those natures is an ethic of self actualization.

### e) Ethic of Love for Humanity

This voice and the next focus on the nature of the other for guidance in ethics. The single most important ethical determinant is not the situation, not the self, but the Other. We must care for all human beings--at least those we are in a position to help. What is important is not one's own character but simply the welfare of the other. It is the presence of the other that makes us human to begin with; therefore, regard for the Other--any other--is the starting point for all ethics. This mode of thinking represents a caring (or at least regarding) attitude toward the world. An environmental ethic would be very comfortable here, because some people think we need to develop that kind of relation to the entire world.

8

# A TYPOLOGY OF ETHICAL THEORIES

European philosophers like Emmanuel Levinas and Paul Ricour are good examples of this mode of thinking. Martin Buber's *I and Thou* also takes this position, as well as Victor Frankl's *Man's Search for Meaning*.

## f) Ethic of Personal Relationships

Finally, this "voice" also stresses the importance of others, but not just any other, but specific others--friends, family, loved ones, community. How can one love the world at large? Don't we really love those to whom we are somehow connected? This position would argue that I have greater moral obligations toward my own children than to others' children, toward my own community than some distant community, and so on. Moral training and obligation begin at home.

Recent writers expressing this point of view include Carol Gilligan, for example. This view would also be especially important for understanding business as it is conducted in China, perhaps, or Iraq, where personal relationships help to define the nature of moral obligation.

## 4. Quandaries in Ethics

This matrix of ethical theoretic categories represents just one way of systematically exploring the landscape of ethical theory. There are other ways. A historical review of developments in ethical theory is one frequently used method, for example. But there are significant advantages to a "theory of theories" above a merely historical approach. One is that it shows us how theory could have developed as opposed to how it did develop. Utilitarianism, for example, plays a less important role in this matrix than in most historical reviews, while theories of caring play a more important role. It also dulls the temptation to adopt one theory as dominant or inclusive by emphasizing the complexity of human nature and recognizing the contributions of markedly different theories in ethics.

One virtue of this approach is its ability to provide an organizing principle for better understanding quandaries and conflicts in ethics. According to this matrix, there are fifteen combinations of categories taken two at a time (not counting conflicts within each category type). Therefore, it should be possible to illustrate fifteen kinds of ethical dilemmas or quandaries, corresponding to the potential conflicts among six different kinds of ethical theories. I won't take the time here to develop and illustrate those possibilities, although it is a worthwhile exercise. I would like to illustrate just one ethical dilemma, however, which adds support to the earlier argument that Caring be adopted as a category on the same level with deontology and teleology. The quandary is posed by Cicero in his *De Officiis* (Book 3, XII, 50). The city of Rhodes has been stricken with a severe famine, and an opportunistic ship captain has loaded his ship with food from the city of Alexandria and has set sail for Rhodes, hoping to make windfall profits. As he sets sail, he notices that several other ships are also loading food and will apparently set sail on the next day's tide. When the ship arrives in Rhodes, is the captain under any moral obligation to disclose what he suspects about other ships arriving the next day?

From the deontological point of view, it is not easy to point quickly to any obvious duty. In fact, Aquinas argues that the captain has no duty to disclose (*Summa Theologica*, Part II, Question 77, Article 3, Obj. 4) Our moral intuitions tell us, I believe, that the "finer" thing to do is at least to disclose what you know, if not several other options, such as selling your food at a reduced price to those in need or even giving it away. But altruism has been a notoriously difficult phenomenon to deal with in modern deontological and utilitarian theories. One might be able to prescribe altruism in an appropriate teleological theory of some sort. For example, one could look forward to better relations between Rhodes and Alexandria and be generous with that goal in mind. Or one could appeal to the captain's personal development by asserting that generosity is a worthy human trait which we all should try to acquire. In that case, the captain would act generously with the end in view of becoming a more generous person. But even that perspective seems too individualized and egocentric. The point of an ethic of Caring is that one should care about others regardless of any upshot, including personal development. And without the third category of Caring, it is impossible to account for the conflict we frequently feel in such a case.

There are significant benefits derived from thinking systematically about the major variants of theory in ethics. For one thing, it helps us to appreciate the difficulty of identifying any ethical universals across cultures. Nevertheless, the papers of this volume take that task seriously, and in what follows, I provide a few glimpses of what is in store for readers of this volume.

## II. Conclusion and Following Chapters

It may not be too surprising that in a volume titled *Ethical Universals in International Business* five of the papers speak from the perspective of universal principles. Three of them are quite similar. Professor Velasquez discusses four possible arguments against relativism and then considers the possibility of a "deep structure" to ethics, one that supports ethical universals while allowing for diverse forms of expression of those universals from culture to culture. Although we observe considerable moral diversity among the cultures of the world, the diversity may only be apparent at the surface, while a deeper analysis reveals a common structure.

Some of that deeper analysis is provided by Professor De George, who focuses on the question of justice in business dealings and the challenge that bribery presents. He suggests that we adopt the notion of "overall justice" as a criterion for just activities in business. That is, when all involved in a transaction regard that transaction as just, it is just, although each party might regard it as just for different reasons. Therefore, if no one objects to bribery it is just, although each person might have different reasons for feeling the way one does. One could speculate about the existence of some deeper invariant which nevertheless allows for the differing rationales; but from a practical point of view, at least, it is sufficient simply to have general acceptance.

Professor Koslowski objects to the Cartesian dualism which underlies modern tendencies to undervalue the natural world. He writes, "In this dualistic view of reality nature has neither aesthetical nor ethical value but only a subjective-economical value which is defined only by its exploitability for the spirit, for the subjective demands of humanity." These conclusions are motivated by an analysis of justice in economic interactions: justice as proper conduct, justice as fairness in exchange, and justice as ecological fairness. His analysis takes us beyond classic social welfare policy toward a new policy of "ecological equalization" which recognizes the inability of the natural environment to assert its interests against human interests.

Professor Bird provides the most thorough look at moral universals in his paper "Moral Universals as Cultural Realities." In all, he lists and defends thirteen universal principles, which comprise three categories of principles. The first category, "Moral Principles that Make Morality Possible," is very Kantian. It includes such prescriptions as promise-keeping, truth-telling, mutual respect, and reciprocity. The second set, "Moral Principles that Make Morality Credible," has a different status. They function to facilitate social cooperation and manage disputes. These principles establish criteria for the fitting enjoyment of various human goods, such as sexual intercourse, self protection, and various material goods; and they institute guidelines for appropriate patterns of cooperation. The third set, "Moral Principles that Make Morality Worthy of Esteem," comprises principles that may not always have been recognized in all cultures at all times but have now come to possess an intrinsic credibility. They include principles regarding human rights, respect for the natural environment, development of character, and practical reason.

One paper argues for ethical universals, not in the form of principles, but in the form of human character traits. Professor Hart speaks with authority from "Voice

11

Three--" Character Ethics. He appeals to the term "sodality" as capturing the Aristotelian notion of friendship based on good character. In modern society, fraternity is a trait worthy of universal emulation, but it fails to capture the gender-inclusive spirit of modern corporations. By making good character a defining characteristic of "sodality," Prof. Hart safeguards against perverted sodalities, such as dens of thieves, which also experience a form of commonality in their relationships. As for inter-organizational relationships, which tend to express competition rather than cooperation, Prof. Hart appeals to the notion of "fair play." Competition does not damage human natures so long as it is fair.

One paper defends stakeholder theory as an ethical universal. Professor Cochran reviews several theories of the firm, concluding that stakeholder theory is a superior theory of the firm and its obligations. I suspect that stakeholder theory represents a kind of "universal care" (Voice Five) approach to business ethics. Businesses care about making a profit for their stockholders, of course; but they also should care about the effect of their activities upon a wide range of other people, including customers, suppliers, the community, employees, and the general public.

Three papers emphasize ethics from the particularist perspective. Professor Paul, for example, reports of her studies of the social responsibility (SR) investing and evaluation schemes in three countries--the United States, South Africa, and Great Britain. The contrasting schemes illustrate significant variation in what is meant by "social responsibility" from country to country. Perhaps Prof. Paul speaks from the perspective of Situation Ethics (Voice Two). The judgment of social responsibility depends on the context.

Professor Suzumura provides a somewhat technical discussion of three related observations. The first warns against the danger that the restriction of competition through socially responsible corporate behavior might simply be a disguised promotion of the interests of the producer, to the detriment of the consumer. The second observation involves an argument that unilateral ethical behavior is not necessarily self-sacrificial; nice guys don't necessarily finish last. The third observation calls attention to the "fractal" or multi-layered structure of competition which makes difficult the imposition of universal codes of behavior. Taken together, these observations appear to profess classic liberal themes which promote freedom and liberty over conformity and uniformity.

The contribution by Professor Lee may be the only one of this collection that assumes an ethical orientation of personal relationships. Although his theory of the firm is a blend of Kantian, utilitarian, and Confucian themes, it is the latter that receives emphasis. Recognizing that the activities of any modern firm must conform to principles of rationality and fairness, Prof. Lee regrets the kind of psychological distance and alienation that often accompany modern bureaucracies.

# A TYPOLOGY OF ETHICAL THEORIES

His solution is to adopt a more Confucian approach that often appeals to the family or community as the model for organizing. Thus, ethics does not exist in an organization that lacks close relationships.

Professor Schefold considers the idea that economic and moral progress might be linked. This was the view of certain scholars which historically comprised the "German Historical School," and it is this school which Prof. Schefold reviews in his paper. He reviews the developing views of Hildebrand, Bucher, Schmoller, Spiethoff, Bechtel, Weber, Mises, and Sombart.

Finally, Professor Casson provides an empirical study of the management of corporate culture. He and his associates were interested in studying the effect of consultants upon a firm's culture. Their study looked at firms in ten countries and involved both survey responses and personal interviews. In all, approximately 300 managers from around the world were involved. In brief, they concluded that national differences in culture are significant and that the "standardized package" sold around the world for the management of corporate culture tends to be blind to these differences. Consequently, consultants in corporate culture rarely provide a quick fix; corporate culture cannot be faked. Morality and corporate culture cannot, it seems, be privatized and converted to a marketable commodity by consultants.

One participant in our conference, Professor Thomas Donaldson, presented a paper that is not included in this volume. He was unable to release the copyright to the publishers, and the chapter had to be deleted just prior to publication.

As this collection of essays shows, the discussion of ethics in international business is multivocal--and irreducibly so, I believe. Not only do the positions taken here sometimes conflict, they also speak different languages, as it were. Some scholars are more impressed with the possibility of ethical universals, such as principles and character traits; others are more impressed with concrete particulars of human experience, such as situational differences, personal goals, and interpersonal relationships.

As editor of this volume, I express little optimism regarding the articulation of some solution to the problem of multiple orientations in ethics. On the other hand, I'm reluctant to call this phenomenon a "problem." Most of us have a feeling that we are closer to moral union than to division, even though our forms of expression differ strongly. We may need to learn to appreciate the capacities of each other's language in ethics, but that achievement may make unnecessary the acquisition of some common language to which all others are reduced. I believe we can appreciate our human similarities while preserving our differences. Both are important.

13

## References

AQUINAS: *Summa Theologica*, London (Burns Oates and Washbourne, Ltd.) 1929.

CICERO: *De Officiis*, Walter Miller, Trans. Boston (Harvard University Press) 1990.

JAMES, W.: *The Will to Believe*, New York (Longmans, Green, & Co.)1919 (originally published in 1863).

KAUFMAN, W.: "I and You: A Prologue", in M. BUBER: *I and Thou*, New York (Charles Scribner's Sons) 1970.

MURDOCK, I.: *The Sovereignty of Good*, London (Routledge & Kegan Paul) 1970.

NODDINGS, N.: *Caring: A Feminine Approach to Ethics and Moral Education*, Los Angeles (University of California Press)1984.

STOCKER, M.: "The Schizophrenia of Modern Ethical Theories", *Journal of Philosophy*, 73, No.14 (Aug. 12, 1976), pp. 453-466.

Chapter 1

# Ethical Relativism and the International Business Manager

MANUEL VELASQUEZ

The most fundamental ethical problem that the manager of an international business faces is the problem of moral diversity.[1] Many oil companies, for example, operate in the United States which professes that men and women should be treated as equals and where bribery is considered wrong, while simultaneously operating in several Middle Eastern countries where women are regarded as subordinate to men and bribery is widely accepted. How is the manager to deal with such differences?

It is often thought that the logical implication of such moral diversity is ethical relativism,[2] the view that the only standards determining the ethical quality of a particular act or type of act, are the moral norms present in the society within which the act takes place.[3] I want in this essay to examine ethical relativism. In particular, I want to reexamine the arguments that have been offered to show that ethical relativism is mistaken. I want to show that some of these arguments provide little help to the problems the international manager faces. Nevertheless, I will argue, other arguments point the way to an approach to moral diversity that can help the manager struggling with the problems of moral diversity.

Before we begin, I believe it is important to have before us a concrete case of the kind of ethical problems that moral diversity poses for the international business manager. The case of cultural diversity that I will describe, then, is one that involves two cultures that are relatively familiar to us. The case has been frequently cited before and so I expect it is familiar to many. [4]

15

# MANUEL VELASQUEZ

During the late 1960s an American bank set up a subsidiary in Italy with an American manager in charge. At the end of the year, when it was time to file the subsidiary's tax return, the American manager was told by the bank's local lawyers and tax accountants that he should understate the bank's actual profits. The local lawyers and accountants explained that when filing their tax returns, every Italian company understated its profits by a sizable amount. They said that the Italian government expected companies to do this, and would later counter with a higher tax assessment. The company and the government would then meet to negotiate a final tax somewhere between the government's estimate and what the company had claimed on its return.

The American manager, though, rejected the advice of his lawyers and accountants on the grounds that knowingly understating the bank's true profits would be deceptive and a violation of company policy. So he filed an honest return following American standards of disclosure. A few months later the manager received a notice from the government requesting a meeting to discuss the taxes the bank owned. The American manager decided that instead of meeting in a face to face negotiation with government officials, he would get everything in writing. So he replied with a letter stating that the bank's original return was accurate and asking the government what specific items it questioned.

A few months passed. Then the government sent the bank a tax assessment based on profits three times higher than what the bank had stated on its tax return. Eventually, the bank was forced to pay this triple tax and the American manager was sent back to the United States.

The Italian tax case makes quite clear that even relatively similar cultures may nevertheless have quite different moral norms that challenge the international business manager. The ethical relativist holds that such cases demonstrate that beyond local moralities, there are no universal moral principles that can be brought to bear on moral issues. Since there is nothing beyond local norms, the relativist would hold, the American manager should have simply gone along with the prevailing Italian norms, as he was in fact counseled to do by several local lawyers and local tax accountants. The view is neatly summed up in the saying that could have been offered to our American banker: "When in Rome, do as the Romans do."

## I. The Non-sequitur Argument Against Relativism

The most common objection that philosophers make to the position of the relativist, is the objection that ethical relativism is based on a non-sequitur. The objection is quite simple: when people disagree about some matter, it does not follow logically that there is no objective truth about that matter, much less that all beliefs about that issue are equally acceptable. When two people or two groups have different beliefs, philosophers are fond of pointing out, at most all that follows is that at least one of them is wrong.[5]

There are, of course, some theoretical difficulties with this reply of the antirelativist. In particular, it assumes that the concepts of truth, falsity, and mistake are applicable to moral beliefs, a point that is not clear. But the problem that concerns me at the moment is that this reply of the antirelativist does not take the manager very far toward a practical solution to the problem of moral diversity that he or she faces. How, for example, does this reply help the American banker operating in Italy in the 1960s to deal with the normative conflict he faced? It is well and good to be told that since the Italian and the American norms on financial disclosure differ, at least one of them must be mistaken. But in what sense are either of these norms supposed to be "mistaken?" And how does the bare assertion that one of these beliefs is mistaken help the struggling manager who has to decide which norm to follow?

## II. The Argument from Moral Universals

A second philosophical objection to ethical relativism is one which challenges the factual accuracy of the claim that there are no universal moral norms recognized by all cultures. In fact, the philosopher will argue, commitment to certain, quite specific norms seems to be a necessary condition for the survival and well being of any society. In all societies we find those norms that the members of a society must adhere to for the sake of social cohesion and the maintenance of certain common institutional forms, such as the institution of promises and of language. These include norms prohibiting violence against fellow citizens, as well as norms against breaking one's promises and lying. Professor Norman Bowie puts the matter as follows:

> What follows from this is that there are certain basic rules that must be followed in each society; e.g., don't lie, don't commit murder. There is a moral minimum in the sense that if these specific moral rules aren't generally followed, then there won't be a society at all.[6]

17

Bowie's point seems accurate enough, and it is a point that is often made in philosophical discussions of ethical relativism. Moreover, it is clear that if there are some universally recognized moral norms, then ethical relativism must be wrong. But, again, it is difficult to see how this point helps the business manager who must struggle with the conflicting norms that confront him in different cultures. Bowie may be correct in claiming that there are some norms that are found in all cultures. But the norms that give the manager problems are precisely those that are not found in all cultures. When the international manager is confronted with host country norms that conflict with his personal norms or with those of his home country, he or she is not helped by being advised that there are other norms that are accepted in both countries. It is not the similarities between cultures that give the manager problems, it is the differences between cultures that create difficulties.

## III. The Argument from Deep Structure

A third, more penetrating objection to moral relativism is the objection that apparent moral differences between societies often mask deeper more fundamental moral similarities. Consider that a moral principle or moral value can have one set of implications when applied to one set of circumstances, and can have a very different set of implications when applied to a second very different set of circumstances. Take, for example, the high moral value that we attribute to life and the associated moral principle that life is to be protected and not wantonly taken. In everyday circumstances that principle would imply that killing is morally wrong. Yet in extreme circumstances that very same principle can sanction or even require the taking of life. When a person, for example, is being threatened by an attacker, his duty to protect his own life sanctions killing the attacker in self-defense. Thus while in everyday circumstances the principle prohibits killing, the very same principle in extreme life-threatening circumstances permits killing.

Now what is true of individuals and their individual circumstances is also true of societies and their circumstances. A moral principle can impose requirements on a society in one set of circumstances that are very different from those that the same principle imposes on a society that finds itself in very different circumstances. Societies that exist in harsh physical environments, for instance, may sanction infanticide, but do so for the sake of the same fundamental moral values that underlie prohibitions on infanticide in societies that exist in more benign physical environments, namely, to ensure that the society is able to survive and flourish over the long term. The relativist is wrong, then, in claiming that the different norms

18

found in different cultures shows that there are no universal values recognized in all cultures. For underlying the norms that differ on the surface, may lie deeper values that are universally recognized even among cultures whose norms at first sight look so different.

Although this argument is common in philosophical discussions of ethical relativism, philosophers have failed to explore its implications, and it is these I now want to examine. The argument implies that morality has an important feature: namely that morality has a structure. The relativist assumes that there is nothing more to the morality of a culture than the surface norms that prohibit, require, or allow certain acts. But what the present argument against ethical relativism shows is that in addition to the surface norms prohibiting, requiring, or allowing certain behaviors, morality must also be seen as encompassing an underlying structure of cultural rationales or justifications of these norms. This underlying structure of cultural rationales consists of two things. It consists, first, of the culture's understanding of the acts that the norm regulates. These cultural understandings include the expectations and beliefs that the culture holds about the act and its circumstances. Secondly, the underlying structure consists of the values that justify the prohibition or requirement of the act thus understood. These may be values such as survival, truthfulness, friendship, equality, liberty, and so on. It is crucial to look at this underlying structure since that structure may impart a meaning to a surface norm that is not obvious by simply inspecting the norm in isolation from its underlying structure of justification.

In the Italian income tax case we have been considering, an examination of the circumstances surrounding Italian tax practices suggests that these practices may not really conflict with American values. The case makes clear, for example, that in the 1960s it was known and expected by all parties that businesses would understate their profits by a substantial amount when filing their income tax returns. Knowing this, the Italian government was never deceived, and it would automatically inflate each company's income statements by a compensating amount and levy taxes on this more accurate estimate. In the Italian context, then, the practice of understating income was not understood as a deception but as a mutually recognized signal of a starting point for negotiation. Moreover, in a culture such as that of Italy, which values personal bargaining over following written, impersonalized and rigid rules, such a signal was commonly understood to be but a first stage in a culturally familiar and valued process of regulatory decision making.[7] In this case, then, a surface norm that appears to sanction straightforward lying, is revealed by an examination of its underlying structure to be a norm based on nondeceptive signaling within a culturally valued decision making process.

The managerial implications of recognizing that morality has a deep structure are important. When the manager is confronted with apparent moral diversity in

19

a culture, the first step toward dealing with the diversity is to get clear about the deep structure that underlies the apparent moral diversity that he confronts. What is the underlying structure of cultural understandings and cultural values that justify the norms of the culture? Achieving clarity about such issues, of course, is not easy. But it is a necessary first step toward dealing with moral diversity.

## IV. The Transcendental Argument

Perhaps the most trenchant argument against relativism, however, is what I will call the transcendental argument. The transcendental argument claims that if ethical relativism were correct, then the only criteria that we can appeal to when making moral evaluations are those moral norms that prevail in one's society. But if the only criteria by which we can make moral evaluations are the moral norms that prevail in our society, then it would make no sense for us to say that these moral norms are themselves morally wrong. It would have made no sense, for example, for a member of pre-Civil War American Southern society to be morally critical of the prevailing view of his society that slavery is morally legitimate; it would have made no sense for a German member of Nazi society of the 1930's to morally criticize the prevailing view that discrimination against Jews was morally permissible; it would have made no sense for a white member of white South African society of 1970 to criticize morally the prevailing view that apartheid was morally justified. Nor, for that matter, would it make sense for an outsider to criticize the moral norms of these societies. It should make no sense for an insider to evaluate the moral norms of his own society, according to relativism, because the insider can have no other standards to which he can appeal in making such evaluations. And it would make no sense for an outsider to evaluate a society's moral norms, because all moral evaluations must be based on the moral norms of the local society and so they should be immune from evaluation by any external set of norms.

But, of course, contrary to the relativist position, we are able to make sense of, and understand, the internal moral criticisms we make of our own moral norms as well as the external criticisms of outsiders. Southerners understood all too well what their own native abolitionists were saying when they claimed that the moral norms of the South were morally wrong and they understood, also, the external moral criticisms of Northern abolitionists; similarly, criticisms of the Nazi Holocaust and criticisms of South African apartheid, whether launched by insiders or outsiders, were not seen as irrational nonsense, but were seen instead as challenges that had to be answered. We understand what it means to say, and it makes perfectly good sense to say, then, that the moral norms of our own society, or of other societies, can be morally mistaken. It follows that ethical relativism is mistaken since it implies that such moral evaluations of local moral norms are not possible.

Although the transcendental argument against relativism is common, philosophers have failed to notice the implications of the argument, implications that, I now want to show, are critically important for the international business manager.

I have said that, contrary to the claims of ethical relativism, we are able to understand both internal and external moral evaluations of our moral norms. This recognition that our own moral norms, as well as those of other societies, can be subjected to coherent moral evaluation implies that local cultural norms are not the only criteria we have available for making moral evaluations. For if we can evaluate the moral norms prevailing within our own society as well as the moral norms that prevail within other societies, there must be some criteria that we rely on to make such evaluations, criteria that must transcend the local moral norms of our society. The practice of moral criticism, then, not only shows that ethical relativism is mistaken in holding that there are no moral criteria that transcend local norms, the practice itself reveals the existence of transcultural normative criteria.

This point, that the possibility of moral criticism of local norms reveals the existence of transcultural normative criteria that are used to evaluate the moral norms of societies, while highly abstract, has important implications for international managerial practice. For the problem that confronts the manager operating in different cultures is the problem of engaging employees across cultures, the problem of communicating about moral issues with employees of different cultures. Somehow, the American manager operating in Italy has to be able to transcend the limits of his own culture and attempt to talk to the members of Italy's culture about the differences between their cultures and how those differences are to be resolved. Ethical relativism would make this transcultural moral task impossible since it holds that each person can talk only from one culture or another, and there are no transcultural norms that enable one to criticize and evaluate the moral norms of a culture in a way that transcends the differences between cultures. But in fact, the transcendental argument shows that transcultural norms do exist and that transcultural conversations, though perhaps difficult, are nevertheless possible. The transcendental argument implies, then, that the manager who is confronted with moral diversity is not forced to remain alone and to make arbitrary choices between conflicting and ultimately irreconcilable moral differences. Instead the transcendental argument implies that there is another possibility: the possibility of working with members of other cultures and together with them appealing to transcultural normative criteria to help resolve and evaluate conflicting moral norms.

What are these transcultural criteria to which the manager can appeal? We can identify some of these criteria by being attentive to the various kinds of considerations that emerge when we evaluate the moral adequacy of the norms of our own or other cultures. Consider, for example, the kinds of questions that an American manager can raise about the norm on understating income in the Italian tax case. He could ask, first, whether that norm is consistent with the other basic norms Italian society accepts. We have assumed that the norm allowing the understating of income on tax returns is generally accepted among Italians and that understating is not seen as shady or improper. But is this assumption correct, or is the norm allowing the understating of income on returns in reality felt to be inconsistent with the basic norm against lying?

These kinds of questions suggest that consistency is one of the criteria a manager can use to evaluate the adequacy of a culture's moral norms. The manager could also ask of the beliefs that form part of the underlying structure, whether these beliefs are true: what publicly accessible evidence can be brought forward in support of those beliefs? For example, we have suggested that in Italian society both government and business officials knew that overstating of profits would take place and so the practice was seen as justified on the grounds that there was no deception involved. But is this construal of the facts correct? Questions of this sort suggest that publicly ascertainable truth is another criterion to which the manager can appeal in evaluating a culture's moral norms. In addition the manager could also ask whether the norm that allows systematic understating of income is in the long range best interests of the country? Does acceptance of the norm, for example, encourage or discourage outsider investment? Does acceptance of the norm encourage or discourage economic efficiency? These and other similar questions suggest that contribution to the collective welfare of society is another criterion against which the international manager can measure the moral adequacy of local norms and their associated practices. The manager can also ask whether the norms that allow understating of income and negotiated agreements treat everyone fairly, or whether they are in practice an invitation to arbitrary treatment. Do these norms unjustly heap burdens on the poor that the rich are able to escape? These sorts of questions suggest that fairness and justice are a third criterion against which the manager could weigh the adequacy of his own norms or those of other cultures.

Finally, the manager could ask whether the Italian norm violates the basic rights of anyone? He might ask, for example, whether the norm has been forced on businesses by government bureaucrats intent on lining their own pockets, or whether the norm is one to which all Italians give their willing consent? If the system of income tax assessment was put to a vote, for example, would most

Italians choose to continue or discontinue it? In short, is the norm consistent with basic rights of self-determination. These sorts of questions suggest that the manager could also evaluate moral norms through considerations related to moral rights.

There are, then, a number of criteria that the manager can invoke when evaluating the norms of, and these criteria would be easily understood by a person from an Italian as well as from an American culture. The criteria that I have pointed to--consistency, publicly ascertainable truth, the collective wellbeing of society, justice, and moral rights--are not specific moral principles or moral norms. I am not suggesting that there is some privileged set of moral principles to which all cultures must bow. Instead, what I am here calling criteria, are really categories of moral considerations in the form of questions that can be asked about our moral practices. The questions point to forms of reasoning that bring various categories of moral considerations to bear on the evaluation of norms. As such they indicate the kind of transcultural criteria that can allow members of different cultures to collaborate in evaluating the moral adequacy of the norms of the culture.

Why are such transcultural conversations important to the international manager? For two reasons. First, they are important because they enable the foreign manager to engage his or her local group in a conversation aimed at determining whether they as a group should accept the local norm. When the manager, like the banker in our Italian case, is confronted with a norm with which he is uncomfortable, he is not forced to make an arbitrary choice to either accept or reject the norm. He can, instead, engage his local managers in a conversation aimed at discovering what can be said for or against the norm (and its underlying structure) on the basis of transcultural considerations that he as well as locals can understand.

Secondly, such transcultural conversations are useful because they enable the manager, together with locals, to decide whether the issue is important enough that the company should work to change the norm. A company, perhaps, has no general obligation to engage a nation in cultural change, and in many cases its obligation is exactly the opposite: to refrain from interfering in local cultural customs. Still, when a local practice is a serious violation of basic moral values that even locals recognize, then the company may have an obligation to do what it can do to work with locals to change the practice. In the Italian case before us, for example, the American manager, together with its Italian employees, might conclude that the practice of understating income is seriously corrupting the local society, and then the manager may choose to have his company start working with other local companies to change the practice. Cross-cultural moral evaluations of the sort that I have described, then, are part of a process of collaborating with locals to improve and develop the moral environment within which the company operates.

# MANUEL VELASQUEZ

An important question that transcultural criteria of the sort that I have identified above raise, of course, is what are their limits? Although the kinds of criteria that I have identified can take members of different cultures some distance toward understanding, communicating about, and evaluating the moral norms on which they differ, I am not claiming that they provide grounds for evaluating the adequacy of all cultural norms. Let me suggest just one important kind of limitation. Underlying all moral norms, and constituting part of their deep structure, are metaphysical beliefs and assumptions about the nature of reality. Some Hindu norms of inequality, for example, are justified on the basis of the doctrine of Karma. The doctrine of Karma holds that the sufferings a person undergoes in his station in life are the result of the karmic guilt he accumulated through evil deeds committed in past incarnations and which must now be expiated through suffering. The sufferings of disadvantaged social castes, then, are simply the deserved and natural result of their own past misdeeds, and so should arouse no moral concern. This doctrine is based on the metaphysical assumption that the course of nature is influenced by the moral qualities agents acquired in past lives. Western metaphysical outlooks of course, reject the belief that natural events are influenced by the moral qualities of agents. Now I have suggested that when the manager encounters different cultural norms, one criterion for evaluating such norms is the requirement that the norms should be based on publicly ascertainable truth. What the example of Hindu metaphysics suggests is that the truth or falsity of some claims underlying moral norms simply cannot be evaluated on the basis of publicly ascertainable evidence. In particular there is just no way to prove or disprove the assumption that the course of nature is influenced by the moral qualities agents acquired in past lives. The truth or falsity of such claims lies beyond our ken. The manager, then, who is confronted with local Hindu norms that permit discrimination against employees who belong to lower social castes, will be limited in his ability to discuss the moral adequacy of such discriminatory norms because the norms are ultimately based on metaphysical assumptions that cannot be evaluated by traditional tests for truth.

There are, then limits to the extent to which the transcultural criteria we have identified can be used by international managers when attempting to collaborate with locals to evaluate the adequacy of moral norms about which they disagree. On some specific issues the members of two different cultures may find little common ground for discussion. Nevertheless, the criteria we have identified provide the basis for transcultural collaboration and communication about ethics on most issues. They can bridge the differences between the members of many different cultures, even if there are some cultural norms that nonnatives may ultimately find themselves unable to understand or evaluate in terms of these criteria. The criteria provide at least the starting point for transcultural understanding and collaboration, and it may be that even where their applicability is limited, they can still take us a long way toward the kind of transcultural resolution of differences that the international business manager must achieve.

# V. Conclusion

Let me conclude. I have tried to show that some of the standard philosophical arguments against relativism do not provide helpful guidance to the international manager. But I have also tried to show that if we look more closely at the implications of other important arguments against relativism, some significant conclusions emerge about the methods and approaches that managers should take in dealing with cultural diversity. In particular, I have argued that one argument against relativism reveals that morality has a deep structure, and that an examination of this structure must be the starting point of cross-cultural moral evaluations. And I have argued that another argument against relativism reveals that there are transcultural criteria of moral adequacy that the manager in collaboration with locals can use to evaluate the adequacy of local norms and their underlying structure. Reflection on our own practices of cross-cultural evaluations of norms suggests, I have argued, that such transcultural criteria are not specific moral principles, but general categories of moral questions indicative of the kinds of moral considerations and reasonings that can be brought to bear on culturally diverse moral norms.

**Endnotes**

1   A comprehensive, although somewhat dated, account of the socio-ethical problems managers face in different cultural contexts is provided by THOMAS N. GLADWIN and INGO WALTER: *Multinationals Under Fire*, New York (John Wiley & Sons) 1980.

MANUEL VELASQUEZ

2    This view is advanced particularly by cultural anthopologists. See M. HERSKOVITS: *Cultural Relativism: Perspectives in Cultural Pluralism*, New York (Vintage) 1972. However, the view has recently been defended by philosophers. See, for example, GILBERT HARMAN: "Moral Relativism Defended", *Philosophical Review*, 84 (1975), pp. 3-22.

3    Two useful collections of writings on ethical relativism are: JACK W. MEILAND and MICHAEL KRAUSZ (Eds): *Relativism, Cognitive and Moral*, Notre Dame, IN (University of Notre Dame Press) 1982, and MICHAEL KRAUSZ (Ed.): Relativism: Interpretation and Confrontation, Notre Dame, IN (University of Notre Dame Press) 1989. For a historical overview of the debate over ethical relativism, see the pieces collected in JOHN LADD (Ed.): *Ethical Relativism*, Belmont, CA (Wadsworth Pub. Co.) 1973.

4    Kelly's account has been reprinted in numerous texts. See, for example, ARTHUR L. KELLY: "Italian Tax Mores", in THOMAS DONALDSON and AL GINI: *Case Studies in Business Ethics*, Englewood Cliffs, NJ (Prentice Hall) 1993, pp. 67-69.

5    JAMES RACHELS: "Can Ethics Provide Answers", *The Hastings Center Report*, 10, No. 3 (June 1980), pp. 33-39; a more recent presentation of this argument can be found in JAMES RACHELS: *The Elements of Moral Philosophy*, New York (Random House) 1986.

6    NORMAN E. BOWIE: "Business Ethics and Cultural Relativism", *Essentials of Business Ethics*, ed. by P. Madsen and J. Shafritz, New York (Penguin Books) 1990, pp. 366-382.

7    See LUIGI BARZINI: *The Italians*, New York (Grosset & Dunlap) 1964. See also FELIX KESSLER: "Bribery of Politicos is Routine in Italian Business", *The Wall Street Journal*, (4 April 1976), section 4, p. 1. Italy is said to have a "high context culture" in EDWARD T. HALL: *Beyond Culture*, Garden City, NY (Anchor Books) 1977. Hall defines a high context culture as one in which in interpersonal exchanges much information is implicit rather than explicitly stated, in which verbal agreements are preferred over written contracts, in which personal interactions and loyalties are valued over impersonal ones, and in which great distinctions are made between insiders and outsiders.

Chapter 2

# Corporate Social Monitoring in the United States, Great Britain, and South Africa: A Comparative Analysis[1]

KAREN PAUL

## Abstract

Corporate social monitoring in the United States, Great Britain, and South Africa provides a way of evaluating corporate social performance on a systematic and comprehensive basis. A comparison of the schemes used in these three countries is presented including key constituencies, methods of evaluation, and dimensions being evaluated.

The object of this paper is to compare approaches to evaluating corporate social performance (CSP) developed in the U.S., Great Britain and South Africa. The choice of these three countries derives from their position in the social investing movement. Only in the United States, Great Britain, and South Africa do we find a highly developed social investing community mature enough to have developed formal rating systems for publicly traded corporations. In each of these countries, groups formed to develop monitoring systems have attempted to identify

---

1   This research was supported by a grant from the Aspen Institute Nonprofit Sector Research Fund.

which companies would be ethically suitable for investment in portfolios screened according to social criteria as well as financial criteria. This analysis is based on interviews conducted with groups doing corporate monitoring in each country.

In the U.S., measures of corporate social performance include the Toxic Release Inventory (TRI) now published annually by the Environmental Protection Agency, in which companies disclose the extent of their toxic emissions, and the Community Reinvestment Act (CRA) data, in which banks reveal the extent to which they serve their various communities. Both measures have good reliability but each is limited in that only one aspect of CSP is being evaluated. Another database provided by *Fortune* magazine has been used by academic researchers, but not by social investors, and has been widely criticized (Fryxell & Wang, forthcoming).

In recent years a new database has become available for measuring CSP on approximately one thousand publicly traded U.S. corporations rated on eight dimensions of corporate social performance, assigning ratings for five of these dimensions on a five-point scale and three on a three-point scale. This database has been developed by KLD, an investment advisory firm in Cambridge, Massachusetts. Investors use the ratings to guide a number of social investment funds, including TIAA-CREF's Social Choice Fund, thus it has attained somewhat more than academic significance for the corporate community. Researchers in a number of universities are using the database to explore both antecedent and consequent variables related to CSP (Graves & Waddock, 1992; Ruf, *et al.*, 1993; Sharfman, 1993).

## I. How Does Social Investing Affect Corporations?

Corporations are responsive to a number of different constituencies or stakeholders. Pressure for social goals can come from many different sources, including government, the media, and consumers. However, with respect to social investing, two sources of pressure of particular interest are investors and employees. Investors can pressure corporations insofar as they monitor social dimensions and put forth their expectations by means of shareholder resolutions, public statements, and actions such as divestment from portfolios of stock in companies considered to be falling short of ethical expectations.

Employees can pressure corporations to maintain certain standards of social performance in several ways. As individuals they can monitor and report on ethical transgressions. Indeed, many recently developed organizational structures and codes of ethics are designed to facilitate this type of conduct. Employees can also put forth social expectations through caucuses and other employee groups. The lists of best companies to work for, best companies for women to work for and best companies for blacks to work for, that are compiled and published annually in the United States appear to be influencing corporate decision-making in the area of employee policies. In addition, trade unions have historically put forth a number of goals relating to working conditions and the treatment of employees.

Investors and employees are important sources of influence for corporations in identifying and measuring various elements of social performance. The case of South Africa demonstrates that managers take CSP as an important priority when they know that their companies will be evaluated according to some systematic set of criteria, that they will be compared with other companies, and that the results will be made public. Investors are important in this process, because it is they who supply the continuing interest and the continuing means of supporting the information-gathering along with the publication and distribution of ratings received by corporations (Paul & Lydenberg, 1992).

## II. Social Investing in the United States

The social investing movement consists both of the individuals and of institutions whose investments are reported as amounting to about $600 billion in 1993. This amount of assets declined, however, as sanctions against companies investing in South Africa were lifted in the latter part of 1993 and 1994. More than fifty mutual funds offer socially screened products. Our main interest here is in institutions that engage in social investing, because they can support an organizational infrastructure that can exercise a regular monitoring program. In the U.S. the institutional investors who have been most visible in formally presenting social demands at shareholder meetings are religious activists, mainly coordinated through the Interfaith Center on Corporate Responsibility (ICCR). Pension funds such as the TIAA-CREF Social Choice Account, and the pension funds of California (CalPERS) and New York Municipal Employees have been especially aggressive in putting forth ethical demands. The Investor Responsibility Research Center (IRRC) is an organization that puts out research reports and monitors corporate social activities, providing information about what companies are doing in several social areas without making actual value judgements as to whether companies are doing what they should be doing.

The most elaborate system of investor monitoring of corporate social performance yet evolved was created around the issue of South Africa. The Sullivan Principles provided U.S. companies active in South Africa with a set of well defined, measurable goals, and allowed ratings to be made of companies along a three-point scale. Codes of conduct have also been put forth relating to U.S. companies active in Northern Ireland (the MacBride Principles) and to U.S. companies regarding conduct on environmental issues (the Ceres Code of Conduct, based on the Valdez Principles). However, corporations have been reluctant to accept codes other than the Sullivan Principles (and their successor Statement of Principles), and especially reluctant to submit to external monitoring other than that required by government agencies.

A new database for evaluating CSP has been made available since 1991 by KLD, a firm that evaluates approximately one thousand publicly traded U.S. companies for inclusion in their own portfolio as well as other social funds. The KLD scheme of evaluating CSP merits particular importance because it is the most systematic approach yet developed, and it is being widely used by a number of investment funds including the TIAA-CREF Social Choice Account. Eight dimensions of CSP have been identified: community relations, employee relations, environmental performance product development and liability, women/minority policies, and generation of revenues from the military, nuclear power, and South Africa (discontinued since the elections of 1994). Each company is rated on a five-point scale for each of the first five dimensions. For the remaining three dimensions, companies are rated only on the negative side, on a three-point scale. Previous research has suggested that the last three dimensions are considered to be significantly less important than the first five dimensions for a number of different constituencies (Ruf, *et al.* 1993).

In order to arrive at ratings of these dimensions of CSP, KLD uses a number of data sources selected in order to enable company ratings to be accomplished whether or not companies provide cooperation. The availability of this database makes it possible for researchers to conduct systematic research programs to explore the relationship between CSP and other variables, as well as to design a portfolio that will test whether a socially screened fund can be as profitable as a comparable fund that does not employ social screens.

## III. Social Investing in Great Britain

Ethical investing dates from the late 1800s, with the concern of the English Quakers and Methodists that they should not profit from "sin stocks" such as those whose profits came from tobacco, alcohol, or gambling. However, in recent decades the investment bodies of religious groups in Great Britain have been somewhat more reticent than their counterparts in the U.S. in limiting investing by ethical criteria. Currently there is a separation between the ethical advocacy groups in British churches and the mainstream church finance groups.

However, two church groups might be mentioned as active at least in raising consciousness on ethical investing issues. The Christian Ethical Investor Group has developed around the effort of the Bishop of Oxford to get the British courts to allow the Church of England to use ethical criteria in screening its investments, an effort which thus far has not been successful. Indeed, the courts have ruled that the church would be remiss in allowing social criteria to influence investment decisions.

The second British church group active in monitoring corporate social performance is the Ecumenical Committee for Corporate Responsibility (ECCR), associated with the Council of Churches for Britain and Ireland. It has just completed a study of the multinational chemical manufacturer, ICI, for which the research was actually done by the Pensions Investment Research Consultants (PIRC). PIRC generally works for the British municipal councils to determine fitting companies for investment of their pension funds, so we see here the potential for churches and trade unions to work together in monitoring CSP (*PIRC Services* ..., 1993).

PIRC has the philosophy that comparisons should be made within an industry rather than between companies in dissimilar industries. It uses both very basic "yes or no" type questions, and very detailed, more qualitative information gleaned through detailed interviews with company principals. Trade unions work with PIRC, but they are very conservative with their investments and have tended to emphasize workplace issues, not expressing much concern with more general aspects of CSP. Most of PIRC's support comes from municipal councils and their pension funds (*The Corporate Governance Service*, 1993).

Another British organization active in providing guidance for ethical investors is the Ethical Investment Research Service (EIRIS) established in 1983. EIRIS attempts to provide three services. First is research on corporate finance, along with social and corporate governance activities. Their database tracks information such as investment and the composition of boards of directors including the presence of women on the board, generates research reports, and performs detailed studies on particular issues such as environmental topics. Secondly, they are registered as financial advisors in order to provide financial advice to clients. Third, they manage shareholder coordination in proxy contests and solicitations and give advice on exercising votes.

31

EIRIS is now attempting to expand its monitoring program to 100 European "company groups" which will be monitored on six criteria that many ethical investors wish to avoid: fur products, gambling, sale or production of strategic goods or services for military users, nuclear power, tobacco production, and South Africa. It attempts to maintain an objective and value neutral position somewhat comparable to the IRRC in the United States. PIRC and EIRIS attempt to provide information so that strategies for socially responsible investing can be developed by interested parties such as trade unions, religious groups, or municipal councils. They do not focus overtly on avoidance of companies with poor ethical standards, and indeed might face a legal challenge if they attempted to do so. Their emphasis is simply on the reporting of facts, and trying to mobilize stockholders who are interested in exercising the responsibility of ownership. Much of the information they provide may be compared with that made available in the Community Reinvestment Act (CRA) reports filed by banks in the U.S.

In Great Britain pension funds representing municipal employees have been the most active group in supporting the development of CSP monitoring schemes to support social investing. Their concern, like their counterparts in the U.S., *e.g.,* CalPERS, is to create a systematic scheme for evaluating CSP in order to judge which companies merit investment of pension funds. More than twenty unit trusts are also marketed to individual investors in Great Britain, a number considerably fewer than in the United States. Ethical unit trusts in Great Britain comprised about £900m in mid-1994, with church-sponsored unit trusts (comparable to mutual funds in the U.S.) and environmental funds dominating.

## IV. Social Investing in South Africa

In South Africa social investing has just gotten started in the past few years, mobilized by the black trade unions, mainly in the mining industry, that have substantial pension funds accumulating and wish to direct investments into equities of companies traded on the Johannesburg Stock Exchange that exemplify the kind of CSP which trade union leaders would like to support. When black trade unions were made legal in 1979, pension benefits were a central part of the negotiations resulting in the National Union of Mineworkers (NUM) collecting pension funds since 1987. Consequently, the NUM and other trade unions in both Congress of South African Trade Unions (COSATU), an African National Congress (ANC) affiliated congress of trade unions, and National African Congress of Trade Unions

# CORPORATE SOCIAL MONITORING

(NACTU), a Pan-African Congress (PAC) affiliated congress of trade unions, started to consider where this money was being invested.

The unions were basically entrusting their funds to insurance companies who were reluctant to divulge how it was being invested. Was it being used to support companies offering poverty wages? To companies who were union busters? To companies going in for privatization? All these actions would be against the trade union's own policies. The unions were concerned that their own investments not be used to support economic positions that were contrary to their interests. Thus developed the impetus for social screening of companies being considered for investment.

The Labour Research Service (LRS), an economic consulting firm located in Cape Town which supplies information for trade unions to use in wage bargaining, was formed in 1986 to provide data on company profits, the comparative position of one company versus another in wages and benefits, and other similar information needed for effective negotiating. Since 1990 it has also provided data relating to the social performance of companies being considered for investment purposes.

In 1991 at the instigation of the NUM, the trade unions started to investigate the possibility of having a union controlled investment fund, rather than just passively assigning their accounts to investment advisors. The unions wanted the right to have a trustee on the Board of Directors of companies in which they invested and national boards for each industry such as retail trade or banking. In this connection they authorized the LRS to investigate criteria for investing. LRS recommended that the unit trust, comparable to the mutual fund in the U.S., would be the appropriate investment vehicle, because it could function as a collective fund where both individuals and union pension funds could invest as opposed to an insurance company portfolio, or an investment trust. The unit trust is a well-regulated form in South Africa with extensive requirements as to information reporting requirements. There is full disclosure of the holdings of unit trusts, and they are listed in the newspapers daily, giving a degree of transparency. This contributes to the confidence that trade union members can have in the security and the performance of the fund. The management company is 50% controlled by Syprets, an investment firm that uses financial criteria to select companies to be considered for investment, and 50% owned by Unity, a nonprofit organization set up to represent the unions' interest. Unity approves the companies against the social criteria (*Report on Companies ...,* 1992).

Seventeen social criteria are used with the following weights: job creation (14), industrial relations (14), conditions of employment (13), training (7), equal opportunities for women (7), health and safety (6), product (5), opposition to privatization (5), practicing profit retention rather than reinvesting profits (5), affirmative action (5), location of jobs within South Africa (4), environment (4), worker participation (4), disclosure (4), political profile (2), social spending (1). Racial discrimination is used as a further test of every other dimension. In other words, a company will be screened for each of the aforementioned dimensions such as job creation, then screened again on each dimension to see if the dimension stands up to the racial discrimination test, *e.g.*, is job creation occurring for all racial groups, or is job creation limited to those jobs where only whites are employed?

Individuals can invest in the Community Growth Fund (CGF), and several hundred have done so, but it is only actively marketed to the unions. Investment from outside South Africa is possible, but has not been solicited. There are about 350 investors, including individuals, unions who have group savings plans in the workplace, and stock companies. By April 1994 the fund had R210 million (about $30 million) in assets, and was increasing at the rate of R4.5 million (about $1.5 million) per month (Community Growth Fund, 1994). The fund only invests in shares of companies listed on the Johannesburg Stock Exchange. Another associated fund, the Future Growth Fund (FGF) was of equal size, and focused on investment in infrastructure projects.

When evaluating a company, LRS begins with public data, then interviews shop stewards and union leaders. Then management is interviewed with the labor leaders present. A report is prepared in which the company is scored using the criteria listed above. Unity receives the resulting report, which may be approved, rejected, or referred back to LRS for additional investigation. In the first year of active screening, twenty of the first thirty companies investigated were approved. Once under consideration, companies are monitored continuously.

The main elements of the rating scheme focus on the workplace, specifically whether or not the company is creating jobs, and its industrial relations practices, including the conditions of employment and wages paid. LRS tries to identify companies having good CSP within an industry, and to make comparisons based on industry practices. An important element is the training component, as well as affirmative action for blacks and women. Programs aimed at women have the same weight in the rating scheme as training blacks. Also considered are the company's record in health and safety, and worker participation. Companies are asked if any workers are on the Board of Directors. They are asked if they make any political contributions, but since South African companies are not legally obliged to give this information, they often refuse to divulge it. The disclosure of information is a variable considered in the evaluation system, including data revealed for union negotiations, for the LRS report, and available in public reports. As noted above, every other criterion is tested against racial disclosure where it is appropriate. For example, "Is there a training program?" is followed by "How well are blacks represented in the training program?"

In general, the assessment of the LRS is that the biggest problem in the country is jobs; therefore, the biggest priority for company social performance is job creation. With unemployment at about 40%, LRS expects that financial institutions should go out and proactively search for investments rather than being content to build big office blocks and manage money, or to use resources for acquisition and control of other companies and holdings, especially those located outside South Africa.

It may come as a surprise to observers outside South Africa that of one hundred total possible points, corporate social responsibility programs funded by corporations are worth only a single point in the South African scheme. The unions are more interested in job creation, the conditions of employment, and training opportunities.

## V. A Comparison of the U.S., British, and South African Approaches to Corporate Social Monitoring for Social Investing

One obvious point of comparison is that labor unions have been the main force supporting social investing in South Africa, while they have been less important in Great Britain and in the United States. Religious investors have been more important in the United States, but less important in Great Britain and in South Africa. Municipal councils and their associated investment funds have been very important in Great Britain, but not in South Africa. In the United States CalPERS and the public pension funds of New York City and New York State have been important, and may be compared to the British municipal councils and their funds.

In South Africa the pension funds of the black trade unions are being coordinated in a way so as to provide a continuing source of added investments for the fund being screened by the LRS. In a very few years this investment fund will constitute a very significant portion of the investment capital available in that country. No comparable influx of funds is being managed in such a coordinated way in the United States or Great Britain. Indeed, in both countries trade unions are relatively reticent to become very involved in social investing.

The legal status of social investing is better established in the United States than in Great Britain, where initial court decisions place severe limitations on ethical investing. In the U.S. the courts have affirmed the legitimacy of using ethical considerations in directing pension fund investments, but in Great Britain the courts have ruled that a church may not use ethical criteria for its investments. In South Africa there has not yet been a legal challenge to using social screens for pensions funds or other investment funds.

In South Africa the emphasis in corporate social monitoring used for ethical investing focuses on job creation and on the treatment of black workers. In the United States there is a more inclusive concern with issues including both "internal" dimensions like product liability and employee relations and "external" dimensions like the environment and community relations. In Great Britain investment practices of companies and corporate governance are important, along with the environment including a concern with factory-style farming, animal rights, and the construction of large retailers that draw business to outlying areas of towns.

The institutional infrastructure of corporate social monitoring and ethical investing is most formally developed in the United States, with the ICCR and the IRRC playing lead roles in coordinating social investors and providing information to them, while the data available from the TRI and the CRA, as well as the database maintained by KLD, make a large amount of quantitative information widely available. In Great Britain EIRIS and PIRC provide information to ethical investors, with the former organization playing a more "value-neutral" role, and the latter adopting more of an advocacy approach. In South Africa the information provided by LRS is put forth on an advocacy basis, sponsored by trade unions and designed to serve their purposes. Both the British and the South African systems use both qualitative and quantitative data, with company interviews providing a significant portion of the data used to evaluate. In the U.S. the emphasis is more on quantitative data such as that contained in the CRA, TRI, and KLD schemes. This allows a larger number of companies to be evaluated, and comparisons to be made over time and between a large number of widely varied companies. However, the detail that comes from qualitative analysis is more apparent in the British and South African systems than in the U.S. We might note that qualitative data and other material derived from interviews can be included in the U.S. schemes, but then not be readily apparent due to the refinement and distillation of this information to a set of numerical scores.

## VI. Conclusion and Implications

CSP is being monitored by social investors in the U.S., Great Britain, and South Africa. Social investing is having an impact on the corporate community in each of these countries, because companies are being systematically and routinely evaluated, the evaluations are being made public, and comparisons are being made between companies to assess their suitability for ethical investing. In the United States the availability of a large body of quantitative data provides the means whereby continuing and comprehensive studies of CSP can be accomplished, with religious groups and individual investors providing the main sources of support for social investing and the monitoring of CSP. In Great Britain a more qualitative approach is supported by municipal councils. In South Africa the massive inflow of funds into ethical investing, combined with the necessity that corporations address social issues in post-apartheid South Africa has created a powerful momentum for social investing and CSP monitoring, supported mainly by trade unions.

Each country's way of evaluating CSP can be further refined with possible improvements suggested by examination of the other models. For example, in the U.S. there is ample quantitative data, but qualitative data are hardly represented in corporate social monitoring; the South African example might be instructive in this regard. In the U.S. religious groups and mutual funds, individual investors, and public retirement funds are the main forces behind social investing and corporate social monitoring. In Great Britain municipal councils are the main force, while in South Africa the black trade unions play this role. The courts in the U.S. have approved the use of social screens as well as financial screens for retirement funds, whereas in Great Britain they have ruled against this idea. The question has not yet been presented to the judiciary in South Africa. In Great Britain if the churches and the courts could both become better informed about the merits of social investing, they might constitute a new force for putting pressure on corporations to pay attention to social goals. In South Africa other investing groups besides the unions might be mobilized to use the same scheme developed by the LRS to guide their investments, or they might be encouraged to develop other schemes of monitoring CSP that would more precisely reflect their own priorities.

Social investing, and the corporate social monitoring which it requires, provide a strategy whereby the ethical dimension can be institutionalized in the management process. Virtually all managers operate with a certain level of knowledge of marketing objectives and financial objectives, and not just abstract knowledge but also internalization and acceptance. When managers are held to the same degree of scrutiny on social goals and ethical principles, they will also develop the same knowledge and acceptance of these ideals. Social investing and the corporate social monitoring required for its practice are of critical importance for the institutionalization of CSP as a managerial objective.

# KAREN PAUL

## References

COMMUNITY GROWTH FUND: *Half-Yearly Report*, June 30, CapeTown, South Africa (Labour Research Service) 1993.

FRYXELL, G.E. and WAND, J.: "The Fortune Corporate 'Reputation' Data: Reputation for What?", *Journal of Management*, forthcoming 1993.

GRAVES, S. B. and WADDOCK, S.A.: *Responses of Institutional Investors to Corporate Social Performance Measures*, ed. by J.W. Wall and L.R. Jaunch, 1992 (Academy of Management Best Paper Proceedings).

PAUL, K. and LYDENBERG, S.D: "Applications of Corporate Social Monitoring Systems: Types, Dimensions, and Goals", *Journal of Business Ethics*, 11 (Winter 1992), p. 1-10.

*PIRC Services for Local Authority Pension Funds*. 1993. London: PIRC Ltd.

*Report on Companies Assessed for the Community Growth Fund*, Second Half of 1992. 1992. Cape Town, South Africa: Unity Incorporation.

RUF, B., MURALIDHAR, K., and PAUL, K.: "Eight Dimensions of Corporate Social Performance: Determination of Relative Importance Using the Analytic Hierarchy Process",ed. by D.P. Moore, 1993 (Academy of Management Best Paper Proceedings 1993).

SHARFMAN, M.: "A Construct Validity Study of Kld Social Performance Ratings Data", *Proceedings*, 1993 (Annual Meetings of the International Society for Business and Society).

*The Corporate Governance Service*. 1993. London: PIRC Ltd.

# CORPORATE SOCIAL MONITORING

| | United States | Great Britain | South Africa |
|---|---|---|---|
| Approximate Number of Funds | 50+ | 20+ | 3 (all LRS) (1 major) |
| Approximate Amount of CGF | $500b; | £900m | R210m |
| Assets FGF | estimate | (£37b with statement on env't) | R210m |
| Lead Groups Supporting Monitoring | Religious groups; Public pension funds | Municipal Councils | Trade Unions |
| Organizations Monitoring | IRRC; ICCR; EPA; CRA; KLD | EIRIS; PIRC | LRS; Unity |
| Legal Status of Social Criteria for Portfolios | Affirmed for public pension fund | Denied for Church of England portfolio | Presumed (Untested) |
| Type of Data Published | Mainly Quantitative | Both Types | Mainly Qualitative |
| Number of Companies Monitored | Over 1,000 by social investors; thousands by TRI; hundreds by CRA | Dozens | Thirty (More in process) |

**Table 1. Comparison of United States, Great Britain, and South Africa on Corporate Social Monitoring for Social Investing**

Chapter 3

# On the Social Responsibility of Corporations under Competition

KOTARO SUZUMURA*

" ... Perhaps you are mixing up morality and legality."
"I'm sure you can explain the difference."
"I don't suppose so.
I'd just say that morality doesn't change when you cross a frontier."

—— Gavin Lyall, *Midnight Plus One.*

# I. Introduction

In a recent article published in one of the leading Japanese newspapers, Mr. Ryuzaburo Kaku of Canon Inc. asked for wide acceptance by Japanese corporations of the ethical code of corporate behaviour proposed in July 1994 by the Caux Round Table of business leaders from Europe, Japan and the United States.[1] According to Mr. Kaku, this code of behaviour is drafted on the basis of the following three value premises:

**Human Dignity**: The dignity of an individual human being working in a corporation or a business group should not be violated or sacrificed even for the sake of promoting the benefits of the corporation or the group as a whole.

**The Minnesota Principles:** A corporation or a business group should pay due attention to the benefits of all stakeholders taken together, which include not only customers and employees, but also investors, suppliers, competitors, and local community.

**Philosophy of Co-Existence**: A corporation or a business group should aim at striking the proper balance between healthy and fair competition, on the one hand, and mutual prosperity through co-existence, on the other, thereby contributing to the promotion of benefits and happiness of the whole human beings.

According to Mr. Kaku, each one of these value premises stands, respectively, for the traditional sense of values in European, American and Japanese societies. The Caux guidelines for ethical behaviour are meant to be universally applicable, not only to the developed economies, but also to the economies in transition as well as the developing economies. In particular, it is emphasized that the idiosyncracy and lack of transparency of Japanese corporations, which have been the target of harsh foreign criticisms of late, will become less conspicuous if this universal code of behaviour is duly observed.

The social responsibility of corporations designed by this code of behaviour, which is universal as well as extensive, is in sharp contrast with the traditional view expressed by Milton Friedman (1982, p.133): "[T]here is one and only one social responsibility of business--to use its resources and engage in activities designed to increase its profits so long as it stays within the rules of the game, which is to say, engages in open and free competition, without deception or fraud." In view of the large gulf that exists in between these two views on social responsibility of corporations, three critical observations will be made in this paper on the role and necessity of social responsibility of corporations engaging in market competition.

The first observation is on the welfare effects of competition. It is on the basis of a widespread belief in the welfare-improving effects of increasing competition that Friedman expressed his parsimonious view on social responsibility of corporations. However, there exists a second conventional wisdom on competition and economic welfare, which is held by a large group of people outside the standard academic circle, asserting that the adage "doing in excess is just as bad as not doing enough" applies to the role of competition as well, and free working of competition should be checked either by public regulation or by socially responsible business ethics.[2] The infamous concept of "excessive competition," which appears ever so often in the general discussion on competition and economic welfare, is an expression which symbolizes this view of competition.[3] Capitalizing on the recent work by Suzumura (1995a), we pose and settle the following two questions:

(a) Can competition ever be excessive in a welfare-theoretic sense?

(b) Can socially responsible voluntary restraint on competition be justified in the name of keeping "excessive competition" under due control?

The second observation is on the fate of a socially responsible agent--an "ethical" agent, for short--in a decentralized socio-economic system. It is widely presumed that an ethical code of behaviour may be of value to all agents, yet it may be to the disadvantage of any one agent to maintain it unilaterally. However, we will show that the nice ("ethical") guy, who follows an ethical code by his own, need not be sacrificed in the sense that unilateral adoption of "ethical" code of behaviour does not necessarily hurt the "ethical" agent himself. In order to give substance to this unorthodox claim, we will exemplify our point in terms of the resolution of the Pareto libertarian paradox due originally to Sen (1970; 1976) through the existence of at least one ethical individual. This resolution scheme is due to Sen (1976) and Suzumura (1978; 1983).

The third observation is based on the nature of competition in Japan. It will be suggested that there exists a clear distinction between insiders and outsiders in the perception of Japanese corporations, but the boundary that separates insiders and outsiders is anything but fixed. Depending on the way we circumscribe the competitive arena, the insider-outsider demarcation changes quite radically. We will try to crystallize an insidious implication of this feature of competition in Japan on the possibility of a universal ethical code of behaviour in a competitive arena.

# II. Welfare and Competition: Consequentialist Evaluation of Market Performance

With the purpose of crystallizing the welfare effects of increasing competition as simply as possible, thereby shedding a new light on the limitation of the Friedmanian view on corporate responsibility, suppose that there are $n$ identical firms in an oligopolistic industry, where $n$ $(2 \leq n < +\infty)$ will be determined endogenously by entry and exit of firms in accordance with profit incentives. This industry produces a single homogeneous good. The inverse demand function and the cost function of each firm are $p = f(Q)$ and $C(q_i)$, respectively, where $p$ is output price, $q_i$ is output of firm $i$, and $Q = \Sigma_{i=1}^{n} q_i$ is industry output. It is assumed that $f(Q)$ is twice continuously differentiable with $f'(Q) < 0$ for all $Q \geq 0$ such that $f(Q) > 0$, and $C(q_i)$ is twice continuously differentiable with $C(q_i) > 0, C'(q_i) > 0$ and $C''(q_i) \geq 0$ for all $q_i \geq 0$.[4]

The profit function of firm $i$, $i = 1, 2, ..., n$, is given by $\pi^i(q_i, Q_{-i}) = q_i f(q_i + Q_{-i}) - C(q_i)$, where $Q_{-i} = Q - q_i = \Sigma_{j \neq i} q_j$. It is assumed that firms choose their outputs so as to maximize their profits. When all competitive firms are simultaneously maximizing their profits, hence $(\partial/\partial q_i)\pi^i(q_i, Q_{-i}) = 0$ holds for all $i \in N = \{1, 2, ..., n\}$, we are at the *Cournot-Nash equilibrium* $q^N(n) = (q_1^N(n), ..., q_i^N(n), ..., q_n^N(n))$ among $n$ firms. This is what we expect to observe at the equilibrium of intra-industrial competition.

By definition, $q^N(n)$ may be characterized by $(\partial/\partial q_i)\pi^i(q_i^N(n), Q_{-i}^N(n)) = 0$ for all $i \in N$, where $Q_{-i}^N(n) = \Sigma_{j \neq i} q_j^N(n)$. Our subsequent analysis will be focussed on the *symmetric* Cournot-Nash equilibrium, so that $q_i^N(n) = q_j^N(n) = q^N(n)$, say, for all $i, j \in N$.

With the purpose of introducing the crucial condition of *strategic substitutability* at this juncture of our analysis, we define $\beta_{ij}(q_i, Q_{-i}) = (\partial^2/\partial q_i \partial q_j)\pi^i(q_i, Q_{-i})$ for all $i, j \in N$, where $i \neq j$. Let us say that strategic substitutability prevails if and only if $\beta_{ij}(q_i, Q_{-i}) < 0$ holds for all $i, j \in N$ such that $i \neq j$. The meaning of this condition can be made clear in terms of the *reaction function* $q_i = r_i(Q_{-i})$ of firm $i \in N$, which is to be defined implicitly by $(\partial/\partial q_i)\pi^i(r_i(Q_{-i}), Q_{-i}) = 0$. Differentiating this equation with respect to $q_j$, where $i \neq j$, we obtain

$$(1) \quad r_i^1(Q_{-i}) = -\frac{(\partial^2/\partial q_i \partial q_j)\pi^i(r_i(Q_{-i}), Q_{-i})}{(\partial^2/\partial q_i^2)\pi^i(r_i(Q_{-i}), Q_{-i})}.$$

Since the denominator of (1) must be negative by virtue of the second-order condition for profit maximization, (1) implies that $r_i^1(Q_{-i}) < 0$ holds if and only if $\beta_{ij}(r_i(Q_{-i}), Q_{-i}) < 0$ holds. Thus, *strategic substitutability holds if and only if the reaction function is downward sloping*, which is commonly assumed in the literature on Cournot oligopoly. In particular, strategic substitutability necessarily obtains if the inverse demand function is linear.

Using the reaction function $q_i = r_i(Q_{-i})$, we now define the *cumulative reaction function* $R_i(Q)$ by $q_i = R_i(Q)$ if and only if $q_i = r_i(Q - q_i)$. It is clear that $R_i(Q)$ is downward sloping if and only if $r_i(Q_{-i})$ is downward sloping. This fact can be verified by noting the relation that $R_i^1(Q) = r_i^1(Q - R_i(Q))/\{1 + r_i^1(Q - R_i(Q))\}$.

It is clear from the definition of $r_i(Q_{-i})$ that the Cournot-Nash equilibrium $q^N(n)$ may be characterized by $q_i^N(n) = r_i(Q_{-i}^N(n))$ for all $i \in N$. Equivalently, $q^N(n)$ may be characterized by $q_i^N(n) = R_i(Q^N(n))$ for all $i \in N$. Adding this last equation over all $i \in N$, we may obtain $Q^N(n) = \Sigma_{i=1}^n R_i(Q^N(n))$. Thus, the industry output at the Cournot-Nash equilibrium $q^N(n)$, viz. $Q^N(n)$ is nothing other than the fixed point of the aggregate cumulative reaction function $\Sigma_{i=1}^n R_i(\cdot)$. Figure 1 uses this useful fact to describe the change in the Cournot-Nash equilibrium when a change $\Delta n$ in the number of firms takes place. Letting $\Delta n$ converge to zero, we may confirm that

(2) $\quad (d/dn)q^N(n) < 0; (d/dn)Q^N(n) > 0$

holds. More precise proof of this property may be found in Suzumura (1995a, Chapter 1).

Turning to the long-run performance of the Cournot market, let $\pi^N(n)$ be the profits earned by each incumbent firm at the Cournot-Nash equilibrium among $n$ firms, viz. $\pi^N(n) = q^N(n) f(Q^N(n)) - C(q^N(n))$. The equilibrium number of firms $n_e$ is formally defined by $\pi^N(n_e) = 0$. It is clear that the Cournot-Nash equilibrium among $n_e$ firms, viz. $q^N(n_e)$, is what we expect to observe at the equilibrium of inter- industrial competition.

In order to gauge the welfare performance of the long-run Cournot-Nash equilibrium $q^N(n_e)$, let us introduce consumers' surplus measure $CS^N(n)$ and producers' surplus measure $PS^N(n)$, which are formally defined, respectively, by

(3) $\quad CS^N(n) = \int_0^{Q^N(n)} f(Z)dZ - Q^N(n)\, f(Q^N(n))$

and

(4) $\quad PS^N(n) = \sum_{i=1}^{n}\{q_i^N(n)\, f(Q^N(n)) - C(q_i^N(n))\}.$

By adding $CS^N(n)$ and $PS^N(n)$ together, we obtain a measure of potential social welfare defined by net market surplus, viz.,

(5) $\quad W^N(n) = CS^N(n) + PS^N(n).$

Suppose that an exogenous change in $n$ takes place. It is easy to verify that the change in social welfare may be reduced into

(6) $\quad (d/dn)W^N(n) = \pi^N(n) - Q^N(n)f'(Q^N(n))(d/dn)q^N(n).$

Evaluating (6) at the equilibrium number of firms $n = n_e$ and noting that $\pi^N(n_e) = 0$ holds by definition of $n_e$ we obtain

(7) $\quad (d/dn)W^N(n_e) < 0,$

where use is made of (2). Thus, a marginal decrease in $n$ at $n = n_e$ unambiguously improves potential social welfare.

The implication of this simple result seems to be quite serious. If there is no intervention into free competition in the Cournot market, the spontaneous outcome of long-run competitive forces will be the Cournot-Nash equilibrium at the equilibrium number of firms, viz. $q^N(n_e)$. If competition is the decentralized mechanism for efficient resource allocation, it should be socially better to let the competitive forces to bring out $q^N(n_e)$ rather than to prevent the occurrence of this spontaneous outcome. Yet the result we have arrived at tells us that it is socially better to *decrease* the number of firms at $n = n_e$ than to stay at $n = n_e$. In other words, the spontaneous working of long-run competitive forces results in a socially *excessive* number of firms at the margin. This is a version of *excess entry theorem* due to Mankiw and Whinston (1986).

Should we conclude on the basis of this analysis that the Suzumura and Kiyono (1987), and Suzumura (1995a).[5] traditional view on competition in Japan is right, and free working of competition should be checked either by public regulation or by socially responsible corporate behaviour? For at least two reasons, it seems to us that we should not rush to this conclusion.

To explain our first reservation, we observe that $CS^N(n)$ and $PS^N(n)$ behave in response to a marginal change in $n$ as follows:

(8) $\quad (d/dn)CS^N(n) = -Q^N(n) f'(Q^N(n))(d/dn)Q^N(n),$

and

(9) $\quad (d/dn)PS^N(n) = \pi^N(n) + Q^N(n) f'(Q^N(n))\{(d/dn)Q^N(n) - (d/dn)q^N(n)\}.$

Note that we may recover (6) by simply adding (8) and (9). Note also that we may conclude from (2) and (8) that $(d/dn)CS^N(n) > 0$ holds for all $n$, not just at $n = n_e$, hence it is always to the benefit of consumers to increase the number of firms $n$, thereby making the Cournot market more competitive. On the other hand, evaluating (9) at $n = n_e$ and invoking (2) once again, it follows from (9) and $\pi^N(n_e) = 0$ that $(d/dn)PS^N(n_e) < 0$. Thus, it is clearly to the benefit of producers to decrease the number of firms at $n = n_e$, thereby making the Cournot market less competitive. The reason we have obtained an unambiguous conclusion to the effect that $(d/dn)W^N(n_e) < 0$ is that the positive effect $(d/dn)CS^N(n_e) > 0$ is overwhelmed by the negative effect $(d/dn)PS^N(n_e) < 0$. Put differently, behind the clear verdict that $(d/dn)W^N(n_e) < 0$ lies an uncompromising conflict between producer's benefit and consumer's benefit.[6] It should be clear now that the

45

restriction of long-run competitive forces in the name of marginally improving potential social welfare is insidious to say the least. This recommendation may well be a disguised promotion of producer's benefit at the sacrifice of consumer's benefit.[7]

Our second reservation is that the restraint of competition may produce distortions of its own, and the potential increase in social welfare may well be swallowed up by the concomitant increase in social cost. As Hayek (1948, p.100) acutely observed, "[t]he basis of comparison, on the grounds of which the achievement of competition ought to be judged, cannot be a situation which is different from the objective facts and which cannot be brought about by any known means. It ought to be the situation as it would exist if competition were prevented from operating. Not the approach to an unachievable and meaningless ideal but the improvement upon the conditions that would exist without competition should be the test." At the very least, it is premature to assert that striking the proper balance between healthy and fair competition, on the one hand, and mutual prosperity through co-existence, on the other, is within the easy reach of socially responsible corporations.

## III. On the Consequence of Unilateral Ethical Behaviour

A strong presumption seems to prevail, according to which unilateral adoption of an ethical code of behaviour is always self-defeating.[8] If this presumption is vindicated without exception, nobody has any reason whatsoever to accept any ethical code of behaviour unilaterally and the sustainable ethical code must be the one that is universally accepted in advance. To take an exception to this widely held presumption as concretely as possible, let us examine Sen's (1970; 1976; 1992) *Pareto libertarian paradox* and its resolution.

Sen's paradox may be illustrated by the following example which is called the *Lady Chatterley's Lover* case. There is a single copy of *Lady Chatterley's Lover*. Everything else remaining the same, there are three social states: Mr. A (the prude) reading it ($r_A$), Mr. B (the lascivious) reading it ($r_B$), and no one reading it ($r_0$). Mr. A prefers $r_0$ most, next $r_A$ (wishing to take the hurt of this "vulgar" book upon himself), and lastly $r_B$ for fear of the misbehaviour of Mr. B). Mr. B prefers $r_A$ most (in order to educate the reactionary Mr. A), $r_B$ next (for his own fun), and lastly $r_0$ ("what a waste of Lawrence's great work!"). On the ground of individual's libertarian right of reading, $r_0$ is socially better than $r_A$, because $r_0$ and $r_A$ differ only in whether or not Mr. A reads the book, and Mr. A does not want to read it. By the same reasoning, $r_B$ is socially better than $r_0$, since B wants to read the book rather than wasting it and Mr. A does not read the book in $r_B$ as well as in $r_0$. On the other hand, $r_A$ is Pareto-superior to $r_B$, so that the Paretian society should judge that $r_A$ is socially better than $r_B$. Thus, any society which respects the *Pareto principle* and the *libertarian principle of respecting individual rights* cannot choose anything from the whole set of social alternatives $S = \{r_0, r_A, r_B\}$. This is an example of the Pareto libertarian paradox.[9, 10]

The logical conflict between the welfaristic Pareto principle and the non-welfaristic principle of social respect for individual libertarian rights, thus exemplified, is deep and hard to find a reasonable way-out. The resolution scheme developed by Sen (1976) and Suzumura (1983, Chapter 7) assigns a pivotal role to the "ethical" individual who adopts a unilaterally liberal attitude towards other individuals. The crucial fact we want to emphasize is that the existence of *at least one* ethical individual is enough to resolve the social conflict which is crystallized in the Pareto libertarian paradox and that, in sharp contrast with the widely held presumption, this unilateral ethical attitude does not in fact hurt the ethical individual himself.

To substantiate our claim, let us show how our resolution scheme may cope effectively with the *Lady Chatterley's Lover* case.[11] The crucial idea behind this scheme is that "the guarantee of a minimal amount of personal liberty may require that certain parts of individual rankings should not count in some specific social choices, and in some cases even the persons in question may agree with this" [Sen (1976, pp. 237–238)]. As an auxiliary step in formalizing this idea, we say that a pair $(x, y)$ of social states belongs to an individual $i$'s *protected sphere* if and only if the only difference between $x$ and $y$ is the personal matter of $i$. Thus, A's protected sphere in the *Lady Chatterley's Lover* case is given by $D_A = \{(r_0, r_A), (r_A, r_0)\}$ whereas B's protected sphere in the same case is specified by $D_B = \{(r_0, r_B), (r_B, r_0)\}$ An individual is said to be *liberal* if and only if he claims only those parts of his preferences that are compatible with all individuals' preferences over their respective protected spheres to count in social choice. An ethical individual, to whom we referred earlier, is the one who is liberal in this sense. Note that a liberal individual never drops his preferences over his own protected sphere, so that a liberal need not die a martyr for his unilateral faith in the ethical code of behaviour.

The formal definition of a liberal individual in the concrete context of the *Lady Chatterley's Lover* case may proceed as follows. Given the specified profile of individual preferences and the profile of individual protected spheres $(D_A, D_B)$, the crucial parts of individual preferences over their protected spheres are: $r_0$ is better than $r_A$ for Mr. A, and $r_B'$ is better than $r'$ for Mr. B. Since a liberal individual claims only those parts of his preferences that are compatible with everyone's preferences over their protected spheres to count in social choice, Mr. A (resp. Mr. B) claims that $r_0$ is socially better than $r'$ (resp. $_B r$ is socially better than $r$), whereas he refrains from claiming that $r_0$ is socially better than $r_B$ and $r_A$ is socially better than $r_B$ (resp. $r_A$ is socially better than $r_B$ and $r_A$ is socially better than $r_0$).[12]

Suppose that Mr. A is liberal and Mr. B is not liberal.[13] Then the social choice of $r_B$, viz. to give the copy of *Lady Chatterley's Lover* to Mr. B, is the resolution of the Pareto libertarian paradox in accordance with the Sen–Suzumura scheme. Two features of this resolution are worth emphasizing. First, it is clear that nobody's libertarian right is violated by this social choice. Secondly, although the social choice of $r_B$ violates the Pareto principle with respect to the bare preferences of Mr. A and Mr. B, it does *not* violate the Pareto principle with respect to those parts of individual preferences which they claim to be counted in social choices. Thus, the existence of a liberal individual does play an essential role in changing the Pareto libertarian paradox into a possibility result on rational social choice.

To understand the meaning of this resolution intuitively, it may help to follow the succeeding monologue of Mr. A: "Although I find Mr. B's tastes for books disgraceful, it is his own reading which is at stake and not mine, and I, as a rational liberal, respect his personal choices within his protected sphere. Therefore, I will not claim my preference for $r_0$ against $r_B$ as well as for $r_A$ against $r_B$ to count in social choices. As a result of this unilateral restraint on my part, $r_B$ turns out to be socially chosen. It is true that $r_B$ is actually the worst choice in accordance with my bare (socially unconscious) preferences. However, I don't feel sacrificed for my ethically conscious act as a rational liberal in a way I would have felt, had the social choice been $r_A$, which is in square contradiction with my preference for $r_0$ against $r_A$ within my protected sphere $D_A$."

A modest conclusion we want to draw from this exercise is this: There are cases where the unilateral adoption of an ethical code of behaviour by socially concerned agents may resolve social impasse. Furthermore, by following this act, the agent in question may not, and need not, die a martyr for his unconcerted ethical behaviour.

## IV. Defining the Competitive Arena

In his F. de Vries Lectures on *Economic, Legal, and Political Dimensions of Competition*, Demsetz (1982, p.1) rightly and agreeably pointed out that

# SOCIAL RESPONSIBILITY OF CORPORATIONS

"[c]ompetition occupies so important a position in economics that it is difficult to imagine economics as a social discipline without it. Stripped of competition, economics would consist largely of the maximizing calculus of an isolated Robinson Crusoe economy." But to agree on the universal *importance* of competition is one thing, and to agree on the universal *meaning* of competition is quite another. Indeed, there are strong claims by those who have studied competitive strategies of corporations from comparative viewpoint that the concept of competition cannot possibly be neutral, inorganic and universal. In other words, the meaning of competition depends crucially on the cultural context, and it is meaningless to talk abstractly about competition in general. According to this view, even the source of escalating trade frictions should be attributed, at least partly, to the cultural difference in the perception of what constitutes the rule and limit of competition.[14]

One aspect of this cultural relativism on competition seems to be relevant in our present context. There exists a clear distinction between insiders and outsiders in the perception of Japanese corporations, and insiders band together against outsiders so as to protect and promote their common interest as far as competition between insider group and outsider group is concerned. However, members within the insider group may be strongly opposed to each other in other aspects of business and social relationships.

Note, however, that the boundary that separates insiders and outsiders is anything but fixed, and the insider-outsider demarcation changes flexibly in accordance with the way the competitive arena is circumscribed. Thus, corporations within a specified industry compete fiercely with each other under "normal" circumstances. But they may form a business organization (with or without the auspices of the ministrial bureau, division, or section under whose jurisdiction the industry in question falls) so as to protect or promote their common interest against other industries. They may also form a cooperative R&D association under the Law on Technological Research Associations in Mining and Manufacturing Industries and collaborate in the pre-competitive R&D stage, subject to a clear understanding that they compete in the product market, with the purpose of coping effectively with foreign competitors.[15] In the latter case, not all competing firms are inducted into the insider group, so that the outsider group used to consist of competing foreign firms and domestic outsider firms. Even within a corporation, there are many factions which compete with each other for corporate control, but they unite power to compete effectively with outside corporations. Each member of a faction within a corporation takes part in rank-order competition with other members, but the faction behaves monolithically against other factions. This multi-layered structure of competition and cooperation in Japan may be called the *fractal structure of competition*. In the presence of this fractal structure, how

49

the insider-outsider demarcation is decided hinges squarely on how we specify the competitive arena. If the competitive arena is broadly (resp. narrowly) circumscribed like international competition for high-technology products (resp. intra-firm competition for employee promotion), there may be orderly cooperation among otherwise competing firms with the shared purpose of competitive survival in international arena (resp. rat race among candidates without restraint).

With this background in hand, let us make our third observation on the role and necessity of the universal code of corporate responsibility. If the code of ethical behaviour is meant to be universally applicable in the unspecified competitive arena, which is in fact the case in the Caux code of ethical behaviour, there is a strong case for agreement among Japanese corporations, at least in principle. But the actual implementation of the ethical code is always in the context of specific, narrowly circumscribed, competitive arena where outsiders and insiders are clearly demarcated. It is too optimistic, if not taking too much risk, to expect that the agreement in principle is a sure guarantee for the smooth implementation thereof in the specific context. In many contexts we are overly used to hearing people say that "I'm not against the principle, but I can't agree with each item."

## V. Concluding Remarks

Three observations we have made in this paper with respect to the Caux ethical code of corporate behaviour are in fact meant to be of much wider relevance. Our first observation warns against the danger that the call for orderly restriction of competition through socially responsible corporate behaviour may well be a disguised promotion of producer's benefit at the sacrifice of consumer's benefit. Our second observation is that, contrary to the widespread perception, *unilateral* adoption of an ethical code of behaviour need not be detrimental to the ethically concerned agent. Thus, we do not have to establish unanimous agreement on the ethical code of corporate behaviour in order for the code to play a crucial role in resolving social conflict in a competitive arena. Our third observation is that the general agreement on a universal code of ethical behaviour does not really guarantee its actual implementation in the concrete context which is of necessity specific. This is particularly so in the presence of the fractal structure of competition.

Note that our observations are not intended to be a criticism against the proposal of a universal ethical code of behaviour. Quite to the contrary, they are meant to serve the role of litmus paper for testing the viability thereof in the context of an actual competitive arena.

**Figure 1:**
**Response of the Cournot-Nash Equilibrium $q^N(n)$ to aChange in $n$**

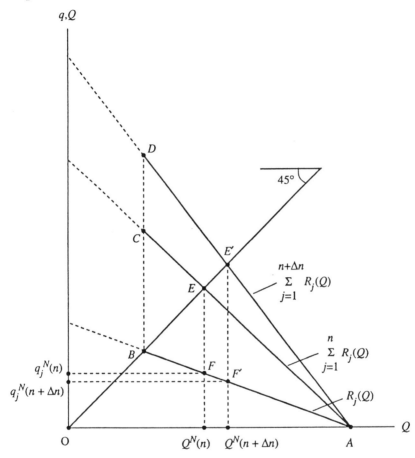

**Figure 2:**
**Excess Entry Theorem at the Margin**

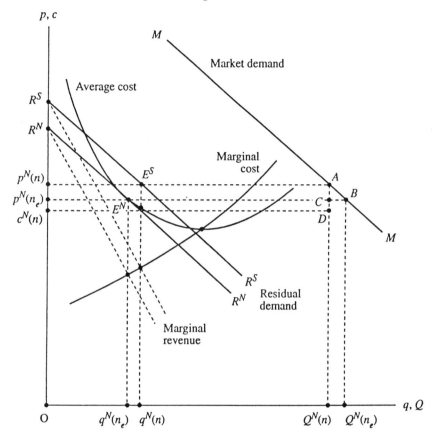

# SOCIAL RESPONSIBILITY OF CORPORATIONS

**Endnotes**

\*    Paper presented at The Third Annual SEEP Conference held at the Marriott School of Management, Brigham Young University, March 30 - April 1, 1995. Thanks are due to Professors Mark Casson, Richard De George, and Thomas Donaldson for their helpful comments on the first draft of this paper.

1    See *Nihon Keizai Shimbun*, January 19, 1995. It would not be out of place to point out that Mr. Kaku used to be one of the Vice Presidents of the Federation of Economic Organizations, and the CAUX ROUND TABLE was formed in 1986 as an attempt to reduce then escalating trade frictions with Japan. The full text of the Caux ethical code of behaviour is available as Caux Round Table (1994), and an article by TIM DICKSON in *Financial Times*, July 22, 1994 provides us with a neat explanation of the substance and background of this ethical code.

2    This second conventional wisdom has been widely and persistently held in Japan. Thus, it is quite to the point that Mr. Kaku attributed the third traditional value premise, viz. philosophy of co-existence, to Japanese society.

3    See ITOH *et al.* (1991), KOMIYA (1975), KOMIYA *et at.* (1988), and SUZUMURA (1995b) for the concept of excessive competition in Japan.

4    Note that the industry we are visualizing in this section is characterized by the existence of fixed cost, homogeneous product, and oligopoly. As KOMIYA (1975, p.213) aptly pointed out, the so-called "excessive competition" in post-war Japan tended to develop in industries featured precisely by these three characteristics. In this sense, our simple model seems to be quite appropriate for the purpose of examining the theoretical possibility of "excessive competition" from the viewpoint of potential social welfare.

5    Although market failure in the presence of increasing returns is well known, the problem we have identified in the main text is of quite a different nature. For an account of the standard market failure argument, the readers are referred to ARROW (1983, Chapter 7), HAHN (1982) and SEN (1993).

6    This conflict between consumer's benefit and producer's benefit is brought into relief in Figure 2, where MM denotes the inverse demand curve for the whole industry, whereas RR denotes the residual demand curve for the individual firm. It is clear that $q^N(n_e)$ and $Q^N(n_e)$ are, respectively, the individual firm output and the industry output at the long-run Cournot-Nash equilibrium. By definition, we must have $Q^N(n_e) = n_e q^N(n_e)$. To verify these facts, we have only to observe that the marginal cost curve crosses the marginal revenue curve derived from the residual demand curve RR at $q^N(n_e)$ and that profits at $q^N(n_e)$ are zero.

    Suppose now that the number of competitors is decreased marginally from $n_e$ to $n$. Since smaller number of firms are sharing the same market demand, the residual demand curve for the individual firm must shift up to $R'R'$, so that the new Cournot-Nash equilibrium to be defined by $q^N(n)$ and $Q^N(n) = nq^N(n)$ must satisfy $q^N(n_e) < q^N(n)$ and $Q^N(n_e) > Q^N(n)$.

    It is clear that this decrease in the number of firms from $n_e$ to $n$ brings about two conflicting effects on the potential social welfare measured by net market surplus. The first is the effect on *allocative efficiency* due to the concomitant decrease in consumers' surplus, which results from the increase in equilibrium price from $p^N(n_e)$ to $p^N(n)$. In Figure 2, this negative effect is measured by the area $Ap^N(n)p^N(n_e)C$. The second is the effect on *production efficiency* due to the better exploitation of residual scale economies, which results from the increase in individual output from $q^N(n_e)$ to $q^N(n)$. In Figure 2, this positive effect is measured by the area $Ap^N(n)c^N(n)D$. The net effect on social welfare is given by the difference between the two, viz. the area $Bp^N(n_e)c^N(n)D$ less the area ABC. Since the latter is clearly of higher order infinitesimal in comparison with the former, the net effect turns out to be positive, vindicating the excess entry theorem.

7   Our analysis has focussed on the consequential evaluation of long-run market forces. For fuller evaluation of the pros and cons of intervention into market mechanism, we should also pay due attention to the non-consequential (deontological) evaluation of market mechanism. See, among others, BROOME (1992), KNIGHT (1923), MATTHEWS (1981), MCNULTY (1968), NOZICK (1994), and SEN (1993).

8   A classical statement of this presumption is due to ARROW (1973), who asserted that "[i]t provides some assurance to any one firm that the firms with which it is in competition will also accept the same responsibility. If a firm has some code imposed from the outside, there is some expectation that other firms will obey it too and therefore there is some assurance that it need not fear any excessive cost to its good behavior . . . . After all, an ethical code, however much it may be in the interest of all, is . . . not in the interest of any one firm. The code may be of value to the running of the system as a whole, it may be of value to all firms if all firms maintain it, and yet it will be to the advantage of any one firm to cheat—in fact the more so, the more other firms are sticking to it." According to this view, the competitive firms are trapped by the impasse of prisoners' dilemma with respect to the adoption of an ethical code of behaviour.

9   For more general account of the Pareto libertarian paradox, the readers are referred to SEN (1970, Chapter 6*; 1976) and SUZUMURA (1983, Chapter 7).

10   There is a recent controversy concerning the formal method of capturing the contents of libertarian rights. For our present purpose, however, it is not necessary to go into details of this controversy. The interested readers are referred to GAERTNER, PATTANAIK and SUZUMURA (1992), NOZICK (1974), PATTANAIK and SUZUMURA (1994; 1995), SEN (1992) and SUZUMURA (1990).

11   Needless to say, the workability of the Sen-Suzumura resolution scheme is far beyond this example. See SUZUMURA (1983, Theorem 7.3) for more general account of the effectiveness of this resolution scheme.

12   The reason why Mr. A (resp. Mr. B) should refrain from claiming his preference for $r_0$ against $r_A$ (resp. for $r_B$ against $r_0$) to count in social choice is straightforward and requires no further comment. Less obvious is the reason why Mr. A (resp. Mr. B) should refrain from claiming his preference for $r_A$ against $r_B$ to count in social choice. Note, however, that Mr. A's (resp. Mr. B's) preference for $r_A$ against $r_B$, if it were claimed to be relevant for social choice, would entail his induced preference for $r_0$

# SOCIAL RESPONSIBILITY OF CORPORATIONS

against $r_0$ (resp. for $r_A$ against $r_0$) in view of his expressed preference for $r_0$ against $r_A$ (resp. for $r_B$ against $r_0$), coupled with the transitive rationality of his preferences, thereby contradicting his liberal refrainment on $(r_0, r_B)$ [resp. $(r_A, r_0)$]. Thus, strictly speaking, our liberal individual should be called a *rational* liberal.

13   The case where Mr. A is not liberal and Mr. B is liberal, or the case where both Mr. A and Mr. B are liberal, can be discussed in a similar way.

14   See, for example, ITAMI, KAGONO and ITOH (1993).

15   SUZUMURA and GOTO (1995) crystallize some salient features of cooperative R&D among firms competing in the product market with special reference to post-war Japanese experience. See, also, SUZUMURA (1992) for the theory of cooperative R&D.

## References

ARROW, K. J.: *Social Choice and Individual Values*, New York (John Wiley & Sons), Second Edition, 1963.

ARROW, K. J.: "Social Responsibility and Economic Efficiency", *Public Policy*, 21 (1973), pp.303-317.

ARROW, K. J.: *General Equilibrium*. Vol.2 of Collected Papers of Kenneth J. Arrow, Cambridge, Mass. (The Belknap Press of Harvard University Press) 1983.

BEAUCHAMP, T. L. and N. E. BOWIE: *Ethical Theory and Business*, Englewood Cliffs, New Jersey (Prentice Hall) Third Edition, 1988.

BROOME, J.: "Deontology and Economics", *Economics and Politics*, 8 (1992) pp.269-282.

CAUX ROUND TABLE: *Principles for Business*, Minneapolis (Minnesota Center for Corporate Responsibility) 1994.

DEGEORGE, R. T.: *Business Ethics*, New York (Macmillan Publishing Company), Second Edition, 1986.

DEMSETZ, H.: *Economic, Legal, and Political Dimensions of Competition*, Amsterdam (North--Holland) 1982.

FRIEDMAN, M.: *Capitalism and Freedom*, Chicago (The University of Chicago Press) 1962.

GAERTNER, W., PATTANAIK, P. K. and K. SUZUMURA : "Individual Rights Revisited", *Economica*, 59 (1992), pp.161-177.

HAHN, F.: "Reflections on the Invisible Hand", *Lloyds Bank Review*, 144 (1982), pp.1-21.

HAYEK, F. VON: *Individualism and Economic Order*, Chicago (The University of Chicago Press) 1948.

ITAMI, T., KAGONO, T. and M. ITOH, (Eds.): *Readings in Japanese Corporation System*, 4 vols., Tokyo (Yuhikaku) 1993. In Japanese.

ITOH, M., KIYONO, K., OKUNO-FUJIWARA, M. and K. SUZUMURA: *Economic Analysis of Industrial Policy*, San Diego (Academic Press) 1991.

# KOTARO SUZUMURA

KNIGHT, F, H..: "The Ethics of Competition", *Quarterly Journal of Economics*, 37 (1923), pp. 579-624.

KOMIYA, R.: "Planning in Japan", in: BORNSTEIN, M., (Ed.): *Economic Planning: East and West*, Cambridge, Mass. (Ballinger) 1975, pp.189-227.

KOMIYA, R., OKUNO, M. and K. SUZUMURA, (Eds.): *Industrial Policy of Japan*, San Diego (Academic Press) 1988.

LABICH, K.: "The New Crisis in Business Ethics", *Fortune*, 125(8), April 20 (1992) pp.167-176.

MANKIW, N. G. and M. D. WHINSTON: "Free Entry and Social Inefficiency", *Rand Journal of Economics*, 17 (1986), pp.48-58.

MATTHEWS, R. C. O. : "Morality, Competition and Efficiency", *Manchester School of Economic and Social Studies*, 49 (1981), pp.289-309.

MCNULTY, P. J.: "Economic Theory and the Meaning of Competition", *Quarterly Journal of Economics*, 82 (1968), pp.639-656.

NOE, T. H. and M. J. ROBELLO: "The Dynamics of Business Ethics and Economic Activity", *American Economic Review*, 84 (1994), pp.531-547.

NOZICK, R.: *Anarchy, State and Utopia*, Oxford (Basil Blackwell) 1974.

PATTANAIK, P. K. and K. SUZUMURA: "Rights, Welfarism and Social Choice", *American Economic Review: Papers and Proceedings*, 84 (1994), pp.438-439.

PATTANAIK, P. K. and K. SUZUMURA: "Individual Rights and Social Evaluation: A Conceptual Framework", Working Paper, The Institute of Economic Research, Hitotsubashi University (1995). Forthcoming in *Oxford Economic Papers*.

SEN, A. K.: "A Game-Theoretic Analysis of Theories of Collectivism in Allocation", in T. MAJUMDAR, (Ed.): *Growth and Choice*, London (Oxford University Press) 1967, pp.1-17.

SEN, A. K.: *Collective Choice and Social Welfare*, San Francisco (Holden-Day) 1970.

SEN, A. K.: "Liberty, Unanimity and Rights", *Economica*, 43 (1976), pp.217-245.

SEN, A. K.: *Resources, Values and Development*, Oxford (Blackwell) 1984.

SEN, A. K.: "Minimal Liberty", *Economica*, 59 (1992), pp.139-159.

SEN, A. K.: "Markets and Freedoms: Achievements and Limitations of the Market Mechanism in Promoting Individual Freedoms", *Oxford Economic Papers*, 45 (1993) pp.519-541.

SUZUMURA, K.: "On the Consistency of Libertarian Claims", *Review of Economic Studies*, 45 (1978), pp.329-342.

SUZUMURA, K.: *Rational Choice, Collective Decisions, and Social Welfare*, New York (Cambridge University Press) 1983.

SUZUMURA, K.: "Alternative Approaches to Libertarian Rights in the Theory of Social Choice", in K. J. ARROW (Ed.): *Issues in Contemporary Economics*, Vol.1, *Markets and Welfare*, London (Macmillan) 1990, pp.215-242.

SUZUMURA, K.: "Cooperative and Noncooperative R&D in an Oligopoly with Spillovers", *American Economic Review*, 82 (1992), pp.1307-1320.

SUZUMURA, K.: *Competition, Commitment, and Welfare*, Oxford (Clarendon Press) 1995a.

SUZUMURA, K.: "Formal and Informal Measures for Controlling Competition in Japan: Historical Overview and Theoretical Evaluation", Working Paper, The Institute of

Economic Research, Hitotsubashi University (1995b).

SUZUMURA, K. and A. GOTO: "Collaborative R&D and Competition Policy: Economic Analysis in the Light of Japanese Experience", Working Paper, The Institute of Economic Research, Hitotsubashi University, 1995.

SUZUMURA, K. and K. KIYONO: "Entry Barriers and Economic Welfare", *Review of Economic Studies*, 45 (1987), pp.157-167.

Chapter 4

# Ecology and Ethics in the Economy

PETER KOSLOWSKI

It is the task of the economy to efficiently organize the satisfaction of consumer demand. Economic theory gives criteria by which efficiency can be measured. The task of ethics in the economy is to guarantee that justice is observed in the interactions of the economy and in its relationship with the natural environment. The ethical principle of justice calls also for open and fair chances to enter contestable markets. It requires the impartial distribution of the opportunities to develop themselves between the individuals. The addressee of the ethical demands might be an individual in the market as well as the lawmakers and politicians in the state. In the economy, ethics is neither limited to entrepreneurs nor to the government but directed towards private commerce and industry as well as to the legislature and the state's economic actions.

# ECOLOGY AND ETHICS IN THE ECONOMY

## I. The Theoretical Foundations: Theory of Ethics in the Economy: Ethical Economy

Ideas about the role of ethics in the economy must combine considerations from economic theory as well as from ethical theory. An ethical theory about the cultural system called economy that does not include economic arguments stays precocious. An economic theory about the economy that does not include ethical arguments about fairness and justice will fall victim to economism. It presents efficiency, which is only part of the aspects of the good, as *the* entire definition of the good. Economic and ethical theory must unite to form the theory of ethical economy.[1]

In the market there are not only economic but also ethical expectations and standards for action. Therefore, a complete and realistic market theory cannot only be „economic economics" but must extend to an ethical economy as the theory of the ethical framework and the ethical prerequisites for cooperation and trade in the market.

### 1. Ethical Economy as a Normative Theory of Business Ethics

Ethical economy as an ethical theory of market transactions generates the synthesis of ethics and economics. It stands between the pure economic theory on the one hand and political economy on the other hand. The theory of political economy tries to understand the state-constructed framework of the market economy and the conditions of the market exchange enacted by state and law. Ethical and political economy expand the economic theory of the market to an extensive theory of the social market economy in which the ethical and political preconditions of the market economy as well as those of social welfare are portrayed.

---

1   See also P. KOSLOWSKI: *Prinzipien der Ethischen Ökonomie. Grundlegung der Wirtschaftsethik und der auf die Ökonomie bezogenen Ethik* (Principles of Ethical Economy, Foundations of Economic Ethics), Tübingen (J.C.B. Mohr [Paul Siebeck]) 1988, 2nd ed. 1994; and P. KOSLOWSKI: *Ethik des Kapitalismus* (The Ethics of Capitalism), with a commentary by James M. Buchanan, Tübingen (J.C.B. Mohr [Paul Siebeck]) 1982, 5th ed. 1995. Abridged English translation in: S. PEJOVICH (Ed.): *Philosophical and Economic Foundations of Capitalism*, Lexington (Lexington Books) 1983, pp. 33-64. Unabridged English translation Berlin (Springer) 1996.

# PETER KOSLOWSKI

The role of ethical standards in the economy is to regulate the market and fence off market failure caused by unethical operations. Ethical economy shows that the alternative to market failure is not the immediate transition to state-controlled coordination and allocation, which bears the danger of the same mistakes being repeated by the state but that ethics is a remedy for market failure, whether caused by the state or by the market itself. The ethical economy and the role of ethics in the state as well as in commerce and industry prove that, as Aristotle knew, economics, ethics and politics are not incompatible and hostile but complementary and that economical, ethical and political theory must be brought to a synthesis.

The system of right laws, created by the state according to ethical and economical consideration, is not only an order of constraints but also an order of willingness. The order of the market economy is not only an order of free discretion, under which everybody does as he pleases and maximizes his profit but is also an order of obligations and „oughts" that tries to realize fairness and justice in the economy. In the perspective of an extensive social theory, a "Complete Social Science," it becomes clear that the market cannot be a zone free of ethics and the state not a realm without economizing[2] but that ethics *and* economics must be considered by the decision makers in politics as well as in business and industry.

Ethical economy is the theory of the synthesis of the economic criterion of efficiency and the ethical criterion of justice in exchange and pricing. It adopts from economics the microeconomic theory of rational action and from general ethics the ethical theory of justice as the virtue and duty in exchange relationships. The allocative or efficiency criterion is only one aspect of the good and must be supplemented by the fairness criterion *within* the analysis of economic action and exchange.

In addition to the criterion of efficiency, the ethical principle of justice demands a) proper conduct and b) fair exchange in economic actions and interactions. The efficient *and* fair solution must be realized in the marketplace. Proper conduct means doing justice to the nature of the matter of the economy. Fair exchange demands that the just price and mutually beneficial exchange are realized.[3]

---

2   See P. KOSLOWSKI: *Gesellschaft und Staat. Ein unvermeidlicher Dualismus* (Society and State: An Inevitable Dualism), Stuttgart (Klett-Cotta) 1982; and P. KOSLOWSKI: *Die Ordnung der Wirtschaft. Studien zur Praktischen Philosophie und Politischen Ökonomie* (The Order of the Economy. Studies on Practical Philosophy and Political Economy), Tübingen (J.C.B. Mohr [Paul Siebeck]) 1994.

3   See P. KOSLOWSKI: *Wirtschaft als Kultur. Wirtschaftskultur und Wirtschaftsethik in der Postmoderne* (The Economy as Culture. Economic Culture and Economic Ethics in Postmodern Times), Wien (Edition Passagen) 1989; and P. KOSLOWSKI: *Gesellschaftliche Koordination. Eine ontologische und kulturwissenschaftliche*

# ECOLOGY AND ETHICS IN THE ECONOMY

The theory of ethical economy assumes that the ethical motivation and selective criteria of ethics are of higher rank and obligation than the economic motivation and selective criteria. They overlie the economic motive and goal of efficiency and utility maximization. In normal business there is no conflict between ethics and economics provided that the economic institutions are just. Thus, in normal business, ethics usually need not be emphasized. It is just a matter of course. In a perfectly competitive market, the market price is the just price that the traders must follow, and realizing the market price means realizing the just price. In other imperfect markets, the prevailing price has the presumption for itself to be just. There are, however, situations under which the market price is not just since the conditions of its formation violate higher ethical norms like human rights or vital interests of the population etc. Under these circumstances, the theory of ethical economy must demand the change of market conditions on the institutional level and the ethical consideration of fair exchange by the individual and his or her adaptation of the individual price to the just price on the personal level.

## a) Overdeterminedness of Economic Decisions

Ethics and economics co-determine the conditions of ethico-economic rationality in production and consumption decisions. They are normally not mutually exclusive or contradicting each other but complementary. To use the term "overdeterminedness" from Freud's interpretation of dreams[4], one could say that human action is "overdetermined" by ethical, economic, and aesthetic determining factors that are usually not in conflict with each other but in coexistence and complementarity.

It must also be emphasized that ethics as well as economics are usually not an order of the ought or compulsion (*Sollensordnung*) but an order of intention and affirmation (*Wollensordnung*). It is only in situations of conflict between economic utility or profit maximization and ethical demands of justice that the ethical is felt as a constraint on the pursuit of economic action since it than overrules economic self-interest. The aim of economic ethics must be to form economic institutions in which the ethical rules are felt as motives and ethics is considered to be an order of willingness, not of compulsion.

---

*Theorie der Marktwirtschaft* (Social Coordination. An Ontological and Cultural Theory of the Market), Tübingen (J.C.B. Mohr [Paul Siebeck]) 1991.

4   S. FREUD: *Die Traumdeutung* (1900) (The Interpretation of Dreams), Frankfurt a. M. (S. Fischer) 1982.

61

# PETER KOSLOWSKI

## b) Economic Ethics as Inducement to Economic Law

Economic ethics is the inducement to economic law. It prepares and tests new law and it persuades to comply with existing law. Ethics demands and furthers the attention and respect for the principles of fair and efficient business, the *attentio* to the rules and attitudes, and it requires and strengthens the intention and inclination to follow these principles, the *intentio recta* to realize good business and management. Economic ethics aims at the right intention or *intentio recta* of business.

The right intention plays as vital a role in business as in all professions. The acting person must have the intention to use his or her knowledge and expertise in the proper way since the professional has better knowledge then the non-professional about the possible misuses of his or her expertise. The stock exchange broker or banker can use his or her knowledge to stabilize or destabilize a currency or market. "Everything depends on the right economic intention."[5] This intention is, however, not controllable or enforceable from the outside and by the law. The law can only aim at the external behavior, not at the inner motives. Since the inner motives matter, ethics matters and cannot be substituted by the law. According to H. Kantorowicz, the law is the totality of social rules that prescribe external behavior and are seen as justiciable. Justiciable rules are rules that are apt to be applied by a branch of the judiciary in due process.[6] Business ethics formulates norms that can shape the inner motives and it includes norms that are not justiciable and therefore transcend the law.

Business ethics forms an order of obligation, of internal and nonjusticiable obligations, that lies between the rules of economic efficiency, the rules of the economic game, and the rules of economic law. Not everything that is not justiciable is allowed or at the free disposal of the acting persons. The law formulates only an ethical minimum that must be supplemented by ethically sound practices and attitudes in the economy. Plato writes in his *Laws* that the laws are of two kinds: the law in the proper sense and the proemium or introduction to the law (*Leges*722e). The former is a tyrannical prescription, the latter, the proemium of

---

5   Cf. TH. BRAUER: *Produktionsfaktor Arbeit. Erwägungen zur modernen Arbeitslehre* (Factor of Production Labor. Reflections on the Modern Theory of Labor), Jena (Gustav Fischer) 1925, p. 190: *"Es kommt alles auf die Wirtschaftsgesinnung an."* Brauer's sentence is also quoted as motto in O. VON NELL-BREUNING: *Grundzüge der Börsenmoral* (Principles of an Ethics of the Stock Exchange), Freiburg im Breisgau (Herder) 1928, p. 1.

6   H. KANTOROWICZ: *Der Begriff des Rechts* (The Concept of Law), Göttingen (Vandenhoeck & Ruprecht) 1963, p. 90. Original: *The Definition of Law*, Cambridge (Cambridge University Press) 1958.

the ethical rules to the laws, formulate propositions of persuasion that try to persuade to the free acceptance of and compliance with the rules and virtues.[7] To the different kinds of rules, the different kinds of sanctions correspond, economic, ethical and legal ones. The violation of the economic rules is sanctioned by financial losses. The violation of ethical rules, of moral and cultural rules, is sanctioned by bad conscience and reputation, the violation of laws by legal penalty.

### 2. Ethical Economy as a Positive Theory of Social Coordination

The sequence of economic, ethical and legal rules and sanctions leads to the second part of ethical economy that is formed by the positive theory of social coordination.[8] Ethical economy as an ethico-economic theory of social coordination analyses the coordination of self-interested action, particularly in markets, by means of economic, ethical, and legal motivation, rules, and sanctions. The question is here under which conditions social coordination by the pursuit of self-interest succeeds and where it breaks down. Ethical economy gives the conditions under which economy failure occurs in situations of prisoners' dilemma, under which conditions this economy failure can be corrected by ethics, and under which conditions ethics failure occurs and can be compensated by law and religion. To give an example: applied to the capital market or stock exchange, ethical economy analyses under which conditions business ethics can correct unethical practices like insider trading, under which conditions the business ethics of financial markets breaks down itself, and under which conditions business ethics must be corrected by criminal law.

## II. Compensating Market Insufficiencies

The twofold focus of ethics on the economy and on the state becomes visible at the problem of justice and of the fair balancing between burdens and rewards in state and society as well as at the problem of balancing between human needs and those of nature in the ecology.

In the following this problem of counterbalancing certain market processes shall be illustrated by the example of a government institution dedicated to the

---

7   Cf. KOSLOWSKI: *Gesellschaft und Staat* (1982), p. 42-46.
8   P. KOSLOWSKI: *Prinzipien der Ethischen Ökonomie* (1988), p. 20-45.

financing of measures counterbalancing certain effects and insufficiencies of the market process. In Germany, a large federal government institution is dedicated to the financing of the fair balance of burdens. It is called *Deutsche Ausgleichsbank*[9] (German Bank for Equalization and Compensation). Its foundation and task as a financing institute, originally for the compensation paid to individuals for damage and losses during and immediately after World War II, reveal the following: equalizing between economic interests and the protection of the natural environment creates a permanent ethical task of balancing - for the private sector as well as for the state's economic actions. According to its definition, stated in § 4 of the Law Concerning Tasks and Business of the *Ausgleichsbank*, the bank shall become active "equalizing within the social market economy in those situations of the economical process where important economic tasks are handled only insufficiently by the free market forces."[10] The bank is a government institution for balancing market failures or insufficiencies.

The first market insufficiency the bank had to fight was the compensation for the refugees from those parts of Germany occupied by the Soviet Union and Poland at the end of World War II. For the market, the new and unequal distribution of wealth between the West Germans and the refugees who had often lost everything through war and expulsion was just one of the many different possible distributions of wealth. The market cannot afford different price policies for refugees and non-refugees but must maintain equal prices for everyone. So government and society were challenged to conduct the redistribution of property between the penniless refugees and the happy well-off. The "burden-balancing" tried to equalize unequal damages, no matter who the guilty party was. The nation as liable party for the dangers of the war emphasized solidarity and tried to equalize the unequal burdens caused by the lost war and by shifting wealth from those who had resources to those who had lost everything.

That process has long since been completed and the legislature has assigned new equalizing duties to the former Bank for Equalization and Compensation of Burdens of the War. These new assignments of an equilibration of burdens include the balancing of financial burdens that arise from the problem of facilitating the

---

9   The German word *Ausgleich* comprises six aspects of balancing: 1. counterbalancing, 2. equilibration, 3. right reciprocation, 4. compensation, 5. equalization, 6. levelling.

10   DEUTSCHE AUSGLEICHSBANK: *Kreditinstitut des Bundes für Mittelstand, Umweltschutz, Soziale Aufgaben*, Schriftenreihe Heft 1, Bonn o.J., S. 7 (GERMAN BANK FOR EQUALIZATION AND COMPENSATION: Federal Credit Institute for Middle Sized Enterprises, Environmental Protection, Social Tasks, Series of brochures, vol. 1, Bonn, p. 7).

access to markets, from the task of environmental protection and from the political goal to facilitate the integration of immigrants, asylum seekers and homeless foreigners. The remarkable similarity of these new tasks is that they describe three areas in which, according to the lawmaker, the market principle does not fail completely but is definitely insufficient.

The legislature figures that market allocation is failing or insufficient for opening the access to market for new middle-sized enterprises and for more precarious undertakings („venture capital"), for environmental protection and for the integration of immigrants and foreigners permitted residence. The three cases may not show complete market failure, yet do display market insufficiency and inadequacy. Thus the bank proves by its very existence the necessity for correctives to market insufficiencies. The term "market insufficiencies" is used rather than the term "market failure," for the latter gives the wrong impression of a total market collapse and the availability of a failure-proof alternative, this being the state. Especially in recent years, however, it has become clear that state failure and misconceptions are as frequent and create even more critical impacts than it is the case with partial market failure. There is a considerable asymmetry between market and state failure: market failure is correctable by the state - state failure is only correctable with more difficulty since the state is the highest order institution. Ever since the collapse of the Real Existing State Socialism in Eastern Europe, the scientific term "market failure" can no longer be used as carelessly as a few years ago.

Still, the tasks of the Bank for Equalization and Compensation show that counterbalancing and compensation are necessary for certain weaknesses in the market coordination. These compensations of the market allocation, though, are not done only in the social welfare field - the classic area of government policy - but also by equalizing insufficiencies of market coordination that occur because of measures in environmental protection and the facilitation of market access for new small and middle sized enterprises. Adding equalizing state interaction in the fields of environmental protection and market access expands the pure market economy not only to a "social market economy" but to an "ecological and contestable market economy." The bank equalizes insufficiencies of the market economy in market access and environmental protection by using political means that are nevertheless compatible with the market process, the means of providing easy credit and investing programs.

The bank's business shows that the separation of autonomous market allocation and the government-directed framework of social welfare policy that used to be the basic concept of the social market economy no longer does justice to the interaction between the market process and government action on the one hand and between both of them with the ecology on the other hand. The new interactions between the market forces and the state in facilitating market access and the furthering of environmental protection demonstrate a new pattern of cooperation between business and government. They furthermore make visible that, in the theory of the social market economy, the ecological and ethical dimensions must be added to the social dimension of the market economy. The "social market economy" (*soziale Marktwirtschaft*) must be extended to the "ecological and ethical market economy." The term "eco-social market economy" (*ökosoziale Marktwirtschaft*) used by some authors should be avoided, since it is a rather ugly Greek-Latin-hybrid.

The effects generated by market allocation on the ecological equilibration and on the accessibility of markets must be included in a complete theory of the ecological, ethical and social market economy. There are needs for the compensation of market insufficiencies not only in social welfare but also in the ecological and the ethical-cultural field. The ecological and ethical-cultural needs for counterbalancing, particularly under conditions of a larger formation of private wealth, are as important for equalization as the social welfare needs.

Since the collective bargaining between unions and employers takes care of the income distribution and the welfare needs, social welfare needs not be the main objectives of governmental corrective actions anymore. Rather, "ecological and ethical justice" must find an equitable place next to social justice or might even replace it. Classical social welfare policy looked for the social balance between the rich and the poor, the employed and the unemployed, the healthy and the sick, and between young people and senior citizens by means of social security and by progressive taxation. In this sense, balance meant chiefly compensation of income losses. Social welfare policy is equalization as compensation for society's weak and financially challenged. The new ecological policy is ecological equalization, compensation for the inability of the natural environment to assert its interests against human interests.

### III. Just Equalization as Compensation and Reconciliation

Right reciprocation and compensation are basic phenomena of human existence individual and societal. Without them a society cannot survive.[11] The term "equalization" can have two main different meanings. On the one hand, it means the

---

11 About the term "compensation" see O. MARQUARD's article "Compensation" in: *Historisches Wörterbuch der Philosophie* (Historical Encyclopedia of Philosophy), ed. by J. Ritter and K. Gründer, Basel (Schwabe) 1976, vol. 4, p. 912-981.

equalization of differences or contradictions by levelling and removing them. Air and water entering a vacuum equalize the different pressure levels between the vacuum and its environment - the incongruity is levelled and disappears. Levelling is not to be considered good in itself but is a rather ambivalent thing.

In the social sciences, the term equalization rather means compensation for damage or a disadvantage than levelling and balancing. Here, equalization means reimbursement or restitution, restoration of integrity. In general, social equalization does not make discrepancies disappear but alleviates them and turns them into reconciled discrepancies. Social equalization means easing disadvantages and reconciling discrepancies. Equalization is at once compensation and reconciliation, compensation being mostly the prerequisite for reconciliation.

A social discrepancy requiring equalization usually remains even after compensation and reconciliation. Social and economical equalization is not on a mechanical-energetic level of making differentials vanish but it is a mediation between *rights*. Every social or economical equalization refers to existing rights. No equalization is possible without taking into account existing rights or, if they need to be defined first, ethically and legally justifiable rights: no compensation without justification, no redistribution without reasons, and no eminent domain without at least partial or symbolic compensation. The social problem of equalization is a question of fairness and not of levelling quantitative differences.

Not all disadvantages can be balanced; not all drawbacks can be compensated. A comprehensive compensation for coincidental adversity and the fate of birthplace and biography would be totalitarian. The fate of a human individual and his/her possessions must be acknowledged and cannot be completely equalized with that of other people. Even the compensation for the refugees could not be more than partial reimbursement for lost belongings and could neither lead to the restitution of the *status quo ante* nor provide equation with the citizens of West Germany.

The insight that compensations can never be complete must also be applied to the aim of developing equal conditions of living in the newly united Germany. The West Germans cannot reimburse the East Germans for all property losses and welfare cutbacks generated by forty years of socialist rule in the former German Democratic Republic (GDR). Equalization between East and West Germany can only be similar to that between refugees and non-refugees. It can balance the losses caused by the lesser economical output in the former German Democratic Republic only as far as it is absolutely necessary for the existence of East German individuals and families. In all fairness, in the new "Lands" the equalization can only guarantee savings and pension entitlement and only to a certain extent. If the Federal Republic of Germany wanted to equalize the financial gap between West and East Germany by governmental redistribution, the equalization as well as the people's solidarity would be overtaxed. The Federal Republic of Germany cannot take the blame for this gap since it has been generated by history. Only by economic growth and promotion of commerce and industry can the differences in wealth be levelled, not by transfers. It is not an ethical or moral statute but a problem of economic policy and financial balance that all German Lands have to solve together on a long-term basis.

A total compensation of human sufferings and detriments is only possible in the theological-transcendent belief in remuneration for injustice and suffering by divine justice. Therefore, theology develops the theory of redemption and reconstruction in terms of exchange, retribution and fair remittance.

Equalization between conflicting interests and claims is a question of justice. Reimbursement must be fair. This is the same for human interaction with the natural environment as well as for the access to and the exchange in markets. The development of the tasks of the German Bank of Equalization and Compensation from the social to the ecological equalization and the emphasis on environmental protection shows that the claims for ecological and ethical justice become equal to the needs for social justice and it reveals that ecology and ethics play an ever-growing role in the economy.

## IV. The Inevitability of the Question of Justice

A fair action or solution is one that can claim approval. "A fair decision" in colloquial language means that the decision can claim approval and demand approval of the involved parties and observers. The statement "That is a fair decision" indicates that claims and conflicts were mediated in such a way that every impartial observer or judge ("the impartial spectator in everybody's breast") could agree even when asked to change the roles between plaintiff and defendant.

Fair is a solution that anticipates consensus, i.e., seeks approval of all those who have an undistorted perception of the situation. Justice does not mean actual approval of all empirical subjects at all times, for the perspectives of the involved parties are always distorted and one-sided because of their interests. A fair decision must be made under conditions of impartiality and objectivity by well-informed individuals who are willing to create these conditions and try to anticipate a consensus under these conditions.

Justice is the characteristic of a wise judge who weighs up the claims of all parties and then decides impartially, trying to create a balance between the diverging interests. Accordingly, justice demands that the economic decision makers impartially, objectively and benevolently weigh up the claims deriving from the rights and performances of the others they do business with.

# ECOLOGY AND ETHICS IN THE ECONOMY

Justice demands from all decision makers that they investigate and decide impartially and seek the approval of all involved parties. Justice demands from those concerned by the decision that they agree to the decision and follow it when they have considered it to be fair. These two claims form a constant factor and a dilemma in human societies and economic systems that cannot be resolved, contrary to the hopes of the Marxist and the Libertarian utopia. The question of justice is permanent; it will not vanish even in a perfect economic organization. Justice would only become unnecessary if there were no more economic scarcity.

Marxism claims, or one should say, claimed, to provide the solution to this problem. Achieving affluence in the perfect communist society through the reorganization of the means of production makes conflicts, equalization of interests and the demand for justice unnecessary because after elimination of all scarcity there will be enough for everybody to satisfy all claims without any concessions. Marx' motto "To each according to his skills, to each according to his needs" is after the elimination of the scarcity of resources not any longer a problem of fairness but the principle of a perfect society and the "self-realization without justice" generated by that society.

For the present, which is a post-Utopian and post-Marxist age, and for the economy working under conditions of scarcity of internal and external resources, the question of justice remains unabated. The principle of justice cannot be replaced either by the principle of freedom or by the principle of equality. Justice must take aspects of freedom and equality into consideration but is not identical with them.

Fair is a reasonable and agreeable settlement of equalizing--not of levelling-- between conflicting, historically grown and historically caused claims for economic services and goods. There are conflicts that cannot be postponed on the grounds of the expectation that the future growth of the corporation or of the whole economy would bring more wealth for redistribution. There are also historically caused conflicts between individuals that cannot be solved by asking the individuals to give up their historically caused identity in order to become a perfect partner in a discourse free of domination and to transform their historical rights into interests that can be generalized. If there are rights that are historically caused and/or conflicts of interest the resolution of which cannot be postponed to later periods of time in which growth might facilitate redistribution, the only solution is to weigh up the situation fairly and to settle claims by right reciprocation.

# PETER KOSLOWSKI

## V. Justice in Economic Interactions

As far as the private sector, production and exchange in the market are concerned, the demand for justice means that proper conduct and fair trade must be realized in the market.[12]

### 1. Justice as Proper Conduct

Economic ethics demand that decision makers act properly to the nature of the matter, i.e., appropriate to the functions of the economy. Economic ethics in their negative formulation demand the cessation of unethical practice such as unfair competition, bribery and corruption. Positively formulated, they demand: act appropriately to the purpose of the economy! Obey economically proper conduct! The purpose of the economy is to enable the self-realization of the individuals in the economic interactions and to secure the satisfaction of effective consumer demand. This purpose can only be fulfilled by realizing the efficient allocation of all resources and by doing justice to the matter and the persons of the economy. Efficient allocation requires the absence of unethical practices by individuals. It does not come into being automatically even if unethical practice is widespread.

The demand for proper conduct does not only mean obeying the economy's rules and regulations but refers also to the contents of the intentions and plans of people in business. A decision maker in an economy must be oriented towards the purpose of the economy. He or she must bring into his or her intentions the purpose of the economy, the satisfaction of effective demand and the enablement of the self-development of as many people as possible. The economic decision maker must adopt the purpose of the economy as his or her own purpose. The individual must not consider personal profit as the sole content of his or her intentions, because it is only one of the means and incentives by which the market economy tries to achieve the goal of an efficient system of allocation.

One example for the necessity of the correct intention, i.e., the *intentio recta* or the ethically justifiable motivation of doing business, is the problem of mergers and acquisitions, and the problem of a "friendly" or "hostile" takeover of a company by another company. Mergers and *leveraged buyouts* are not unethical in themselves. They become unethical if they aim at only one goal: to buy a company, to

---

12   See P. KOSLOWSKI: *Wirtschaft als Kultur* (1989) and P. KOSLOWSKI: *Gesellschaftliche Koordination.* (1991).

raid its assets, i.e., to separate and cannibalize its capital, then to sell these parts again, all for the sole purpose of gaining profit for the buyer, without wasting a single thought on the company's dedication and contribution to the economy. Take-over-bids and mergers, in case they serve only profiteering by selling out the company or parts of it or only satisfy a power-hungry board, violate the substantial purpose of the economy, because they completely separate the buyer's profit interest from the interests of the company to be bought and thus deny the company's purpose or teleology as a producing social unit.

The example of the *leveraged buyout* is especially interesting in terms of business ethics because it is not always clear in the beginning whether a merger financed by a leveraged buyout serves the economy's purpose or not. A threat of a takeover can awaken a company, put pressure on the management, enhance performance and thus serve the interests of staff and stock holders. Such a takeover can lead to an efficient reallocation of resources. Therefore, leveraged buyouts cannot be condemned in all cases.[13]

Leveraged buyouts, though, might as well be regarded as mere games (of chance) or only satisfy the narcissism of the buyers, the „raiders," who want to gain profits without becoming active in the company themselves. If the company's assets are split up and auctioned without giving consideration to the possibly existing but not yet fully exhausted or hitherto underestimated synergy effects, mere profit harvesting takes place. This is only justified when the company purchased has definitely proven to be unable to use its assets to make profitable business and conduct business contributing to the purpose of the economy, the satisfaction of consumer demand. The intention of the party planning to take over a company cannot be neglected, since in cases of mergers it is the *intentional* deeds only which define which economical and ethical facts are at hand and whether the intended merger is a truly synergetical merger or a mere *asset stripping*.

A merger done for the sole purpose of wrecking the purchased company is not a merger but *asset stripping*. On the other hand, a takeover with the intention to achieve synergies between the two companies strengthens the productivity of both companies and the allocative efficiency of the economy. Only this procedure is worth of being called "merger" in the sense of a synergetic alliance.

Proper conduct of a merger and its *intentio recta*, the right intention objectively aimed at proper economic conduct - in our case the intention of the party planning the merger or takeover - decide whether an act is ethical or unethical.

---

13  N.-J. Weickart notes the positive influence of company takeovers on competition in the article "Firmenübernahme: Festung Deutschland" ("Company takeovers: Fort Germany") in: *Manager Magazin*, 19 April, 1989, p. 128-139.

The example of mergers shows that the economy is not only a formal market context of trading and exchange, on which subjective demands and subjectively defined supplies meet and are coordinated, but that the economy serves an objective purpose that must be realized by the subjective will of the individuals, i.e., according to the will of the people in the economy. The economy does not chiefly serve the profit maximizing purpose of the individuals but its purpose is utilizing the subjective striving of the individuals for the realization of the objective purpose of the economy: the unbiased satisfaction of subjective demands by an efficiently produced and distributed supply that is organized by subjective entrepreneurs.

Bearing in mind that proper conduct is necessary for the economy, the term "profit maximizing" must be seen in relative terms, since it contains a conversion of means and ends. Positive (not maximum) profit is a necessary condition for business, yet maximum profit is not the ultimate goal for an enterprise. Profit, i.e., market success, is the measure for the objective success of an enterprise. Still, profit cannot be the sole and foremost purpose of business. Profit should also not be "maximized," because maximizing the residual profit is not the goal. Profit as surplus is the measure for economic health of an enterprise and functions as a control force for the whole company, including the board of directors or the president. Thus, as one industrialist put it: "Profit is like health: You need it, and the more the better. But it's not the only reason for our existence."[14]

## 2. Justice as Fairness in Exchange

Regarding the price system and trade, the demand for proper conduct of business turns into the following rule: "In a price system, always act correctly in accordance with the objective goal of the price system," i.e., "When trading, give everybody what he or she is entitled to according to the undistorted rules of the price system." Proper conduct of the price system demands that everybody receives what he is entitled to according to the rules of coordination by market price. Fair trade is a distinct case of a general fairness principle: "To each his own" (*suum cuique tribuere*). According to the natural right tradition from the Roman *Corpus Iuris* up to Thomas Aquinas, fairness is the permanent attitude, supported by will and directed by prudence, to give each his own, especially his rights.

In terms of trading and exchange it means: if everybody receives that which he is entitled to, then everybody receives the value equivalent of his goods or services.

---

14  See TH. J. PETERS, R. H. WATERMAN JR.: *In Search of Excellence. Lessons from America's Best-Run Companies*, New York (Harper & Row) 1982.

He receives equivalent money for his goods or service or on the other hand equivalent goods for his money. The exchanging of equivalents represents the equality of services rendered and renumerations paid. Economic interactions must be conducted in such a way that nobody is being taken advantage of and everybody receives what he or she deserves.

Therefore, fair trade includes the fair setting of prices. Fair prices are especially in demand in situations where great leeway for prices exists and where the entrepreneur cannot only adjust his quantities to a given market price but set prices, i.e., where oligopolistic or monopolistic market power exists.

Proper conduct and fair price in trade and exchange are defined by four criteria:

1) The actually agreed upon and finally realized price must correspond with the prevailing price, i.e., in the market economy with the market price.
2) The goods exchanged must be genuine and not fake or of bad quality. One must not sell "bogus wheat" instead of real wheat.
3) The exchange must be of benefit to both parties, i.e., not to the disadvantage in net wealth of any of the involved parties.
4) The exchange should represent a fair equalization of interests. The gains of the trade should not be accumulated on one side only.

The demand for fairness or justice in exchange is inevitable, for every free contract needs and creates creative leeway for all contract partners. Prices and contracts do not emerge "by themselves" from the mechanics of the price system. Adapting individual prices to the market price is one of the crucial aspects of fair exchange and trade. In a market economy, harmonizing market prices and individual prices is also an ethical problem of price fairness.

## VI. Justice in the Interaction with Nature: Justice as Ecological Fairness

Justice is defined here as the determination and endeavor to reach a right reciprocation of rights and claims that is considered reasonable and supportable by all involved parties. Such a problem of reciprocation and balancing of interests does not only appear in human interactions but also in the interactions of man and his natural environment.

# PETER KOSLOWSKI

The "equalization task" of the Bank for Equalization and Compensation in the field of environmental protection reflects the problem of ecological equalization and fairness towards the natural environment. To be fair towards the natural environment in our interactions is an ethical demand on individuals, enterprises and the government.

As in the social field, in our relation to nature the question of justice contains the weighing or balancing of justified claims. In the case of being fair to the natural environment, not the conflict of interests between legal subjects has to be settled. Rather, the human interests in economic expansion and the survival conditions of the natural environment confront each other in the problem of ecological justice. Justice towards nature means consideration of the natural environment in the decision structure of market and democracy. It demands the inclusion of the natural environment with the help of representatives in the decision processes of market and democracy.

Further it demands consideration of the external effects of the economy on the natural environment, i.e., the internalization of external effects on the environment. Fairness towards the natural environment requires respect of certain rights the natural environment has and which are legitimate no matter how humans value them. Humankind must not regard the natural environment only as exploitable raw material but also appreciate the aesthetic, ethical and material value qualities and the creative ideas prevalent in the genetic code of the natural beings and characteristic of them.

The demand for fairness when interacting with the natural environment, as an ethical demand, assumes that there are not only human rights but rights of the natural environment as well. These rights must be defended by humankind, as nature's representative, against humankind itself and its expansionist desires. Fair interaction with nature should protect nature's dignity, integrity and "freedom." Nature's right of "freedom" is its right to behave "naturally." Nature's "freedom" rights must be protected like economic freedom protects the human individual's right for rational behavior and purposeful actions.[15]

Fairness towards nature demands respecting the rights for natural behavior of fauna and flora as worthy of protection or at least as relevant for humankind and calls for their consideration in human decisions in market and democracy, for weighing its rights against the rights of man.

---

15  Cf. F. FORTE: "Tutor of Nature. Comment on Peter Koslowski", in: P. KOSLOWSKI (Ed.): *Individual Liberty and Democratic Decision Making. The Ethics, Economics and Politics of Democracy*, Tübingen (J.C.B. Mohr [Paul Siebeck]) 1987, p. 97.

# ECOLOGY AND ETHICS IN THE ECONOMY

This weighing-up is a problem of weighing goods. Whether to keep a natural environment the way it used to be or establish a nature reserve or to turn it into an agriculturally exploitable area, especially in case of increasing population, is an example of interaction with nature in which nature's rights are always in a weaker position. It is questionable whether the social decision systems of the market and of democracy, which are limited to humans, are able to protect nature's "rights," i.e., to make them part of the discourse. In the discourses of the market and democracy, only creatures who can speak bear rights and are admitted. When the democratic discourse is considered the sole creator of rights, nature has neither voice nor vote, especially when a transdiscoursive "natural right" is rejected by the discourse.[16] Since there is not only social but also ecological exchange, the principle of fair reciprocation demands not only justice in social exchange but also justice in the interaction with the natural environment, demands fair exchange with nature.

According to Jean Baudrillard, exchange is time saving.[17] Every exchange is a gain of time. By trading with others we gain life-span because we do not have to do everything ourselves. The idea of time gain by exchange leads beyond commercial trade to ecological exchange with nature. The theory of time gain by trade transcends social trade to exchange with nature: in the exchange with the nonhuman nature and with nonhuman life we gain our life that we can only receive by exchange, because we cannot do everything by ourselves. In exchange with nature, life is a process that fights entropy and disorder and consumes energy. The exchange of negentropy against entropy, of order against chaos, enables us to gain time that life must fight for in order to avoid decay and the permanent danger of being destroyed by the world's increasing disorder and entropy.[18]

Only by exchange with the natural and social environment can an organism stay on a high level of differentiation and organization. This exchange with nature, the economy of ecological exchange, shows the necessity of ethics for interacting with nature and for equilibrating man's and nature's interests. It becomes obvious

---

16  See P. KOSLOWSKI: "Market and Democracy as Discourses. Limits to Discursive Social Coordination", in: P. KOSLOWSKI (Ed.): *Individual Liberty and Democratic Decision Making. The Ethics, Economics and Politics of Democracy*, Tübingen (J.C.B. Mohr) 1987, pp. 58-92. German translation: "Markt und Demokratie als Diskurse", in: P. KOSLOWSKI (Ed.): *Individuelle Freiheit und demokratische Entscheidung. Ethische, ökonomische und politische Theorie der Demokratie*, Tübingen (J.C.B. Mohr) 1989, Tübingen (J.C.B. Mohr) 1989.

17  J. F. BAUDRILLARD: *Der symbolische Tausch und der Tod* (The Symbolic Exchange and the Death), Munich (Matthes & Seitz) 1982. Original: *L'échange symbolique et la mort*, Paris (Gallimard) 1976.

18  Cf. E. SCHROEDINGER: *What is Life?*, Cambridge (Cambridge University Press) 1944.

that we are in dire need of an "ecological ethics for the economy." An environmental ethics of economic action must consider arguments of justice and fairness
in relation to the exchange partner „nature." This requires the inclusion of environmental protection and environmental damage as real gains and costs in the
economic calculations of the individuals and in the national economic statistics. It
furthermore requires not treating the natural environment as economically irrelevant, as it is considered in classical economic theory. Classical economic theory
regarded nature only as a free and unprotected asset or as raw material, brought to
value by human labour. Only now is the ecological dimension of business considered and appreciated in economic theory.[19]

Considering aspects of fairness towards nature is not forcibly created by
rational economical arguments. Respecting nature and the natural environment is
more a problem of respecting the rights of nonhuman nature. The task is to include
nature's rights and internalizing costs of natural resources and grown natural
structures in the social discourses of the market economy and democracy.
Acknowledging someone as being relevant in his or her rights is always a
phenomenon of freedom and ethical consideration. Careful interaction with the
natural environment is an ethical phenomenon of voluntary respect. Respecting the
right of nature means acknowledging that we have to include and be responsible for
the (side) effects of our interacting with the natural environment exactly as we must
be responsible for the side effects of our actions towards other people, although we
have to include nature to a lesser degree than other humans in our decision making
processes.

The natural species and creatures of life are ideas of creation that possess their
own ethical significance. The theory of the intrinsic values of the ideas of creation
assumes the existence of a creator and a theory of creation. In a theory of creation
without a creator, the idea of creation is inconsistent. The term "creation" is here
used in its original sense. To think that the world is a creation means to include a
creator. There is no creation without a creator.

---

19  See N. GEORGESCU-ROEGEN: *Energy and Economic Myths*, New York (Pergamon
Press) 1976, p. 3-36. Cf. for the relevance of this ecological-economic relationship for
the post-modern state of mind, P. KOSLOWSKI: *Die postmoderne Kultur* (The
Post-modern Culture), Munich (C.H. Beck) 1987, 2nd ed. 1988, p. 12f. Japanese
translation: *Postmoderno Bunka*, Kyoto (Minerva Shobo) 1992, 2nd ed. 1993.

# ECOLOGY AND ETHICS IN THE ECONOMY

## VII. Science and Wisdom in Our Relationship with Nature

The idea of creation and creational wisdom gains new importance under conditions of post-modernity[20] and of the obsolescence of an idea of Enlightenment that is narrowed to materialism. The French philosopher and contemporary of the 18th-century Enlightenment, Louis-Claude de Saint-Martin, wrote in 1782 that "like the individual human being should not only make progress in knowledge but also in wisdom; *l'homme général*, mankind, must develop not only science but also wisdom."[21] Saint-Martin extends the demand that the wisdom tradition since antiquity placed on the individual, to acquire wisdom and not only knowledge, to all of humankind: Humankind must not only make progress in scientific knowledge but must progress in wisdom as well.

Saint-Martin takes up the demand of the Enlightenment of his days for scientific progress and transcends it at the same time to that other or new form of Enlightenment that demands religious enlightenment or illumination in the tradition of wisdom. This other kind of enlightenment demands that mankind must not only proceed in the science of control over nature but at the same time win that relationship with nature which is traditionally described as wisdom. "Otherwise," Saint-Martin says, "looking back on the past centuries, the last humans will recognize the terrible abuse their ancestors have done to the benefactions of nature."[23] Saint-Martin wrote this before 1782 - before the industrial revolution and the ecological problems emerging in its trail.

---

20  For "Postmodernity" cf. P. KOSLOWSKI: *Die Prüfungen der Neuzeit. Über Postmodernität. Philosophie der Geschichte, Metaphysik, Gnosis* (The Trials of the Modern Age. About Postmodernity. Philosophy of History, Metaphysics, Gnosticism), Wien (Edition Passagen) 1989 and P. KOSLOWSKI: „Risikogesellschaft als Grenzerfahrung der Moderne. Für eine post-moderne Kultur" („Risk-taking Society as Borderline Experience of the Modern Age. For a Post-Modern Culture"), in: *Aus Politik und Zeitgeschichte. Supplement to the Magazine Das Parlament* (1989), Nr. 36, p. 14-30.

21  LOUIS-CLAUDE DE SAINT-MARTIN: *Tableau Naturel des Rapports qui existent entre Dieu, l'Homme et l'Univers* (Natural Scheme of the Relationships that exist Between God, Humankind, and the Universe), Edimbourg 1782, 2e partie, p. 211, in: *Oeuvres Majeures*, ed. par R. Amadou, Hildesheim (Olms) 1980, vol. II, p. 211.

22  See P. KOSLOWSKI: "Die Postmodernität der Weisheitstradition" (The Postmodernity of Wisdom Tradition), in: *Scheidewege. Jahrbuch für skeptisches Denken* (Forkways. Yearbook for Sceptical Thinking), 18 (1988/89), p. 110-119.

23  SAINT-MARTIN, *loc. cit.*, p. 212.

This phrase is in absolute contradiction to the parallel development of Goethe's pantheistic understanding of nature. According to Goethe's optimistic pantheistic view of nature, there is no ethical problem because nature can equalize all incongruities. "Nature's drive for formation . . . are the rubrics of its budget prescribed where it must allocate its resources . . . how much it . . . wants to spend on each topic is, however, to a certain degree, its own choice. If it wants to make a greater outlay on one item, it is forced to neglect another; thus nature can never become debtor or even go bankrupt."[24]

Saint-Martin's religious wisdom of nature is closer to us today than Goethe's Pantheism of Nature. Nowadays' people are well aware that nature can go bankrupt. According to Saint-Martin, true enlightenment means using wisdom to regulate the kind of knowledge that longs for domination and turn it into an understanding relationship with the object of that knowledge. If mankind only proceeds in knowledge but not in wisdom, future humans, looking back on their long way of evolution, will find in the world they have influenced only the ruins and the debris of their domination over nature enabled by science and technology.

This Illuminist criticism of Enlightenment and the demand for the widening of its concept of our relationship with nature, voiced not at the Enlightenment's Postmodern end but during its dawn, is even more important today than at the time it was developed. Saint-Martin was convinced that wisdom is the purpose and the perfection of all sciences.[25] Nevertheless, he also perceived that the demand for wisdom, especially in science, can generate resistance, since wisdom as the ultimate scientific goal is less "transparent," less easy to convey and demands more caution and consideration than the goal of control over nature by scientific and technical "knowledge of domination."

Modern scientific-technological domination of nature comes to limits because of its "side effects." New forms of a nonindustrial, non-mechanical relationship with nature must replace industrial control over nature or at least be equally treated. To develop possible new ways of using the natural environment, not only science is

---

24  J. W. V. GOETHE: *Erster Entwurf einer allgemeinen Einleitung in die vergleichende Anatomie, ausgehend von der Osteologie* (First Draft of a General Introduction to Comparitive Anatomy, based on Osteology), (1795), in: J. W. V. GOETHE: *Works*, Hamburg Edition, Munich (C.H. Beck) 1982, vol. 13, p. 176 f.: *Dem natürlichen "Bildungstrieb. . . [sind] die Rubriken seines Etats, in welche sein Aufwand zu verteilen ist, vorgeschrieben. . . , was er auf jedes wenden will, steht ihm, bis auf einen gewissen Grad, frei. Will er der einen mehr zuwenden, so ist er nicht ganz gehindert, allein er ist genötigt an einer andern sogleich etwas fehlen zu lassen; und so kann die Natur sich niemals verschulden, oder wohl gar bankrott werden."*

25  SAINT-MARTIN, *loc. cit.*, p. 121.

78

required but a wisdom which can recognize the wisdom in nature. New forms of symbiosis with nature are possible when the perception of nature changes. New bio-economical and socio-biological designs of natural science and exchange with nature already prove a development in this direction.[26]

Saint-Martin further wrote in 1782: "The wisdom that has created us fulfils its contract, only we humans do not."[27] Humankind does not fulfil their contract with nature and nature's wisdom because they do not act wisely in their interactions with nature; nature in return does not fulfil its contract with them in the way it was intended by Creation. If we conduct interaction with nature with wisdom and fairness and not with the single purpose of exploitation, nature will give us her goods more easily and more generously. The "physicality" of traditional wisdom forms a correcting factor to the Cartesian separation of material without spirit and soul, res extensa, and the body and natureless spirit, res cognitans. This Cartesian separation of spirit and nature has ontologically predominated modern natural science and enabled its development. In this dualistic view of reality nature has neither aesthetical nor ethical value but only a subjective-economical value which is defined only by its exploitability for the spirit, for the subjective demands of humanity.

Such a theory of reality, devaluing nature and spiritually overestimating human subjectivity, is not wise, for it not only neglects nature's wisdom but also the fact that the human being is not only spirit but also body and as such a part of nature itself. The conviction of an irreconcilable dualism of man and nature, spirit and body devalues in its blindness towards the physical world and nature's wisdom not only the nonhuman nature but also mankind itself, since it despises the fact that mankind is part of nature. If organic nature is worthless, the human as a physical being also loses his other value and is reduced to the mind - to a spiritualistic entity. But if only the spiritual part of the human is valuable, he or she loses his or her dignity as a mortal being, a physical individual.

On the contrary, wisdom allows us to recognize nature's inherent value and the ethical value of the integrity of that which nature is in itself. Wisdom enables us to acknowledge the value of nature in our actions. This wisdom is not a hostile competitor but a congenial completion to science. It must complete science and the

---

26   See P. KOSLOWSKI: *Evolution und Gesellschaft. Eine Auseinandersetzung mit der Soziobiologie* (Evolution and Society. A Critical Assessment of Sociobiology), Tübingen (J.C.B. Mohr [Paul Siebeck]) 1984, 2nd ed.1989. English translation Berlin (Springer) 1996.

27   SAINT-MARTIN, *loc. cit.*, p. 101.

quest for knowledge, so that knowledge is not only able to control nature but to recognize and acknowledge its value.

Chapter 5

# Ethical Universals, Justice, and International Business

## RICHARD T. DE GEORGE

Are there ethical universals in international business? Normative theories in general tend to claim some sort of universality. Hence, the short answer that a Mill or a Kant would probably give is yes.[1] For on the most common interpretations the principle of utility applies universally both in that it applies to all actions and in that it applies to all persons. The same is true of the categorical imperative. An affirmative answer to the question will also be given by a number of others. On the other hand, a relativist would probably have an equally short answer to the question: no. For the relativist would deny that any principles apply either to all actions or to all persons. But having said this much is not to have shed any light on the issue that people did not know before. And the point of the question surely is not to ask for one more defense of some normative ethical theory, or one more argument for or against relativism.

The question of whether there are ethical universals in *business* ethics might be taken as a special instance of the question whether there are ethical universals in *general* ethics. There is no reason to think that the answer to the first question will be any different from the answer to the second question. Business ethics is not separable from general ethics any more than business is separable from the rest of human life. Hence no special answer is possible with respect to ethics in international business.

# RICHARD T. DE GEORGE

The question of whether there are ethical universals can be considered a special case of the question of whether there are universals. The problem of universals goes back at least as far as Plato, with many different and subtle positions and variations developed from antiquity through the middle ages to the present time.[2] For a nominalist, there are no universals, and hence no ethical universals. Some non-nominalists might hold there are universals--for instance in the realm of mathematics--yet deny there are ethical universals. But that discussion is not the point of asking about ethical universals in international business.

There are other ways to construe the original question as well. It might be taken to be raising the issue of the difference between subjectivists and objectivists in ethics, although one can be an objectivist without holding ethical universals; or between moral absolutists and moral relativists, although moral universals need not be absolutes; or between moral realists and non-realists, although moral universals do not necessarily demand moral realism.[3]

Finally, raising the question of ethical universals in international business may not seek an answer based on a normative theory, or an answer based on metaethical or metaphysical considerations, but an answer based on empirical findings. Judeo-Christian, Muslim, and Buddhist morality overlap to some extent.[4] But they also differ, and none of them or any other view is in fact held everywhere by everyone. Factual cultural relativity is widely acknowledged.[5] Yet neither it nor factual moral similarities solve the problem of ethical universals any more than did our earlier answers.

All these are familiar debates in the literature of philosophy and of ethics. The many varied responses to these complex and debated issues are well known. There is no last word on any of these issues, and I do not propose either to rehearse the many positions or to attempt to give a final answer to any of them. Rather, I shall argue that we no more need to settle all these questions in advance in order to make moral judgments in the area of international business than we do to make moral judgments in other realms of moral life. I accept the fact that peoples and cultures often differ both on their moral principles and on their particular moral judgments. And I am not sanguine about developing any arguments strong enough to show that certain principles are the only right one or ones, or that particular judgments are infallibly right or wrong.

Nonetheless, for purposes of international business, there are certain basic claims and norms that are necessary for business, and these throw some light on claims to universality in ethics, whether or not they yield what are considered moral universals.

# ETHICAL UNIVERSALS AND INTERNATIONAL BUSINESS

## I. The Particularist Sense of Universality as a Moral Prerequisite

There is one sense in which morality is and must be considered universal for any discussion of morality to take place, and that is the particularist sense of universality. By this I mean that if a particular action in specific concrete circumstances is wrong for me, then it must be wrong for everyone else in comparable circumstances. This is a conceptual point, not an empirical one. But unless we agree at least on that, it is not clear what it means to make a moral judgment, nor does making moral judgments make much sense.

Even on an emotivist account, in which making a moral judgment is simply expressing my emotions, I would have to hold that anyone else similarly placed, and so having the same emotions, would make the same judgment. Someone who had a different emotive response would make a different judgment. But then that person would be differently placed. This simply means that having a negative emotional response to an action constitutes the judgment that the action is wrong. For a utilitarian, if a particular action produces more bad consequences than good consequences, then it is morally wrong. For all others similarly placed, the action will produce more bad than good consequences. Otherwise they would not be similarly placed. This is compatible with different people using different criteria judging the action differently. But for each one, however he or she judges it, the judgment is what it is and not its opposite, otherwise it is contradictory and unintelligible. And if it were not the same for all others similarly placed, it would not be what it is. This much agreement is necessary to even begin discussing ethics in any area, including ethics in international business.

This is true for ethics in general and for ethics in international business as well. Making moral judgments commits one to at least this much. A business that wishes to act ethically makes moral judgments, and in doing so it makes them not only for and about itself but also about any other firm similarly placed as well. Only by assuming this can a business engage in ethical discussion and considerations. Acknowledging this may not seem to commit a business to much, but it does commit it at least to moral discourse and to the restriction of self-consistency within that discourse.

# RICHARD T. DE GEORGE

## II.  Some Norms Required for Business Transactions

Since business involves transactions, we need at least enough agreement among those taking part in the transaction to have the transaction take place. Let us assume this. It is possible for transactions to take place without regard to ethics, and simply with regard to self-interest. One party may force another into certain transactions. The penalty for failing to take part would involve some penalty that the second party would prefer to avoid. For instance one country A may force some neighboring territory B to pay taxes or tribute to A. Failure to do so will mean the destruction of part or all of B and the death of some or all of its inhabitants. This is not yet business, but the step to business is not very great. A strong company or firm may in an analogous manner force some region to sell the firm its minerals at extremely cheap prices that we would term exploitative.

Having said that the transactions can take place without regard to ethics does not mean that the transactions cannot be evaluated from a moral point of view, either by the dominant or the subordinate party, and by some third party (as the description of the transaction as exploitative shows).

What I wish to argue is that if business is viewed not as a set of forced transactions but as a set of relatively free transactions, then some ethical norms emerge necessarily from the very nature of free transactions. To the extent that they are necessary conditions for the transactions to take place they provide the basis for norms or rules of conduct that each of the parties should abide by if they wish the transactions to continue. Violating those rules is possible on a small scale. But doing so presupposes the rules, and constitutes immoral behavior.

Since we are interested in business transactions, let me start with an exchange based on a contract. Part of what it means to make a contract is to agree to abide by the conditions stated. If someone makes a contract but does not consider himself bound by it in any way, then that person does not understand what it is to make a contract. Since it is an agreement to abide by the terms stated, one takes on an obligation to act accordingly. Within a legal system, one takes on a legal obligation to act accordingly, and failure to do so carries with it legal penalties. But whether or not the contract is legally enforced, making a contract binds one morally. For if one denies this, then it is not clear what it means to be bound by a contract. Being bound means that one *should* adhere to it, and the nature of that *should*, whether or not legal, is moral.

Violations of a legal *should* carry with them legal penalties. Violations of a moral *should* carry with them moral sanctions, which in a business context are primarily lack of repeat business. If A does not honor his contract with B, B has no incentive and a strong disincentive to making another contract with A. If A habitually violates contracts he makes, then, unless he can keep this information from potential new partners, and unless his business is such that it does not require repeat business, no one will contract with him. The possibility of his acting as he does, nonetheless, is parasitic on there being the practice of contracts, which involves honoring the commitments made. Thus the practice of making contracts involves the moral obligation to fulfill the terms agreed to.

This obligation, inherent in the very nature of contracting, is universal in the sense that there can be no practice of contracting without it. If contracts are found in international business transactions, as they are, then the obligation to honor the conditions of a contract is an obligation that crosses boundaries, and is an obligation of international business.

Implicit in the obligation to abide by one's contracts are other moral obligations. Contracting in business presupposes that one wishes to engage in the transaction. Hence each party must respect the life of the other. It is understood that a condition for business is that one not kill those with whom one is contracting. Otherwise, clearly there would be no contracts of the sort necessary for international business, and the transactions would have a very different character. Similarly, contracts assume that both parties are truthful and are not making lying promises. A lying promise is no promise and undermines the very nature of a contract.

That respect for the life of those with whom one does business, that truthfulness, and that respect for contracts made are necessary for the flourishing of business activity comes as no surprise. For these are moral norms that are necessary for any society to flourish, and are basic to human interactions of many sorts. As accepted norms in any society, they are norms that are held universally. Nonetheless, they may not be applied universally in every society. In a slave society masters may observe these norms in free transactions with other free people in their society, but they may not respect the lives of their own slaves, whom they dominate by force. Now we may claim that slavery is immoral everywhere, and that this is a moral universal truth or norm. And this may place certain moral requirements on us as we interact with countries that have slavery. But this issue is different from the one with which I am presently dealing. The question of how one should act in an international context when one's own moral beliefs differ from those in another country is different from the question of whether there are certain moral norms that are necessary conditions for certain business practices.

What I have argued so far is that there are some basic moral norms that business transactions require, whatever one's substantive view of morality. Since these are required by business transactions, they are required by international business transactions, and hence are found, because presupposed by the nature of the transaction, everywhere that such transactions take place. If there is some country in which it is considered acceptable to kill one's transaction partner so as to avoid payment after receiving one's goods, or to change the conditions of the transaction in one's favor after the partner has made a substantial investment of time or money, or to lie about what one will do, then business in the ordinary sense cannot and will not take place between that country and other countries; and if transactions do take place they will not be ordinary business transactions but some sort of transaction dependent on force, either unilaterally or mutually applied.

These basic moral norms can and do carry business a long way. In a somewhat similar manner we can argue that human flourishing in various ways requires other moral norms: that societies in which people are free flourish and prosper more than do slave-holding societies; that societies without prejudicial bias against any group based on gender or race flourish and prosper more than societies that promote such bias; that societies in which children are educated flourish and prosper more than societies in which child labor is the norm. And to the extent that we can make out these claims, we can argue that for societies to flourish and prosper, they should acknowledge these norms. If we can also show that societies as societies are such that they wish to flourish and prosper, then all societies should adopt those norms. This is one way to interpret natural law, utilitarian, or Kantian approaches to ethics. But we know that there are societies in which slavery or something very close to it continues, in which gender and racial bias is built into the social practices, in which there is child labor. Stating that all three are immoral or unethical is appropriate for those who believe so. Stating that these are moral universals is also appropriate for those who believe so. And one may produce the best arguments one can in an attempt to convince others. But doing the latter is not clearly an obligation of a business engaged in international transactions.

What is an obligation is to observe those norms that are necessary for and that undergird the kind of transaction--and more generally the kind of activity--in which a business engages. These obligations are not imposed from without by any group or society. Rather they are demanded by the activity itself. To that extent they can be called universal in the sense that anyone wishing to engage in the activity as an ongoing one must acknowledge these obligations or norms. I have suggested some required by contracts. But the technique of deriving the norms required by specific activities can be extended to other practices and even more broadly to economic systems.[6]

## III. Ethical Consistency in International Business

It is not the practices on which businesses agree that pose the problems. It is those on which businesses from different countries or different cultures disagree. For practical purposes the question for business is then: what is the ethical obligation of an international business given the existence of practices in some countries in which it operates that the business views as unethical?

Note that it is not necessary that the practice be thought to be ethical in the host country. Bribery may be widely practiced in some countries. That fact may only show that it is tolerated. It does not show that it is ethical or considered ethical by all or even the majority of those in that country. In fact it is difficult to see how bribery could be *ethically* justified as a practice if it involves special preference based on the bribe and hence undermines both efficiency and fair competition. The practice necessarily involves hurt or harm to some and is incompatible with the ideals of a free market.[7]

Similarly child labor is practiced and tolerated in a good many countries, especially in less developed countries of Asia, Africa, and South America. That it is tolerated by the population does not show that it is considered ethical or morally approved either by those who employ the children or by the children and their families. The children are sent to work by their families, who need the income. This is a form of forced labor. Any inference from that to moral acceptability would be mistaken. The employers hire the children because they are cheap labor-- or sometimes in the rug industry because they have small hands necessary for weaving some rugs. Any inference from the fact that they hire the children to the claim that they think this is ethically justifiable is also mistaken. And if they do think it is, that does not show that they can in fact give a justification of the practice in terms of whatever ethical norms they hold.

Child labor, defined as full-time work in factories by children under the age of fourteen, is illegal in many of the countries in which it is still practiced--which shows that at some level it is considered inappropriate, even if it is still tolerated. Such toleration sometimes shows inability to police one's own laws, ineffective government, public corruption, or other internal deficiencies. It does not show moral acceptability.[8]

What then of an American company that wishes to do business with firms in a country in which child labor is tolerated? Must we argue either that child labor is universally unethical in the sense that it is wrong everywhere or that it depends on the local conditions and beliefs and may be wrong in some countries and ethically acceptable in others? My own view is that it is wrong everywhere in the world today if it in fact--as it almost always does--deprives the children of the possibility of developing their talents in such a way that will prepare them for active and fruitful participation in their societies as adults. If it does, it unfairly cuts off many future possibilities for them, it frequently harms them physically, and it illegitimately deprives them of education to which they have a right. It is a violation of their human rights, both ethically and from the point of view of the Declaration of Human Rights.[9] It fails to treat them as ends in themselves. And it leads to worse consequences than the alternative of educating them both for themselves and for the development and improvement of their society. While I hope my arguments are persuasive, they do not yet completely answer the question of what the American firm should do.

Let us assume that the multinational in question wishes to act ethically. If it does not, then it will not care whether the hiring of children is ethical or not. The question will be beside the point for such a company. Even if it could be shown that hiring children is unethical, and even if the company agreed that doing so is unethical, it would make no difference. The fact that murder is wrong both ethically and legally does not prevent murders from taking place. The fact that lying is ethically wrong does not mean that people do not lie. Whether an action is ethically permissible or ethically prohibited makes a difference only if one cares about being ethical, because it is the right action to take, and/or because it is good business, good public relations, or something similar.

If we assume the firm in question wishes to act ethically, then the important decision is whether it considers child labor ethically justifiable. If it does not, then it cannot hire child labor, nor can it promote the practice of hiring children by the contractors or suppliers with which it deals. For if the practice is unethical, then to help promote and indirectly support the practice is at least indirectly to act unethically.

The situation may not be that clear-cut. An American firm might believe that hiring children is unethical in the United States but not know whether it believes it is unethical in the host country. That is, it might raise the question: are there ethical universals, such that what is unethical in my country is unethical every-where? But raising the question to a high level of generality ignores the real issue. If the company believes it is unethical to hire children in its own country, then it must ask: would it be ethical for it to hire children in the host country if it owned the facility? In answering that question it might well look at local practice. But it could not validly infer from the local practice to the ethics of the practice. It would have to see whether the reasons that lead it to consider the practice unethical in its own country also apply in the host country. It might consider the reasons I gave above for considering child labor unethical. If the answer it finally reaches is that it would be unethical for the company to hire children in the host country, then it cannot claim that it is permissible to buy from local companies that employ children.

Some may claim that the question I substituted begs the question of whether hiring children is universally wrong. And they would be correct. For part of what I am claiming is that that question does not have to be answered to determine how companies should act in international business if they wish to act ethically.

When a company is faced with a local practice that it considers unethical, it must ask itself not only what the local custom is, but whether the practice is ethically justifiable, given the values that the company espouses. This means that the company should act consistently. Consistency does not mean that it must act the same everywhere it operates. Of course it must consider and frequently abide by local custom, so long as doing so is not unethical by its own lights. Where local custom is unethical by its own lights, then a company of integrity, a company that wishes to act ethically, cannot change its ethics as it changes its geographic location. To do so is to give up ethics and to give up any supposed commitment to its values.[10]

## IV. Some Moral Norms Are Relative to Existing Conditions

So far I have argued that certain practices demand or presuppose certain ethical norms (that a viable society precludes the arbitrary killing of its members, lying, and gross dishonesty); that some ethical norms form part of certain practices (such as the practice of making contracts); and that ethics demands that if one considers an action wrong, then one cannot consistently claim that encouraging others to perform the action for one's benefit is ethically acceptable.

Not all actions are of this type, however, and not all actions lend themselves to this type of analysis. So far we have considered actions the descriptions and moral evaluations of which cross borders intact. There are also some actions the morality of which depends on existing conditions, expectations, customs, and particular circumstances.

Morality is a social enterprise, just as law is a social enterprise. Whether one has violated a particular statute is not a question that finds its solution in some state of the world in which the action is found to be illegal, as it were, in nature. The same thing is true to some extent of morality. This does not mean that either law or morality have no foundation in the constitution of people and in the way they live. It does mean that, just as with law, not everything that is called moral has to be the same in every culture. What is moral, for instance, with respect to property necessarily depends on what property relations exist.

Every country has some notion of property. But the notion of property varies widely. It is immoral to steal another's property. But what constitutes stealing depends in part on what constitutes property. Some actions that constitute stealing in one country, for instance that recognizes ownership of land, may not even be possible in another country in which land cannot be owned.[11]

Similarly, lying is wrong in every country and culture. For if lying were the rule rather than the exception, there could be no trusted communication between people. Yet saying this leaves room for interpretation about which acts constitute lying and so are ethically prohibited. In some societies a "yes" or a "no" may mean "maybe" because the people of that society do not like direct questions or answers and prefer to communicate through indirection, nuanced inflection, body language, or other means. Those who do not know the culture may be misled and may feel that have been lied to. But what has in fact happened is that they have interpreted a response to a direct question incorrectly. The person responding may have felt that the question was rude or confrontational because it forced an answer. The answer was not given to deceive, but was given in the cultural context in which the expectation was that the answer would be correctly understood. Since the essence of lying involves the intention to deceive, from the point of view of the person responding the reply was not a lie. The person receiving the answer interpreted it in the light of his own customs, rather than in the light of the customs of the country in which he finds himself. The result is a failure to communicate, and perhaps charges of lying by the outsider. What is important to see is that a very similar act may have one moral character in one culture because of the intention and the accepted background conditions, and have another moral character if interpreted from the point of view of another culture.

This does not mean that whatever any culture believes is moral is in fact moral. Societies may be mistaken about the morality of an action, just as individuals may be mistaken. What it does mean is that in at least one sense some types of outward actions are not universally right or wrong. Rather the morality of the action is relative to existing conditions, expectations, customs and particular circumstances. To this extent it is dangerous, misleading, and false to claim that all ethical judgments at some middle level of generality hold universally, where that means everywhere and all the time; but it does not mean that at the highest level of generality, that is, at the level of general ethical principles, there are no ethical universals. That remains an open question. It may be the case, for instance, that an action is right if it produces more overall good than bad. Yet what can be taken as the same action might produce more good in one context and more bad in another, making it moral in one context and immoral in another. Similarly, respect for persons might be taken as a universal norm, and what constitutes respect for persons in one society may appear as disrespectful in another society because of different customs, conditions, expectations, beliefs, and so on.

Once again, these issues need not be settled definitively to provide guidance to a company on how to act morally in international business. What is important is that the people involved in operating in another culture be sensitive to the ways cultures can influence the interpretation of actions and to the ways in which specific moral judgments are thus sometimes relative to local conditions and cultures.

## V. International Justice

What then of justice? If different people have different views of justice, whose are appropriately applied in any evaluation? If we do not have a universally held view of justice, can we justify international business transactions? What are the implications of the approach I have been developing for issues of justice in international business?

To answer these questions we need to make at least a few distinctions. I have already argued that with respect to property, we cannot generalize what is right and what is wrong without indicating within which system of property we are operating. Although we may hold with Aristotle that justice consists in giving each his due and in treating similar cases similarly, there are many ways of considering what one is due. In many instances what constitutes substantive justice is in part a function of the system, background conditions, understandings of the participants, common and expected practices and expectations, the law, and so on. Hence except for the very broad characterization of justice, whether a particular practice is just is often context-dependent. Moreover, there are many kinds of justice--distributive, commutative, retributive, and compensatory, to name four of the more common types. Given this complexity, how can we judge issues of justice in international business?

Let us assume, as is the case, that there are different views of what constitutes justice in international business. The differences are exemplified, for instance, in charges made by Americans about the unfairness of the Japanese closing many of their markets to American business, and about the unfairness of the Japanese preferring to buy from Japanese companies even when products of at least equal quality are available from American companies. The Japanese do not believe these practices are unjust, and argue in terms of their views of *keiretsu*.[12] In other instances what seem like justifiable business arrangements from one point of view may seem like exploitation from another point of view. Which is the correct point of view, and if there is one, who is to decide and how?

Since we started with international business transactions, I shall deal primarily with justice in such transactions, or with commutative justice. This is what businesses face most directly. Issues of international distributive justice (such as the fair allocation of wealth and the resources of the world) and of global justice (such as the distribution of burdens with respect to lessening global warming) are of undeniable importance, but are more complex and not as tractable for individual firms engaged in international business as are issues of commutative justice.[13]

In discussing international business transactions I restricted the ethical discussion to those that were not forced. I shall similarly restrict the discussion of commutative justice to transactions that take place between two or more parties, each of which takes part in the transaction willingly and to achieve its own purposes. According to Aristotle, equals should be traded for equals. But how one decides what is equal to what is part of the problem. In any transaction, each of the parties wants what the other offers more than he wants what he has. Otherwise, it would make no sense to engage in the transaction.

Given the fact that different people have different views of justice, that they use different criteria to evaluate the justice of a transaction, and that they may well value the items involved in the transaction differently, I shall argue that what constitutes justice is and should be what constitutes justice for all, and that means for all from their points of view whatever they are. A business transaction is just on this view if all affected parties, whatever their view or conception or criterion of justice is, consider the transaction just. To this extent my view might seem to be a consensual view of justice. But contrary to most consensual views, my claim is *not* that the consent of the parties makes the transaction just. A theory that holds that the consent of the parties makes an action just is a substantive theory of justice on a par with other theories of what makes a transaction just. Where there is agreement on what makes a transaction just we do not have a clash of ethical theories or views. But if each of the theories claims to be the only correct view of justice, then it is not clear how to resolve issues in which people or businesses differ on their views of justice.

The position I am defending aims to handle all transactions in which each of the parties already espouses a substantive view of justice. If they hold the same view of justice, then there is no problem on that level. A transaction that is just according to that view of justice should be perceived and accepted as just by all those affected by it. Since the transaction is just according to the criteria they hold, they have no grounds for not claiming the transaction just if it satisfies the criteria. But if all the parties did not hold the same criteria or conception of justice, then what might be considered just using one set of criteria might not be just using another set.

In these latter cases, each can and will judge the action just from some particular point of view or conception of justice. One might ask whether the transaction satisfies Rawls' principles of justice; another might ask whether it is in accord with natural law; a third might ask whether it produces more good than harm to all those affected; and so on. What I am claiming is that it is not necessary that all those affected by the transaction use the same criterion of justice or have the same view of justice. It suffices that they all accept the transaction as just.

If we adopt this approach then a transaction that is viewed as just by one of the involved parties but not by the other would not be *just overall*. To be *just overall* it must be considered just by all those affected. Some third party in another time or place may judge the transaction unjust, and give good reasons for so judging it. But that is compatible with holding that the action is just overall. For purposes of international business, if a transaction is just overall, then it is just for all practical purposes.

This notion of justice may be seen as an ideal. But it is not simply an ideal, for it has practical import. Many transactions take place in international business in which all affected parties--most frequently the buyer and the seller--accept the transaction as just, each from its own point of view. Unless there were many transactions of this sort, at least one of the parties would feel that the transaction is not just, and hence would take part at least reluctantly, and with a constant desire to change the terms so as to make it just. Such transactions take place with less than full freedom, and with at least one party feeling that it is coerced or being taken advantage of because of its need or competitive weakness. Where both parties deal from relatively equal strength, it is unlikely that transactions that are considered unfair or unjust would be continued for long, and it is likely that such transactions will tend to be unstable and short-term at best.

The view of justice overall that I have proposed says that all those directly affected must judge and accept the transaction as just, from whatever perspective they make that judgment. A slave holder may purchase slaves for a certain price that the seller agrees is fair. To that extent, since both transactors agree the exchange is fair, we can call it *transactionally just*. Yet the transaction is *not* just overall because the slave is directly affected, and from his perspective the transaction is unjust. Similarly, a multinational may buy raw materials from a corrupt government and both may look upon the terms of the sale as just, ignoring the fact that the people of the country are being exploited by the government. It too is transactionally just, but from the point of view of the exploited population the transaction is not just, and hence it would not be just overall, because it is not just from the perspective of one of the parties directly affected.

It is of course possible for all those directly affected to judge a transaction just, and for some unaffected third party to judge it unjust. On the view I am presenting, the transaction would remain just overall. For "just overall" does not mean just from every possible perspective, or from some absolute, privileged, or true perspective, although any party may make his judgment from what he considers such a position. What my position entails is that even if someone judges a transaction just from some absolute and even true position, it might not be just overall. If all affected parties do not agree that the claimed absolute, privileged or true position is in fact absolute, privileged and true, and if some affected party disagrees with the judgment, it is not just overall. For practical purposes, it is essential that all those directly affected agree the transaction is just, for they are the ones involved who must live with the consequences of their actions. If some third or fourth party thinks that one of the parties suffers from false consciousness, that it misconceives its own good, or that it suffers some other comparable defect of moral vision, then that party may certainly engage in consciousness raising.

A transaction that is just overall may be reconsidered by the transactors at a later time, and their evaluations may have changed. But this simply says that some judgments are made with incomplete information, or that conditions change, or that judgments are for some other reason unstable. Reconsideration is possible even if one judges from what one considers an absolute or universal conception of justice.

The aim of a company that wishes to act with integrity is to work towards transactions that are not only just from its point of view, but just overall. Where this is not possible to achieve, the transaction may well not take place. The company should not achieve the transaction through force or threat of force, for this would violate the freedom condition for a transaction to be just in the business world. If not forced, the transaction would tend to be at least transactionally just. If a company enters into a transaction that is transactionally just but that is not just overall, then the company has the extra burden of justifying its action. This means it should be able to show why carrying through the transaction is not exploitative, forced, or whatever else it is charged with by whoever is directly affected. It may not be able to convince that party that the action is just. But at least from its own perspective it must be able to justify carrying through the transaction under those circumstances.

To ask more of a firm engaged in international business seems to me to demand the unreasonable, or what it cannot achieve. It can properly be held to transactional justice and to attempting to achieve justice overall. It cannot be expected to act in a way that is either universally agreed to as just or that is just from some privileged point of view and so "truly just" because there is no such position--at least presently--available.

ETHICAL UNIVERSALS AND INTERNATIONAL BUSINESS

## VI. Practical Morality and Open Ethical Questions

The position I have outlined is a limited one. It makes no claim to encompass the complete domain of ethics. It leaves open the possibility that there may be one overarching ethical principle, but it does not require it; and the norms that I have developed are compatible with many different ethical theories. To that extent they are ethically underdetermined. But everyday morality is ethically underdetermined, in that all of the different comprehensive theories attempt to account for it.

The position is also limited in the sense that it leaves open as well the possibility that although some norms are basic to certain kinds of interactions, not all norms are of this kind. Because of differing circumstances an action under a particular description may be morally right in one society and morally wrong in another society. The morality of some actions might be morally relative to a given society because of the different conditions present in that society, because of the social system, customs, laws, beliefs, or because of other factors.

The upshot is that it is possible to give businesses that wish to act ethically in their international dealings some help in thinking through how they should act, given cultural diversity and disputes about moral theories. Because philosophers are unlikely to reach a consensus soon on many aspects of moral universals, the fact that we do not need to settle abstract questions about moral universals in order to provide guidance may be viewed as good news by companies wishing to act ethically and with integrity in international business.

**Endnotes**

1 I say "probably" because Mill and Kant do not specifically answer the question of whether there are ethical universals.
2 For a brief overview of the problem of universals see A. D. WOOZLEY: "Universals", *The Encyclopedia of Philosophy*, 8 (1967), pp. 194-206.
3 The literature dealing with these issues is large. Among other works see GEOFFREY SAYRE-MCCORD (Ed.): *Essays on Moral Realism*, Ithaca (Cornell University Press) 1988; MICHAEL KRAUSZ and JACK MEILAND (Eds.): *Relativism: Cognitive and Moral*, Notre Dame (University of Notre Dame Press) 1982; and GENE OUTKA and JOHN

REEDER, JR. (Eds.): *Prospects for a Common Morality*, Princeton (Princeton University Press) 1993. See also, the 1994 issue of *Social Philosophy and Policy* devoted to "Cultural Pluralism and Moral Knowledge" and the *Ethics* "Symposium on Pluralism and Ethical Theory" (vol. 102, No. 4 [July 1992]).

4    An interesting attempt at capturing some of the overlap is contained in the 1993 Parliament of World Religions's Declaration "Towards A Global Ethic" and its "Principles of a Global Ethic". Both were published and made available by USA Weekend.

5    In addition to the anthropological literature, see *Social Philosophy & Policy*, vol. 8, 1 (Autumn 1990), on "Ethics, Politics and Human Nature"; and JAMES Q. WILSON: *The Moral Sense*, New York (Free Press) 1993.

6    For a discussion of the justice of economic systems, see my *Business Ethics*, 4th ed., Englewood, N.J. (Prentice Hall) 1995, Chapters 6 and 7.

7    For a fuller development of this argument see my *Competing With Integrity in International Business*, New York (Oxford University Press) 1993, pp. 99-105.

8    On child labor see "Danger: Children at Work", *Futurist*, 27, No. 1 (Jan/Feb 1993), pp. 42-43; MARTHA NICHOLS: "Third-world Families at Work: Child Labor or Child Care?", *Harvard Business Review*, 71, No. 1 (Jan/Feb 1993), pp. 12-23; and "Slavery", *Newsweek*, May 4, 1992, pp. 30-39.

9    Art. 26 of the Universal Declaration of Human Rights states: "Everyone has the right to education. Education shall be free, at least in the elementary and fundamental stages. Elementary education shall be compulsory." This is incompatible with child labor as defined. If child labor is actually equivalent to slavery or servitude, as in some cases it is (see "Slavery", *Newsweek*, May 4, 1992, pp. 30-39), then it violates Art. 4 of the Declaration.

10   See *Competing with Integrity in International Business*, especially Chapters 1 and 2, for support for this claim.

11   For a fuller discussion of this point see my article "International Business Ethics: Russia and Eastern Europe", *Social Responsibility: Business, Journalism, Law, Medicine*, XIX (1993), pp. 5-23.

12   See IWAO TAKA: "Business Ethics: A Japanese View", *Business Ethics Quarterly*, 4, No. 1 (January 1994), pp. 53-78.

13   For more on these issues see my articles, "Property and Global Justice", *Philosophy in Context*, 15 (1985), pp. 34-42; and "Rich and Poor: The Ethics of Global Distribution", *Paths to Human Flourishing: Philosophical Perspectives (Proceedings of the International Philosophy Conference)*, Seoul (Korean Philosophical Association) 1993, pp. 25-40.

# Chapter 6

# Moral Universals as Cultural Realities

## FREDERICK BIRD

# I. Introduction

In this essay I argue that it is possible to identify a number of moral universals and that this identification can serve as a resource for addressing the problems that arise from moral diversity. In making this case I assume that this diversity cannot be and should not be ignored; nor can it be overcome or eliminated. However, we can find ways of managing moral diversity and the problems that arise in connection with it. I maintain that the recognition of certain moral universals can assist in addressing these problems. However, I also argue that the recognition of moral universals still plays only a limited role in managing these concerns. Primarily, the problems attendant on moral diversity can be best addressed by an approach which I refer to as the Ethics of Good Deliberations or Good Conversation. This approach assumes the reality of moral diversity and views ethics as the communicative activity by which people seek to reach and honour normative agreements. The recognition of moral universals serves an important but limited role in facilitating the conversations and deliberations by means of which people who may well hold different views of moral goods, utilize different patterns of reasoning, and communicate in different patterns of discourse and rhetoric can still reach normative agreements that matter for particular periods of time.(1)

The argument I develop here owes more to Aristotle, Montesquieu, Durkheim and Weber than to Plato, Aquinas, Rousseau, and Kant. In the end I identify and defend a number of moral universals, whose status as moral universals I defend by arguing both, one, that they have been and are almost everywhere acknowledged as being normative and, two, that they are acknowledged because these standards by their very nature make it possible for moral systems to exist and be treated as legitimate and worthy of respect and deference. I will elaborate on this position in due course. In the meantime it is first necessary to consider moral diversity and the problems it gives rise to.

# MORAL UNIVERSALS AS CULTURAL REALITIES

## II. Moral Diversity

A difference exists between recognizing that people hold diverse moral views and determining what response we will make to this phenomenon. I will first examine how pervasive and deeply rooted this diversity is before analyzing several typical responses.

The moral standards, rules, beliefs, and institutions which human communities have adopted have been indeed diverse. Some moral systems are religiously based, while others are secular; some are articulated in philosophical principles while others are communicated by taboos and ritual codes. Some moral systems foster egoistic self-interest while others encourage altruistic self-sacrifice. Moral systems differ with respect to the norms they endorse, the reasoning processes by which these norms are selected and justified, and the functional objectives they seek to realize. They differ as well in relation to their scope and jurisdiction and the means by which they are taught and enforced. Most importantly, they differ with regard to what they consider really to matter and the imperativeness by which these concerns are communicated. As cultural phenomena the diversity of moral systems reflects and expresses the diversity of human cultures.

Moral diversity exists on at least four different levels, each of which I will examine briefly: one, differences in social norms; two, difference in beliefs about moral ends and moral goods; three, differences in the assumptions about what count as reliable forms of reasoning; and, four, differences in the rhetoric and rituals by which people communicate moral sentiments and expectations. None of these differences are small or trivial: they are all profound.

One, people differ in the social norms they regard as authoritative. It is easy to make a long list of these differences. Different moral communities support and abhor foot binding, female circumcision, abortion, the use of contraceptive devices, indentured labour, and partial censorship of the press in the name of decency or national honour (Velasquez, 1996). Dumont has examined at length the contrasting views in South Asia and Europe regarding hierarchy and equality (Dumont, 1972; Dumont, 1977). Muslims, Christians, and secular Europeans hold or have held very different standards regarding fair interest payments. Europeans' standards regarding fair labour contracts have markedly changed over the past two centuries from master/servant contracts, through prerogative contracts, to what Selznick refers to as constitutive contracts (Selznick, 1969). People clearly differ about whether they think fair corporate tax returns are best achieved through negotiations that take into account specific situations or through impersonal rules for which companies then hire lawyers and accountants to help them adjust to and work around (Velasquez, 1996). Some communities favour democracy and others rule by elders (Bendix, 1978). Differences in social norms are not easily ignored or transcended. People organize their interactions in terms of them, defend themselves aggressively against those who would propose alternative standards (regarding birth control, interest payments, arranged marriages, to name just a few examples), and resist the attempt of those who seek to relativize these standards in relation to shared but more transcendent principles.

Two, people differ, often sharply, in their conceptions of moral goods. Efforts to identify universally shared conceptions of the good have not really proven successful. Although we may note that humans generally seek to promote happiness or human well-being, in practice they mean quite different things. Humans are not indifferent about their particular understandings of what constitute their moral goods. Buddhists who value enlightenment have something quite different in mind than Christians who seek salvation, Marxists who strive to create societies undivided by class, the liberals who seek to promote civil liberties, naturalists who seek to live in tune with nature, others who seek to enhance material well being, and still others who seek to express themselves and create beauty. Our conceptions of moral goods are indeed multiple (Walzer, 1983; Taylor, 1989). There are religious versus secular views, communal versus individualistic views. The attempts at an abstract level to identify a highest good, whether it is identified, as Royce argued, as whatever promotes loyalty or as Nozick has argued as whatever promotes intrinsic value (Nozick, 1981), are unconvincing to those who value their own particular conceptions. It has been argued, for example, that all societies value fairness and hence fairness is a commonly valued moral good. However, this contention can be criticized from a number of different perspectives. It is not at all clear that the way Hindus allocate resources and decide upon fitting shares of rewards and burdens in keeping with notions of auspiciousness and dharma is appropriately thought of as a system of fairness. Concerns about purity and danger, about social rituals, and about honour play a major role. Although notions of justice and fairness have begun to be raised more in modern times as the result of Muslim, British legal, Western philosophical, and modern commercial influences, it is a bit of cultural imperialism to see these concerns as a central underlying theme in traditional notions of dharma (Weber, 1958; Dumont, 1972). Even if we were to argue, as I will later, that each society holds up some normative notions about the fitting allocation of resources, we would still have to acknowledge both that the beliefs about what constitute "fitting" allocations differ markedly and that these differences frequently occur in contention within the same societies. For example, trade unionists, entrepreneurs and corporate capitalists ordinarily hold contrasting ideas about what constitute fitting and fair allocation of resources.

Three, not only do humans differ markedly in their conceptions and rankings of moral goods, they also differ in their views about what forms of reasoning they regard as reliable and valid. Some reason by citing Qu'ranic verses or legal precedents. Others argue by telling stories or invoking abstract principles. Many reason by calculating means to arrive at sought for outcomes. Whether people use intuitive, natural law, utilitarian, de-ontological or social contract arguments often makes a difference in terms of how they interpret particular normative standards, as Rawls has argued at length with respect to standards of justice (Rawls, 1970, Chapters 1,3). Since the Enlightenment philosophers have sought to utilize reasoned arguments in hopes of identifying common and highest moral principles which could be invoked to demonstrate that varying and differing moral standards were relative and less compelling. Hobbes, Spinoza, Hume, and Kant all developed reasons in defense of particular conceptions of moral truths. People like Gewirth have produced modern versions of these arguments. However, as MacIntyre has observed: these attempts to use reason in order to overcome differences in moral beliefs have not produced the hoped-for consensus but only more refined disagreements in part because people hold quite different views about which reasoning patterns they regard as being most truthful, most trustworthy, and most convincing (MacIntyre, 1981). People differ strongly about their view of how to reason correctly and wisely and they resist attempts to subordinate their differences to some particular form of reasoning.

Four, people differ in terms of the rhetoric and rituals by means of which they communicate their moral sentiments and expectations. At one level, we can summarize this point by saying that people use different moral languages and that these differences cannot be eliminated by convincing everyone to use a common moral Esperanto (Stout, 1988). People express themselves inevitably in terms of the symbols and rites of their local cultures. It is impossible to invent a superculture. If we seek to identify common standards we must abstract from local expressions in ways that typically do not do justice to particular formulations and understandings. Geertz has argued at length about the need to respect local knowledge and accordingly attempt to see things as local people themselves do (Geertz, 1973; Geertz, 1983).

For many people and for extensive historical periods the cultural diversity and historical relativity of moral ideas has posed no significant moral concern. Particular communities assumed the validity of their own moral systems. They viewed the moral ideas of other peoples as being clearly inferior or as being a matter of indifference since, it was assumed, the moral ideas of other peoples in no way affected their own lives. With respect to differences in moral ideas within particular communities, most societies have allowed for minimal degrees of diversity so long as the fundamental beliefs and principles of authority were not directly challenged.

In other settings this cultural diversity and historical relativity have raised moral concern, especially because of interactions between peoples with diverse moral ideas and rivalries between moralities within particular societies. People have become concerned regarding the diversity and relativity of moral ideas for several reasons. Thus, one, the recognition that moral ideas are culturally and historically diverse and relative often gives rise to attitudes of comparative indifference with respect to the authoritative claims of any particular moral systems. In these settings individuals are tempted to relativize these claims and to assert their personal discretion in choosing which aspects of their own or other moral traditions seem to them to make most sense. As individuals selectively honour parts of various moral systems, the capacity to create a sense of moral community between groups of people is thereby reduced. Two, the fact that interacting groups of people embrace diverse moral ideas makes it more difficult to resolve conflicts between people by reference to common or even similar moral assumptions. As a consequence resolutions often have to be imposed by those with political, legal, or personal power. Three, the recognition that moral ideas are culturally and histor-ically relative often makes the claims of any particular morality seem more arbitrary and accidental to the individuals involved. Most people adopt the moral ideas of the cultures in which they are raised. In the face of diversity and conflict, some individuals have been encouraged to ask whether these inherited ideas are in fact most fitting or valid. Perhaps they ought to adopt alternative moral ideas or at least modify their own morality in light of these alternative ideas. As a consequence the recognition of the diversity and relativity of moral ideas in some settings has tended to reduce the authority of particular moralities and their capacity to resolve conflicts.

## III. Approaches to Moral Diversity

It is possible to adopt several quite different attitudes towards this fact of moral diversity. I will first consider the views of those who see this diversity as the whole story and then I will consider the views of others who in varying ways have attempted to add to this picture by identifying some kinds of commonalities that transcend these differences. These positions differ not so much in their empirical accounts but in their evaluations and interpretations of these accounts. I will examine briefly four quite different approaches to moral diversity: one, those who adopt a relativist position; two, those who seek to identify common first moral principles; three, those who seek to identify cultural commonalties; and four, those who adopt evolutionary or developmental models.

# MORAL UNIVERSALS AS CULTURAL REALITIES

## 1. Relativistic Approaches

Relativists assume that moral ideas are historically relative and often culturally specific. People may well adopt new moral ideas and be persuaded to accept the moral standards and arguments of others. The degree to which different cultures adopt similar moral ideas is a matter of historical chances brought about by events such as conquests, cultural diffusion, and religious conversions, as well as legal and commercial negotiations. Relativists make several claims about moral diversity, one of which is defensible and others of which are less tenable. One, relativists argue that it is impossible to identify a set of first moral principles which all conscientious humans would recognize as morally compelling if they were thoughtfully to consider the matter. The case against common first or highest moral principles is strong for reasons I have already cited: namely, the fact that people hold quite different views about the status and priority of moral goods and the fact that they assign quite different ranks to various patterns of moral reasoning. However, a convincing argument against common first moral principles does not constitute a convincing argument against other common moral standards not regarded as first or highest principles.

Two, relativists often argue that it is ethno-centric to criticize and judge the culturally legitimate norms and practices of other people. They maintain that it is imperious and moralistic to try to change culturally accepted activities just because they differ from moral standards held by western Europeans. Who are we, they ask, to make judgements about female initiation rites in East Africa, or about exchanges of favours accompanying business transactions in India, or about working conditions in south east Asia factories? This argument can be criticized from several angles. Often in practice those making this argument fail to distinguish between social practices and culturally held norms. While bribery and extortion have been practised for some years by those managing government contracts in India, Italy and the Near East, there has been considerable public and popular opposition to these practices (Gillespie, 1987). While some forms of legitimate reciprocating personal consideration play a role in business practices in a number of countries, the norms governing these exchanges allow neither for bribery nor extortion (Wertheim, 1964). More importantly to tolerate among others practices we ourselves judge to be unfair and devious may be an even more insidious form of ethnocentrism (Klitgaard, 1988). If we genuinely care about the welfare of others, then we ought to voice our concern if we judge they are following practices that in some ways undermine their well-being. Actively voicing our concern is not the same thing as coercively compelling them. They may argue back after all. And both we and they may learn from the exchange. However, not to speak up in some manner is to treat their well-being as of lesser significance.

Three, relativists err both in failing to distinguish between different facets of moral diversity and by claiming too much. Several features of moral diversity can be more easily managed than others. Differences in the rhetoric, discourse, and rituals by which people communicate moral claims and feelings can be handled through sensitive, attentive attempts to listen to others and to translate our concerns into the images, turns of phrase, and etiquette that they are used to using. This is a major undertaking. It requires the ability to listen well, to enter into reciprocating discussions, and the imagination to comprehend the accounts of others. Reaching common understandings is not always either easy or fully possible. However, through give and take exchanges people can begin to see equivalence between superficially quite different moral practices. Through give and take discussions it is possible to identify some common considerations about justice as well as important differences in, for example, negotiated as well as impersonally determined tax rates. In contrast it may be much more difficult to arrive at common understandings with respect to the identity and ranking of moral goods or to gain agreements about moral reasoning. These differences cannot be overcome or reduced by imaginative and artful translations. They are often very intensely held. However, people can still reach agreements in spite of these latter differences (De George, 1996). Many decisive agreements between otherwise antagonistic parties have been reached because each can justify the agreement using their own and different moral logics and invoking their own and different moral beliefs (Zartman, 1976; Zartman and Berman, 1982). Because relativists typically fail to distinguish between the several dimensions of moral diversity, they often view differences as more intractable than they can prove to be. It is possible to arrive at common moral understandings and to reach common moral agreements in ways that both respect differences while transcending them.

### 2. Moral Universals as Common Highest Principles

In response to this recognition of moral diversity and relativity, a number of observers and moralists have attempted to identify some beliefs, assumptions, standards, and/or principles which are common or ought to be common to all moral systems. What they have attempted to identify were not any trivial similarities but rather some universal and invariant principles or features that were integral and essential features of all moralities. They assumed that the moral universals they were able to identify were of such a character that conscientious people who thought about the matter would acknowledge them to be reasonable and

# MORAL UNIVERSALS AS CULTURAL REALITIES

authoritative. Thus, these commonalities were not thought of as being merely empirical generalizations. Rather any commonality that qualified as a genuine moral universal was expected to command the respect, deference, and assent from all those who thoughtfully considered its substantive and formal characteristics. Hence, moral universals, unlike theoretical or empirical generalizations, were expected to possess normative authority. Moral universals have been variously identified with specific rules (Gert, 1966), virtues (Aristotle, 1953), principles (Donagon, 1977; Kant, 1949), and rights (Gewirth, 1978; Edel and Edel, 1968).

Moral universals have been defended as common highest principles using three quite different approaches, which I refer to as neo-Vedantic, apologetic, and Kantian. I will discuss the first two only briefly and consider the third more fully.

## a) Neo-Vedantic Approaches

Neo-Vedantists argue that differences in moral standards, reasons and beliefs represent different pathways to a common highest truth. Moral diversity is acknowledged but treated as not being very serious. One ought to tolerate these differences while at the same time one ought to recognize them as secondary and subordinate to ultimate truths. Neo-Vedantists artfully combine a tolerance for diversity with a firm conviction in their own spiritual view of the world. They persuasively defend virtues of compassion, harmony, self-discipline, self-mastery and tolerance along with the belief in the importance of self development. Jagdish Parikh offers a secular version of these ideas as a guide for successful business men and women. In "Managing Your Self," a guide to detached involvement, "Intuition," which he describes as "the new frontier of management," and "Beyond Leadership," (with Bennis and Lessem) which he views as a guide for balancing economic, ethics, and ecology, Parikh draws upon neo-Vedantic traditions to develop a moral stance for managers in any and all cultures (Parikh, 1992; 1994; Bennis, Parikh, and Lessem, forthcoming).

Neo-Vedantists do not treat the differences in social norms, moral goods, and moral reasons very seriously even while they acknowledge them. Their ethic of tolerance can easily become a justification for simply overlooking or evading these differences. Their position is basically apolitical and personal.

## b) Apologetic Approaches

Apologists assume that their own moral systems can be generalized in ways that allow them to comprehend and incorporate the morally significant aspects of other moral traditions. Apologists avoid the inherently relativistic position of those sceptical regarding moral universals. They recognize the diversity and relativity of moral ideas but then rank various other moral reasons and standards in relation to

# FREDERICK BIRD

their own system. In the process they may discern in the other moralities ideas that can be treated as parallels or as expressions of their own ideas.

This apologetic approach remains a morally appropriate strategy for the proponents of any particular moral system. Rather than viewing all moral systems indifferently as moral equivalents, they attempt to assign greater and lesser validity to other moral systems from the perspective of their own commitments. This apologetic strategy is followed most effectively when apologists are able to identify significant correspondences between moralities and to explain the reasons for diversities in ways that seem comprehensible. This apologetic approach has been persuasively articulated by a number of moralists. For example, Christian mission-aries adopted this stance in their efforts to win converts in Asia and Africa. Alan Donagan has recently defended his own rational ethic by arguing that it reflects the most important, common, non-theistic moral ideas of Stoicism, Thomistic Christianity, Judaism, and Kant (Donagon, 1977, chps 1,2). Herbert Spenser argued for his own utilitarian ethic by asserting that most other moralities represented simply earlier, less historically evolved expressions of the moral ideas that attained fullest expression in his own views (Spenser, 1893).

Apologists often run roughshod over moral dissents and disagreements of others. Their approach is more evangelical rather than ecumenical. They often assume that significant moral agreements can only occur when people also concur in their beliefs about moral goods and set forth their moral arguments with the same patterns of reasoning. They seek converts rather than collaborators.

## c) Kantian Approaches

Kantian approaches argue that it is possible to use human reason to identify moral universals as highest ethical principles. From this perspective moral universals are viewed as fundamental principles which are discovered or discerned by thoughtful reflection. These principles are not viewed as cultural products nor is their authority based upon the accidental presence of popular respect. They are viewed as necessary truths. The most important moral principles for all humans are viewed as being derived from a thoughtful analysis of what reason requires, and/or what must be done to respect the basic character of human life. Because these moral ideas are derived from an analysis of the nature of human life and reason, it is possible in principle for any thoughtful human being to recognize the validity and hence authority of these ideas. One need not be a member of a particular culture to be able to recognize these moral universals. To be sure, some individuals, who are less discerning and more biased, may be able to discern these truths only obscurely and in distorted forms.

Immanuel Kant's moral philosophy well illustrates this approach. He asserted that all humans morally value good will. He then proceeded to identify the formal marks which necessarily characterized good will. He argued that a will is genuinely good if the maxim by which it acts can be universalized (Kant, 1949, p. 18). From this perspective a moral maxim has validity if it is universalizable in the minimal sense that all individual similarly situated ought to be guided by the same standards.

Alan Gewirth has recently elaborated upon Kant's argument. He carefully analyzes the nature of human action and observes that humans inherently seek to realize what they deem to be good. Thus, humans inherently value their own actions and the conditions which make it possible for them to act with intention and choice. If they are to be consistent with their own inherent dispositions to value the conditions which make it possible to act as humans necessarily do act with intention and choice, then they must require that other people not interfere to obstruct or deny those conditions. Hence, they must necessarily demand the right to minimal levels of freedom and well-being so they can in fact act with genuine volition and intention. However, in order to be consistent, they must demand that this right be respected not only for themselves but also for all other human beings. Consequently, by virtue of what he refers to as the Principle of Generic Consistency, Gewirth argues that individual humans must necessarily respect the human rights of all persons to the minimal levels of freedom and well being which make genuinely volitional and intentional human activity possible (Gewirth, 1978, Chapters 1-3).

It is possible to cite a variety of additional examples. Thus, Bernard Gert attempts to identify universal moral rules which all rational humans would necessarily adopt when they consider the pain, unnecessary deaths, the lack of freedom, disability, and lack of pleasure which they all inherently seek to avoid. He then, sets forth as moral universals rules against murder, causing pain, disability, death, the deprivation of freedom and the deprivation of pleasure, unless good reasons can be publicly advocated for acting otherwise (Gert, 1966, Chapters 1,2,4,5).

The ancient Stoics articulated an extremely influential idea about moral universals in relation to a theory of natural law. The Stoic arguments, which subsequently influenced Jewish philosophers like Philo as well as Catholic moral theology and Roman law, assumed that humans could most fully realize the good they sought by acting in keeping with their nature as rational animals. Accordingly, as animals they ought to act to preserve their lives and as rational creatures they ought to act in keeping with reason (Koester, 1968; Troeltsch, 1960, pp. 150-5).

In the 17th century, Thomas Hobbes articulated his own version of natural law based not simply on an analysis of human nature but upon the conclusions which human beings would likely endorse when they reflected candidly upon their own egoistic desires to seek their own advantage, the scarcity of resources, and likelihood of others seeking to deprive them of their advantages. Hobbes argued that in order to protect their own liberty, men and women would endorse moral principles which would limit their own freedom to that which they would be willing to extend to others (Hobbes, 1958, Chapter 14).

Although these several formulations of moral universals differ in a number of ways, still they share several decisive assumptions. Thus, for example, they argue persuasively that any standards or principles regarded as moral absolutes ought to be universalizable. Any standards or reasons that favour particular people or particular interests cannot be regarded as moral absolutes since they are not impartial and consistent with respect to all humans. Furthermore, according to these several theories, humans ought always to act on the basis of principles which they can communicatively defend with intelligible, coherent and logically consistent arguments. We may more generally restate this position by saying that as moral beings, humans ought to act on the basis of principles which they can defend with reasons which are comprehensible and compelling to others no matter what their position or cultural background. Finally, these several theories assume that a primary function of moral principles is to identify the primary duties and basic rights of individual humans.

These several theories have been defended and criticized from various perspectives. From the perspective of comparative, historical studies of moral theories, it is possible to make the following critical observations. One, these natural and rational theories of moral universals focus primarily on individual moral actors, their rights and principles for actions. As a result these theories tend to provide overly atomistic views of human relationships with little analysis of ways social structures and patterns of social organization influence human interactions. Probably with Kant, Rousseau, and Spinoza in mind, Hegel argued that these theories focus far too much on abstract rights and abstract notions of morality and not sufficiently on the moral life as lived in actual social interconnectedness (Hegel, 1952, pp. 138-142; Ilting, 1971). Toennies argued that these moral views were overly influenced by views of human willing as guided by rational principles at the expense of alternative views of human will guided by natural instincts for affectionate interrelatedness (Toennies, 1957, Part III). Two, it can be argued that these several theories have been typically idealistic and utopian. They defend principles which humans ought to be guided by if they act consistent with reason and the essential character of human action. They give less direct counsel regarding relevant moral guidelines under circumstances where human communication is likely to be obscured by misunderstandings, human reasoning distorted by self-interest, and human relations modified by the pursuit of power.

Three, these various natural and rational theories of moral universals fail to account both for the moral authority of conventional moralities and their role in extending human sympathies and resolving human conflicts. These theories often distinguish quite sharply between normative conventions and authentic moral principles. Kant argued that conventional wisdom was typically prudential and utilitarian in character and thus lacked the categorical imperativeness of true moral counsel (Kant, 1949). Gert has more recently argued that it is "a sloppy use of language that has allowed 'code of conduct' to be taken as the equivalent to `morality...'" (Gert, 1966, p 4). From this perspective universal moral principles may be invoked to evaluate the moral worth of particular conventional codes or to propose reformulations of them. However, these principles cannot be used to explain the functions of these cultural codes as authoritative normative guides. Hence, from this perspective a tendency has developed to draw too sharp a distinction between moral codes articulated as natural or rational principles and moral codes articulated as conventional codes of behaviour. No examinations are conducted to analyze the similar status of both as cultural phenomena (Williams, 1972, pp. 76,7). Finally, four, these various natural and rational theories of moral universals presuppose that consent to these principles as authoritative primarily takes place as a result of rational reflection. They fail to observe the ways these ideas are proposed and gain widespread acceptance as historical occurrences influenced both by particular cultural symbols by which they are communicated and by the institutional support they receive (Winch, 1972, Chapter 3).

I have referred to these approaches broadly as Kantian because like Kant they variously seek to identify first or highest moral principles which they view as being rationally defensible and from which other moral standards are derived or to which they are subordinated. These assumptions are problematic. After all, if moral universals are defined in terms of first principles, then it becomes increasingly difficult to identify any such standards that have been universally adopted. Moral systems typically differ with greatest intensity with respect to first principles. The first and highest moral principles of Buddhism, Brahminism, Confucianism, Christianity, liberalism and Stoicism, are decisively different. To live with an enlightened dispassionate compassion, for example, calls for a markedly different orientation to life than attempting to follow one's dharma, or acting in keeping with rational principles of natural law. Moreover, the assumption that moral universals ought to be defined in relation to first principles too readily dismisses the importance of some shared moral assumptions, like the incest taboo, which, even though they are not central to any particular morality, are fundamental and constitutive of moral systems as cultural realities.

# FREDERICK BIRD

### 3. Moral Universals as Cultural Commonalities

Moral universals additionally have been identified by discovering salient, empirically observable commonalities among culturally diverse moral systems. These approaches assume that moral universals exist as cultural commonalities that can be discerned by thoughtful, empirical analysis. These theories treat all moral ideas as cultural phenomena but assume morally significant commonalities can be located among diverse moral systems in relation to their forms, functions, and substantive standards. They recognize that moral ideas are articulated in varied idioms and genres but assume these differences can be overcome by identifying more general principles which the local standards illustrate and general functions which local standards variously perform. The basic assumption of these approaches is that moral systems by virtue of their nature as culturally communicated standards for conduct inherently deal with a common range of issues and make some common assumptions with respect to the ways of handling these issues. The purpose of these cultural commonality theories of moral universals is clearly to identify these common features.

The formulation of the ius *gentium*, the law of peoples by Roman jurists best illustrates this approach to the identification of moral universals. Roman jurists sought to set forth a common set of moral and legal principles to govern the relations of the ethnically, religiously and linguistically diverse peoples that became part first of the Roman Republic and then the Roman Empire. Beginning with careful observations of the other Italian peoples, Roman jurists identified common characteristics in the conventional practices and rules with respect to transference of property, the making of wills, the negotiation of contracts, the definition of civil wrongs, the rules of tenure, the rights and responsibility of parents, and status of corporations. Maine observed "Whenever a particular usage was seen to be practised by a large number of separate races in common it was set down as part of the law common to all nations or Ius *Gentium*" (Maine, 1879, p. 47). Roman jurists did not seek to annul local laws and conventions but rather to incorporate them within a more universal system of law. The latter provided consistent means of interpreting these rules in relation to common principles and common juridical practices.

Other examples of this approach may also be cited. Thus, without undertaking the same kind of detailed scrutiny of other peoples, David Hume still attempted to identify a set of moral universals based upon his observations of those principles which all people approve as the basis for their censure and approbation of human conduct. In general terms Hume observed that all people approve of benevolent affection as a preeminent moral quality. He added that everywhere where resources are scarce but not wholly depleted, they also establish principles of justice and

110

equity to deal with definitions and allocations of property and the establishment of contracts. In addition Hume argued that humans universally seek to protect the unity and security of their communities, establish rules regarding proper forms of government, and develop standards for good manners. Hume deduced that communities agreed to these moral principles because the latter functioned to regulate human interactions and extend human sympathies in ways that were personally and socially beneficial (Hume, 1975).

May and Abraham Edel more recently attempted to discern a set of moral universals on the basis of anthropological studies of diverse cultures. They argued that it is possible to identify a number of moral concerns which are universal. In spite of other differences, local societies everywhere, the Edels argue, insist upon the obligation of mothers to take good care of their children, prohibit what is variously defined as incest, limit and control the exercise of aggression against other members of the community, establish principles with respect to the just distribution of resources, and encourage individual loyalty to the larger community (Edel and Edel, 1968. Chapters 4-7, 9).

These various theories which regard moral universals viewed as cultural commonalities share several common traits. Thus, typically the universals they discern result from making empirical generalizations with respect to observed phenomena rather than theoretical generalizations on the basis of rational deliberations. They attempt to identify common features in the actual codes of behaviour of diverse people. Typically, these cultural commonality theories examine what Hegel referred to as the ethical life, namely, the ways in which typical interactions in families, social groups, communities and societies are in fact guided by normative codes (Hegel, 1952, Part III). These theories have observed a number of morally significant commonalities shared by quite diverse moralities.

However, these formulations of moral universals as cultural commonalities may be criticized for several reasons. One, like the rational/natural theories, these cultural commonality formulations largely treat moral universals as ahistorical realities. To be sure, they recognize them as cultural products but they fail to consider ways in which these universals may have altered with historical developments. They ignore the possibility that the whole set of moral universals might be altered or augmented as a consequence of widespread and influential moral reforms, economic and social developments and changing understandings of human life. Two, these commonality theories are vulnerable to the criticism that in their attempts to identify similarities among moralities they ignore those particular aspects of specific moralities which are viewed by their adherents as being of central importance. The Roman law of peoples intentionally ignored these particularistic features which were often religiously grounded because they represented divisive influences. In the process this approach may become reductionistic. Certainly

Hume's formulation may thus be criticized. He ignored the particular cultural beliefs in which specific moral rules were defined and in terms of which people identified what they deemed to be beneficial. He reduced what was worthy of attention to the formal fact that people adopted normative standards which they judged to be beneficial.

### 4. Developmental Models

Moral universals have also been formulated in cultural terms in relation to developmental models. Two kinds of models have been conceptualized: those which identify the typical stages in the historical development of moral ideas and those which chart the typical stages in the personal development of moral ideas. Both types of models recognize that humans have thought about morality in culturally varied and historical relative ways. Both attempt to demonstrate that this diversity is not entirely random. They argue that identifiable patterns can be discerned because particular ways of thinking about moral issues reflect specific stages that can be sequentially arranged. These theories assume that people will be able to think about moral issues in more developed ways only in so far as they have already learned to think about these matters according to less developed ways. Later stages presuppose and build upon former stages. All these developmental models assume that subsequent stages of moral thinking are more morally fitting than former stages. Although they vary some in their accounts, these models generally assume that later stages are characterized by moral thinking that is less particularistic, less rigid, less authoritarian and more universalistic, more adaptable, and more open to rational interpretation and individual discretion.

Unlike the commonality theories, developmental formulations of moral universals do not attempt to identify standards and forms of reasoning which are authoritative for all peoples. Rather, they first attempt to identify sets of moral ideas of different people which share enough significant similarities in their basic beliefs or reasoning patterns to be grouped together. They next attempt to demonstrate that these sets of ideas are not unrelated. In spite of obvious differences, specific sets of moral ideas may be arranged in an overall developmental pattern. From the perspective of the developmental models moral universals are not strictly to be identified with the most developed moral ideas. The most developed moral ideas may represent the inherent goal towards which less developed moral systems aim as they mature. Still these most developed moral beliefs and patterns of reasoning would be quite inappropriately adopted by individuals or communities which have not already progressed in their moral growth sufficiently to understand and apply them adequately. Nonetheless, the moral universal is essentially to be defined in relation to the developmental models themselves. These models identify the characteristic sequences by which humans learn increasingly more developed and more morally adequate moral ideas.

Hegel formulated his developmental model of moral universals in relation to the overall course of world history. Hegel recognized that moral ideas were parts of cultural ethoi and attempted to analyze moral standards and reasons as aspects of cultural wholes. He therefore attempted to analyze the fundamental orientations of entire moral cultures. He surveyed the moral cultures of varied human communities and arranged them in an historical and developmental order. He observed that the most primitive moral cultures lacked a sense of historical possibility. In these ethoi individuals were dominated by ascriptive ties which bound them to kin groups and their immediate environment. Hegel observed a clear development in moral cultures with the growth of subjective awareness both by individuals and by collectivities. This subjectivity manifested itself, he observed, in the recognition that individuals could dissent from group norms, could create their own distinctive personalities and form their own associations. This subjectivity also manifested itself at the corporate levels as peoples organized themselves as political communities able to extend themselves purposively by discrete political action. Hegel observed that the subjectivity of individuals characteristically clashed with the subjectivity of organized communities. Hegel argued that a final development of moral ethoi occurred as these two opposing subjectivities were integrated in cultural settings where individual discretion was guided by universal reason and collective subjectivity was guided through the state by general will of the people involved (Hegel, 1956).

Kohlberg has conceptualized a theory of moral universals in relation to a sequence of stages which individuals necessarily pass through as they develop their moral thinking. These stages are identified with typical patterns of moral reasoning. Kohlberg argued that individual adopt more developed forms of reasoning because they find them to be more morally adequate, coherent, and comprehensive ways of thinking about moral issues. Kohlberg argued that all the diverse ways of thinking about moral issues can be subsumed under one of the six sequential stages. At the first two pre-conventional stages, Kohlberg argues that individuals view moral guidelines as heteronomously imposed and attempt both at times slavishly and deferentially to follow these guidelines or to pursue their own individual ends. At the conventional levels of stages three and four, moral thinking develops to the point where individuals variously act with regard to others in hopes of reciprocal benefits and honour the conventions of the groups of which they are members. At the post conventional level of stages five and six, Kohlberg argued that individuals initially think of moral issues in relation to basic rights and social contracts and then subsequently think of these issues in relation to universal principles of justice. In his latest formulation Kohlberg maintains that he has discovered considerable empirical data with respect to the pre-conventional and conventional stages but less evidence with respect to the post-conventional stages, the last of which must remain conjectural (Kohlberg, 1984).

Additional formulations of moral universals as developmental models have been set forth by Spenser, Hobhouse, Piaget, Wright, and others. I have briefly described Hegel and Kohlberg's model only in order to discuss the general features of this methodological strategy. The initial appeal of these models lies in their capacity at once to acknowledge the cultural diversity of moral ideas and to find ways of arranging these varied moral beliefs and forms of reasoning into single schema that account in a large part for observed diversity. From the perspective of these models an observer can acknowledge the diversity of moralities without becoming a relativist because differences in moral thinking represent simply less or more developed approaches. These models also recognize that particular individuals have in the past and may in the future learn decisively new ways of thinking about moral matters. Basic moral principles need not be viewed as having been given for all time either by the requirements of human nature or human reason or by the inherent features of human societies: some new principles may be proposed and adopted that significantly add to the accumulated moral wisdom of humankind or of particular individuals. Evolutionary models take seriously the historical contingency of moral ideas. Finally, evolutionary models view particular moral ideas in relation to larger sets of beliefs, reasons, and standards which form cultural wholes. In the attempt to identify moral universals, they do not extract particular standards or reasons out of the larger overall approach to moral matters of which they are part. Rather, they attempt to analyze these overall approaches. In this regard, it is obvious that the historical and individual models of moral development are fundamentally different. The former attempts to explain the relation between distinct moral cultures while the latter seeks to explain differences between the way individuals think about moral issues quite independent of the larger cultural setting.

Developmental formulations of moral universals may be criticized for the following reasons. One, individual models cannot be used to account for the cultural diversity and historical relativity of moral ideas. The adoption of moral ideas by whole societies, led by adults, is quite dissimilar from the adoption of moral ideas by individuals maturing to responsible adulthood. Two, developmental models as a whole remain moralistic and progressivistic. They belittle the commonalties shared by both developed and undeveloped moralities and they fail to recognize the morally fundamental principles which inform the most undeveloped expressions of human morality. They tend to overvalue the virtues of what they refer to as developed moralities and to undervalue the virtues of what they refer to as less developed moralities. Three, most of these models assume moral developments occur teleologically as people seek more closely to think about moral issues in keeping with particular often utopian principles of the highest stages, whose existence are defended not by empirical observations but by value-laden theoretical arguments. The models in turn fail to allow for the possibility that significant developments in the moral thinking of individuals may best be explained not teleologically in relation to ideal objectives but rather more contingently in relation to typical problems confronted and characteristic innovative responses. Four, it is not clear finally whether these developmental models ever really identify culturally created moral universals. What they seem to offer rather are their own formulations of moral development as a moral universal. They identify few universals actually shared by diverse communities and individuals.

## IV. An Alternative, Cultural Approach

Moral diversity constitutes a serious challenge. However, it is important to be clear about the nature of this challenge and about what we can hope to accomplish by identifying moral universals. By means of moralities human create and sustain normative agreements. Creating and sustaining normative agreements involves rendering judgements, invoking beliefs, making arguments, praising and blaming, rewarding and punishing, identifying ends, setting forth rules, and much else. Moral diversity makes the process of creating and sustaining normative agreements more difficult whenever those involved defer to and treat as normative different and competitive social norms, beliefs about moral goods, moral reasons, and forms of moral discourse. The answer to this difficulty is not to create and defend as normative for everyone a single set of social norms, moral beliefs, moral reasons and/or moral discourse. What can and should be done is to discover and encourage ways by which people from varied moral backgrounds can still create and sustain normative agreements between themselves. What is especially helpful are skills, processes, and ideas that help people to bargain and negotiate with others, to translate their ideas into rhetoric and discourse others can comprehend, and to explore empathetically and imaginatively the positions of others. Elsewhere I have proposed viewing ethics like good conversations and I have argued that what is especially needed is to develop skills to perceive and acknowledge what is going on, to listen and attend to the concerns of those involved, and to voice articulately our own positions (Bird, 1991; Bird, 1996).

In this essay I examine what role the identification of moral universals can make to this interactive process. This role is useful but limited. However, how useful the identification of moral universals is depends in large part on our prior assumptions about the nature and status of moral universals.

Each of the four broad approaches to moral diversity and to moral universals are subject to serious limitations. However, the attempt to identify moral universals need not be abandoned. It is possible to formulate a series of moral universals as culturally created phenomena in ways that avoid or meet the criticisms which I have set forth. This can be done by making several critical assumptions.

For example, moral universals need not necessarily constitute first principles from which other moral rules and guidelines should be derived. Often it has been assumed that any authentic moral universals quite naturally ought to exist as first principles like Hobbes's articulation of the first natural law "that every man ought to endeavor peace, as far as he has any hopes of attaining it; and when he cannot obtain it, that he may seek and use all helps and advantage of war," (Hobbes, 1958, Chapter 14) or like the Apostle Paul's counsel to "love your neighbour as yourself" (Romans 13:9). This presumption has frequently been readily embraced because it has characteristically been assumed that the alternative to identifying moral principles in terms of first principles was to identify them in relation to universal standards like the incest taboo that many specific moral systems view as being derivative, or marginal and hence trivial. However, from an historical and soc-iological perspective this stance cannot so readily be assumed. After all if moral universals are viewed necessarily as first principles then it becomes almost impos-sible to identify any such standards that have been universally adopted. Moral systems typically differ with greatest intensity with respect to their first principles. The assumption that moral universals ought to be defined in relation to first principles too readily dismisses the importance of a number of shared moral as-sumptions like the importance of keeping promises, which, even though they are not central to any particular morality, are nonetheless fundamental and constitutive of moral systems as cultural realities.

I presume that these universals are fundamental and authoritative features of the world's varied moral systems. However, I do not assume that they are every-where assigned similar rank or importance or even validity. I recognize that spec-ific moral systems acknowledge as of greatest validity those principles which are often culturally singular and philosophically unique. There is no way in which a formulation of moral universals can displace the high regard which particular peoples assign to the first principles of their own moral traditions. A statement of moral universals as cultural realities can, nonetheless, indicate some decisive features which various moral systems share in common as cultural phenomena.

Two, the purpose of identifying moral universals is not to create a new, universally acknowledged super morality which has priority over other particular moral systems. Rather, recognizing moral universals functions primarily to help us manage this diversity not to relativize it or rise above it. Most of the proponents of moral universals have viewed their own moral philosophies as more basic, more authoritative, and more compelling than other particular moralities. This assumption informs the arguments of Plato, Hume, Kant, Hegel, Spenser, Donagon, and even Kohlberg. In contrast I assume a more ecumenical view. By identifying moral universals we can more easily recognize similarities and equivalences between particular moralities.

Three, I assume that general moral principles can count as moral universals only if they are in fact universally acknowledged as being morally normative and compelling. Imagined or hypothetic principles do not qualify. Arguments about what reasonable or conscientious people would agree to may be ethically persuasive but they do not establish the principles thereby defended as moral universals. Reasonable and conscientious people have embraced a wide range of very different and often antagonistic moral principles. Moral universals exist as cultural phenomena not noumenal intuitions. Beginning with Plato many people have assumed that moral universals exist like the truths of mathematics and could be discovered in the same way by a careful analysis of the nature of human reason, human action, or the good itself (Plato, 1956; Plato, 1960a; Jonsen and Toulmin, 1988, Chapters 1, 2; Nussbaum, 1985, Part II). Along these lines, Bernard Gert has recently argued that "A moral rule is unchanging . . . discovered rather than invented. A moral rule is not dependent upon the will or decision of any man or group of men . . . Thus moral rules have a status similar to the laws of logic or mathematics" (Gert 1966, pp. 67, 8). Arguments like Gert's may be rationally compelling but the rules he thereby discovers can only count as genuine moral universals to the extent that they are also universally regarded as being authoritative. Donaldson makes a case for economic civility as a moral universal. While I think he makes a strong case for the importance of this ethic especially among modern, industrial cultures, historically this standard has competed with at least two others as normative criteria for allocating scare resources (Donaldson, 1996). Compelling arguments have as well been fervently defended for allocating resources in ways that preserve valued patterns of authority and sacrality (cf. Rappaport, 1979) and for allocating resources in terms of the uncoerced choices and transactions of people with legitimate proprietary claims to these resources (Nozick, 1974).

Moral principles can count as universals only to the extent that they have in fact been more or less universally recognized as normative. The words "as normative" are critical in my argument. Principles qualify as moral universals not because people everywhere comply with them but because the diverse moral systems created by human communities acknowledge them as authoritative and compelling standards for conduct and because individual adults correspondingly either seek to comply with them or to offer excuses and reason why they do not. The standards which I identify and defend meet these qualifications.

I do not include several highly valued standards which fail to satisfy these criteria. For example, there is no universally regarded standard that calls for people to act in morally consistent ways. Although philosophers often use arguments of consistency in order to identify conclusions they believe to be entailed by already accepted premises, there are a number of good reasons why it may be morally justified to act in ethically inconsistent ways (cf. Williams, 1985; Nozick, 1981). Similarly, there is no universally accepted standard prohibiting child labour. In fact in pre-modern and early industrial societies child labour was often defended as a means of supporting family solidarity and apprenticing children in the work of their parents. Arguments against child labour have only arisen in fairly recent times correlated with the development of public school systems.

With these several assumptions in mind, in the remainder of this essay I identify a number of principles as moral universals. I use two complementary arguments to defend their status as moral universals. Initially I make an empirical argument, observing the ways in which these principles have been universally recognized as normative standards. That is, people in diverse cultures have attempted to comply with these standards or have felt it necessary to give good reasons for making exceptions. In order to demonstrate that principles are regarded as normative, it is necessary to show that extensive efforts are made either to comply or to verbalize acceptable excuses and rationalizations. For a number of reasons few if any normative standards elicit full compliance even from those who defer to them (Bird, 1996; Aristotle, 1954). The fact that people do not always comply does not render these principles any less normative than comparable non-compliance does with specific social rules. I complement this empirical case with theoretical arguments about the factors that render moral standards normative in the eyes of those who defer to them. While the first defense argues that these standards have been regarded as normative, the second argument examines why and how these particular principles create this aura of legitimacy. In a circular fashion I argue that these standards are recognized as normative because of the intrinsic ways in which they foster the possibility, credibility, and esteem of moral standards more generally and thereby contribute to their legitimacy.

It is possible to identify three distinctly different expressions of moral universals. Each gains its recognition as authoritative standards somewhat differently. Thus, one, there are those normative standards which are presupposed by the existence of moralities as cultural phenomena. I argue that these standards must in some way be acknowledged and respected in order for moral ideas to attain minimal cultural status as authoritative guidelines for judgements and rules of interpersonal conduct. We may refer to these standards as the moral principles that make moral systems possible. The recognition of these standards is found wherever it is possible to identify moral systems as cultural realities. Two, there is a set of moral standards which facilitates minimal degrees of cooperation within human communities. These standards, which provide basic regulations with respect to kinship, in-group violence, and communal allocation of goods, are also universally recognized. Particular moral systems gain in legitimacy and credibility to the degree that they are able to facilitate human interactions and cooperation without recourse to coercion or caprice. Hence, we may refer to these common standards, which facilitate this cooperation in relation to universal sets of typical human needs, as the moral principles which make moral systems credible.

Finally, three, there is a series of moral universals which have not always and everywhere been recognized as authoritative. They have gained authority as a result of historical developments. They have gained authoritative status as various peoples have recognized their importance for their own particular moral systems. These principles and beliefs have been adopted and acknowledged as people have recognized that their own moral traditions ought to be rethought or reformulated in order to incorporate these new principles. These principles and beliefs have not always been readily accepted. Often they have been resisted. Over time, however, the impact of these new principles on traditional patterns of moral discourse and moral judgements can be discerned. These several principles have gained authoritative recognition because they articulate assumptions which have been recognized as being basic and integral to the real essence of morality as a cultural phenomenon. As they are adopted, these principles and beliefs augment the legitimacy of particular moralities. Moreover, once these principles and beliefs have been seriously considered by particular peoples, the culturally transmitted moral systems are likely to decline in legitimacy in the opinions of many if their traditional moralities are not in some ways appropriately modified. Since these principles and beliefs as adopted have functioned to raise the prestige of particular moralities, we may refer to these moral universals as the moral principles that make moral systems worthy of esteem.

## V. Moral Principles That Make Morality Possible

Several principles are basic to the existence of moral systems as cultural phenomena. In order for a set of ideas to be able to function for a group of people in their interpersonal discourse as authoritative moral ideas, these people must minimally acknowledge several normative principles including the following. Thus, individuals must respect the others with whom they enter into agreements; they must keep their promises; they must not intentionally deceive; and they must honour their reciprocal obligations. In various terms, these four principles have been universally recognized as authoritative, even though in many cultural settings they have been presumed and not directly and articulately advocated.

These four principles constitute a moral minimum. Taken as a group, they embody the basic and minimal basis for negotiating, reaching, and honouring agreements between people that can be regarded as obligating and normative. They represent the minimal grounds for transactions that result in agreements. Moral standards exist as cultural phenomena only on the basis of agreements. Moralities cannot be imposed. Compliance is moral only when it is consented to. In order to reach agreements, individuals have to exhibit respect for each other as wilful and self-interested beings. Without this respect conversations leading to agreements are impossible. In order to reach agreements that they can feel obligated to keep, they must be able to assume that the other is not intentionally deceiving. Agreements would not be possible unless people were able to make and keep promises. Agreements matter because people feel reciprocally bound to honour them. Only to the degree that people feel that these principles will be honoured are they willing and able to make and sustain normative agreements and in the process make morality possible. However, there are settings where people find it difficult or impossible to reach morally binding agreements precisely because they cannot assume that these principles will be honoured. Frontier settings are notorious as situations in which it is often impossible to expect people to respect those with whom they are trying to make agreements, communicate honestly, keep promises, and honour reciprocal obligations except with few trusted friends. Hobbes argued that where people were not able to enter into normative agreements life was short, brutish, and nasty (Hobbes, 1958).

### 1. People Ought to Respect the Others with Whom They Seek to Reach Agreements as Willing and Interested Persons

We ought to respect others with whom we seek to make agreements as willing and interested persons (De George, 1996). This principle has been formulated a number of different ways, although many versions claim more than I think is minimally necessary. The arguments that we should treat all persons as ends and not means and that we should be benevolent and sympathetic towards others call for greater concern for others than is required in order to negotiate agreements. It is often quite difficult to express sympathy for others and to treat them consistently as intrinsically valued autonomous selves. However, this principle asks less from us. It calls for us to be attentive to the voiced concerns of others with whom we are interacting whether we agree with them or not. In so far as they are reasonable and responsible adults, it calls for us to seek their voluntary and not forced or manipulated cooperation. It calls for us to recognize that they have interests that may well differ from ours. When we are seeking to reach agreements with others, minimally we must recognize them as unique others and not as extensions of our own interests (Bird, 1996, Chapter 3).

## 2. People Ought to Keep Their Promises

The importance of keeping promises is widely recognized as a basic moral principle (Donagan, 1977, pp. 88-90; Gert, 1966, Chapter 6). Where people keep promises, trust develops and some measure of trust is necessary both for human cooperation and for personal development (Erikson, 1975, Chapter 1). What distinguishes humans from other species is that they can and do make promises (Wilson, 1980). Humans recognize themselves as both the subjects and objects of their own volition and can foresee how as objects of their volition they may act in the future in relation to their present choices. People make promises to each other by communicating in keeping with culturally specific guidelines which may be more or less simple or elaborate (Searle, 1969). Written and oral contracts represent only one formal expression of such promise-making. Basically, a person or group makes a promise by communicating to others at one moment in time their agreement or consent to act in a particular way at another moment in time. This communication may be more or less explicit and may involve more or less clearly articulated stipulations, vows, and threats. Promises undergird practically all human institutions. As members of particular groups, men and women consent to act in particular ways. The corresponding groups promise to recognize their membership so long as they act as agreed.

Promise-making and promise-keeping are only sometimes distinct, deliberate, self-consciously verbal activities. Frequently, promises are elicited and undertaken as part of ongoing affectionate relationships characteristic of family, friendships and community. Individuals respond to the affection, care, and demands of others by explicitly and tacitly consenting to these relationships and expressing their commitments to preserve them. Promise-making and keeping becomes intertwined with the receiving and giving of these relationships. Promise-making and keeping becomes an issue only when something disrupts mutual expectations formed by history and experience. At these points people are called upon to make explicit pledges and vows, as when they form new relationships.

Promise making and promise keeping plays a central role in morality. Men and women use moral discourse primarily in order to persuade others to reach agreements. Agreements represent reciprocal sets of promises whereby individuals make certain promises in return for corresponding promises made by others. These agreements may exist as contracts, as the consent of some to the judgements of others, or as the assent of some to the guidance of others. In order to persuade others to reach agreements, individuals may invoke normative standards, reasoning arguments, valued objectives, or beliefs, all of which are expressed by the symbols which constitute features of culturally transmitted moral ideas. These symbols retain their value as communicative coinage in so far as people honour the agreements they thereby have been persuaded to accept. They lose their value when agreements thereby reached are not honoured. In effect, moral discourse is used in order to identify prior promises and agreements which have already been made tacitly or directly in order to identify these as a basis for new agreements that are to be made or renewed. If individuals have made no promises or commitments - and a commitment is a promise to oneself - then it is correspondingly difficult to persuade them to reach as yet unrealized agreements or consent to as yet unmade promises unless the latter narrowly serve their own interest. When people use moral discourse to persuade others, they presuppose that it is possible to invoke various promises and agreements to which others have already consented by identifying their group loyalties, beliefs, and objectives. Moral communication is best able to facilitate the realization of new agreements, when it can be assumed that people have already made promises and they can be counted upon to keep these promises. Hence, promise keeping is universally invoked as a normative standard not only because of its importance for the existence of social institutions and human cooperation, but also for its central role in making moral discourse possible and credible.

### 3. People Ought to Make Their Communications Honest and Not Deceptive

We ought to communicate honestly and not deceptively. Strictures against lying are found in all cultures. Numerous principled, purposive, utilitarian and traditional arguments have been made against lying. In the context of the present discussion lying is wrong simply because it is impossible to reach any kind of agreements if we think others are lying in their communications to us. As Bok has observed, lying is a parasitic activity. People can get away with it only in settings where everyone is assumed to be speaking honestly (Bok, 1978). Lying involves intentional efforts to deceive others in what we communicate. Not disclosing information that others seek and consider vital constitutes an additional form of intentional deception even if it is not strictly lying as such. A number of forms of communication are similar to lying and the withholding of vital information but do not really constitute instances of intentional deception. Exaggerated statements, puffery in advertising, evasions to avoid public embarrassments are usually communicated much like traditional jocular lies not with the intention of deceiving but of momentarily expressing bravado, or pride, or protecting people who might be unintentionally hurt by more straight forward communication (Bonhoeffer, 1955). Negotiations as instances of bargaining over time typically call for the parties to begin withholding some information, which is then disclosed more fully as the negotiations proceed. There are standards which function to monitor these exchanges, communicated both through legal and moral expectations about bargaining in good faith as well through culturally specific etiquettes. As long as people abide by these "rules of the game" then neither partial disclosures, nor exaggerated claims constitute instances of intentional deception. The moral prohibition against lying is directly connected with the normative principle which forbids the breaking of promises. To break a promise is to make into lies one's communicative utterances regarding promises already made. To break a promise, hence, is to lie with respect to the future. Similarly to make a promise or to enter an agreement on the basis of intentionally distorted information is to lie with respect to the present. Thus, the prohibition against lying is directly related to the strictures against breaking promises or making deceptive promises.

## 4.   People Ought to Honor Their Reciprocal Obligations

Four, the principle of reciprocity is likewise a necessary assumption which undergirds our ability to make and keep normative agreements. This principle calls for us to help and not injure those from whom we have received benefits. In so far as we benefit as members of institutions, we are expected to fulfil certain duties and obligations that are variously spelled out by particular moral traditions. As members of institutionalized groups, individuals accumulate social debts as beneficiaries of these groups which they variously redeem in keeping with particular standards of obligation and reciprocity. Alvin Gouldner has argued: "In sum, beyond reciprocity as a pattern of exchange and beyond folk beliefs about reciprocity as a fact of life, there is another element: a generalized moral norm of reciprocity which defines certain actions and obligations as repayments for benefits received" (Gouldner, 1956, p. 170).

The principle of reciprocity rarely requires rigid symmetry between benefits received or claimed and the obligations and duties thereby occasioned. Typically, the relations between benefits and reciprocal obligations are defined asymmetrically. This fact is most evident in the relationships between parents and children. Children benefit greatly from the care, affection, security, and guidance they receive from parents and elders. They are characteristically expected to reciprocate by deference, loyalty, and by using elders and parents as role models. Their obligations are different in kind and extent. It is characteristically assumed that they cannot ever fully repay their own parents and mentors except in so far as they in turn provide the same kind of parenting and guidance for subsequent generations. Hence the patterns of reciprocal relations remain open-ended and generative of ever new obligations and expectations. Social norms characteristically call for some people to give more than expected. Those who are well placed are expected to provide charity and benefits for those who are in need not on account of any strict obligations to these people but because such acts of philanthropy represent a corresponding duty of their position. Their claims to be honoured as elites correspondingly call for them to act with certain generosity, public-mindedness, and social display. "The paradox of elites," Gouldner further observes, is that "like all dominating social strata, they exploit and take something for nothing. But what transforms them from merely powerful strata into a legitimate elite... is that they can and sometimes do give something for nothing" (Gouldner, 1973, p. 272).

This principle of reciprocity is universally advocated or assumed by particular moralities, not only for its importance for social cooperation but also because a minimal degree of reciprocity is presupposed by any moral system with acknowledged authority. As cultural realities moral systems gain legitimate authority as a consequence of the cumulative effect of several factors. Most of these factors are circular in character. Thus, in any human community individuals are likely to be bound together by a number of complex sets of reciprocal obligations and duties in relation to the ways they interact and help each other. These reciprocal expectations are typically communicated by moral discourse. In the process particular expectations are defined in generic terms. These terms themselves are correspondingly coloured in their meanings by the sets of obligations and reciprocal expectations which they define. In those settings where people tend to evade or ignore their reciprocal obligations, then the moral terms which define these generic expectations correspondingly lose significance and authority. They become merely the expressions of personal feelings. Contrariwise, in those settings where individuals for the most part honour their reciprocal obligations, the moral terms which define these generic expectations gain added meaning and authority. These terms do not reflect merely abstract ideals or subjective feelings. Instead they reflect the commitments, gratitude, and sense of accountability which individuals concretely experience in relation to specific sets of obligations and relationships. The counsel to do one's duty or to follow one's dharma gains authority because it does not merely express an empty and abstract ideal but because it calls to mind sets of relationships in which one has already benefitted and been reciprocally linked to others. Moral systems possess little authority where such interconnecting sets of reciprocal relationships are absent. They gain in recognized authority precisely among those communities of people where such reciprocal sets of relationships to some degree already exist and are understood and guided by these moral terms.

In varied terms all moral systems call for people to respect others with whom they interact, to honour their promises, to communicate honestly without intentional deception and to fulfil their reciprocal obligations. These principles, which may be either directly articulated or assumed, identify patterns of behaviour which, when they are honoured, make it possible for people to create and sustain normative agreements. In so far as people abide by these standards, they foster trust among themselves. Correspondingly, in so far as people experience trust, they are more willing to take risks and enter into further agreements through which they establish and agree to other normative standards. As such they make it possible for moral ideas to possess authoritative influence within particular cultural settings. These principles thereby directly reinforce the legitimacy of moral expressions as cultural realities.

## VI. Moral Principles That Make Morality Credible

A second series of moral universals possesses different status than those just analyzed. Like the standards respecting promise-keeping and reciprocating obligations, these principles are empirically observable, culturally created, and universally advocated. However, they differ from those previously discussed in several ways. None of this second set of principles need to be presupposed in order to make and keep normative agreements. We do not need the following set of principles in order to create and sustain moral standard as such. The following principles function to facilitate social cooperation and manage disputes related to the access and use of sexual intercourse, violence, and valued material goods. They restrict the access and establish criteria for the fitting enjoyment and use of these goods. In the process they institute guidelines for appropriate patterns of cooperation. To the degree that these principles are honoured and to the degree that particular formulations of these principles in fact enable people to cooperate without resort to violence, these principles serve to promote the well-faring of those communities which defer to them. Correspondingly, to the extent that these principles foster cooperation and promote social welfare, they add to the legitimacy of moral ideas generally by making them more credible.

I will examine five very general principles. This list is representative and not necessarily exhaustive. Each of the five principles I will discuss has been formulated in decisively different ways by particular religions, ideologies, and societies. One might well then ask whether it is possible really to identify these principles as moral universals when they are subject to quite different renditions. The defense of their status as culturally recognized moral universals requires that we distinguish between social rules, which are more particular, and general principles, which are more abstract. This defense also reminds us that the identification of moral universals function not to overcome the problems of moral diversity but to provide points of departure for seeking equivalencies to make these differences more manageable. The particular character and status of this second set of moral universals is well illustrated by the incest taboo. The incest taboo is a universally recognized culturally transmitted principle that prohibits sexual engagements with people who are considered to be members of one's own natural family. Although there have been notable exceptions where sibling marriages were favoured for royalty, as with the Ptolemies, these exceptions were allowed and encouraged as exceptions that were royal privileges. What is interesting about the incest taboo is the extremely wide variety of forms which it has assumed, reflecting the extremely different notions of family. At a concrete level, the incest taboo has allowed for great variation in allowable and forbidden sexual relations. Nonetheless, in spite of this variation, the basic principle still exists as a universally acknowledged normative standard. It is not a hypothetical or imagined standard. It is not an analytic construct, an empirical generalization set forth by academic or other interested observers to summarize shared qualities among a number of diverse social mores. It remains a universally acknowledged normative principle in spite of the fact that it is stipulated in different terms and articulated in diverse languages.

These five principles can be stated as follows: One, individuals ought to choose as spouses and sexual partners those persons outside their natural families with whom it is fitting for them to marry and to engage in sexual relationships. Two, parents are expected to care for, protect, and educate their children. Three, people should not exercise physical violence against others except as a means of defending themselves against and disarming those who threaten them or others with physical violence. Four, social goods and burdens ought to be allocated in keeping with publicly recognized rules and procedures that accord to people what is their due. Five, people ought not steal.

These principles have been communicated by many of the most ancient and revered codes. For example, the Ten Commandments include prohibitions against adultery, murder, and theft as well as a command to honour parents (Exodus 20:12-17). The same standards are also reiterated by the New Testament (Luke 18:18-36; Romans 13: 8-10). The Ten Precepts of Buddhism incorporate among their initial five rules prohibitions against improper sexual conduct, taking of life, and the taking of what is not given (King, 1964, p. 140). The same standards are incorporated in the fundamental yanas which mark the preliminary restrictions that must be honoured by all who seek to pursue the discipline of yoga (Sharma, 1965, pp. 208,9). A variation of these standards is expressed in the Confucian teachings about right relationships. On the basis of anthropological studies, Edel and Edel argue that these principles have been universally acknowledged by all human communities (Edel and Edel, 1968, Chapters 4-7, 9; Kluckholm, 1979).

1.  **Individuals Ought to Choose as Spouses and Sexual Partners Those Persons Outside Their Natural Families with Whom It Is Fitting for Them to Marry and Have Sexual Relations**

Individuals ought to choose as spouses and restrict their sexual relationships to people outside their natural families with whom it is fitting for them to marry and engage in sexual relationships. This principle incorporates the basic strictures of the incest taboos and extends them to include other considerations. In all cultures humans have established normative standards to order and regulate sexual relationship and marital choices. The specifics of the rules do differ with respect to who count as natural family members and on the particular relationships between marital and sexual relationships. Nonetheless these general principles incorporate a number of more specific standards which are universally treated as normative. These include strictures against sexual relationships between parents and children, bestiality, rape, pedestry, and incest. Also assumed are strictures against adultery narrowly defined as sexual relations with the spouses of people who would oppose such liaisons if they knew about them. Since some cultures tolerate both affairs and open marriages, a more general understanding of adultery cannot be identified as a feature of this moral universal. The social function of these several strictures has been analyzed at length by Levi-Strauss, Malinowski, Spiro, Wilson, Foucault and others. Although the arguments of these scholars do not all agree, we can summarize their collective investigation by observing that these strictures variously function to strengthen lineage bonds, to set apart parents from children, to foster social cohesion across family lines, to assert and protect the sense of family identity, and to reduce otherwise aggravated social rivalries occasioned by unregulated sexual and marital relationships. Although understandings of who are members of natural families and what constitute fitting choices do vary

127

culturally, the general principle remains authoritative even as it assumes different particular expressions.

### 2. Parents Ought to Care for, Protect, and Educate Their Children

Parents ought to assume responsibility to care for, protect and educate their children. This principle includes as well the corollary that children ought to respect and honour their parents. Again this principle assumes markedly different expressions in local cultures. In some cases male relatives rather than fathers take on the male parenting role and in some cultures grandmothers rather than mothers assume the female mothering roles. In many settings the responsibility for education is delegated to others. Intense debates have been waged both within and across cultures about what constitutes proper care, protection, and education. Debates about child labour arise in this context. Are parents exercising their appropriate responsibilities to care for, protect, and educate their children when they encourage or compel them to work apart (or even with) their adult family members? Although these debates have been resolved in different ways, the general principle still retains its normative force: parents are expected to provide for and foster the physical, mental, and moral growth of their children until the latter are considered adults and are ready to assume this responsibility for themselves.

### 3. People Should Not Exercise Physical Violence to the Injury of Others Except as a Means to Defend Themselves Against, and to Disarm, Those Who Threaten or Exercise Physical Violence Against Them

People ought to refrain from exercising physical violence against other humans except as a means to defend themselves against or disarm those who threaten them with physical violence. I will defend this principle as a moral universal even though I recognize that everywhere people have proposed and defended as morally legitimate exceptions to this standard. Subject to several minor exceptions, this principle is universally viewed as authoritative within the bounds of given political communities. That is, people ought to refrain from committing acts of physical violence against other members of their political communities. This principle thereby prohibits murder and unprovoked violence against others. This principle still allows for communities to use some types of physical violence, often in the form of deprivations, to punish persons who have violated social codes and committed injury to others. In many settings, individuals are allowed to exercise

128

violence, as in duelling, in keeping with specific normative conventions. Political authorities usually claim the prerogatives to control and regulate the uses of violence. Political communities also claim the right to protect themselves against violent attacks both from within and without. This right is the minimum core of what Walzer describes as the right to self determination (Walzer, 1977): that is, the right to defense against those who use or threaten to use physical violence to seize political power, property, and/or other valued goods. The above principle incorporates the right to use physical violence for the purpose of self-defense.

The major exception to this principle about the legitimate uses of violence concerns the exercise of physical violence as conquests and crusades. The right to exercise violence in these forms has been articulated in moral terms by religious and political ideologies. These represent religiously and politically justified exceptions. Apart from these exceptions, the general strictures retain their normative status. Individuals are expected to refrain from asserting physical violence as private or gratuitous acts, except where they are allowed to punish others in keeping with social rules or except when they act to defend themselves against the violence or threatened violence of others. Political communities are bound less strictly by this principle. Acts of gratuitous violence by political authorities are generally condemned. And political communities are everywhere allowed to defend themselves against attack. Although specific moralities interpret this principle in varied ways and allow for a number of exceptions, I still think it is valid to argue that people everywhere invoke as normative a principle that stipulates that exercise of violence ought to be restricted to avoid murder, injury, and harm that are not called for except for self-defense, rightful punishment, and certain political or religiously defined goals. While this principle may seem to be riddled with holes, it is neither trivial nor insignificant. In its various particular culturally specific renditions, this principle has served to restrict and regulate the exercise of violence generally, to limit private acts of violence, and to guide the morally sanctioned acts of violence between political communities.

## 4. Social Goods and Burdens Ought to Be Allocated in Keeping with Publicly Recognized Rules and Procedures That Accord to People What Is Their Due

Social goods and burdens ought to be allocated in keeping with publicly recognized rules and procedures that accord to each person and group what is their due. All societies have established normative standards to identify and to regulate proper claims to, and exchanges of, valued goods and burdens. These valued goods include specific roles and statuses as well as personal possessions and real property. Burdens include work, especially onerous labour, taxes, military service, child care and much else. Typically valued goods are scarce. The desire for them extends beyond the number of those who can reasonably obtain or share them. Hence, some rules have to be established to delineate who may rightfully claim title to what kinds of roles, possessions and properties. Those who violate these rules correspondingly are identified as usurpers or thieves. The rights to particular valued goods may be variously defined as by-products of lineage, prerogatives of elites, or just deserts of labour. Locke, for example, defended the rights of individuals to make proprietary claims over any goods that they were able to transform from useless substances into usable commodities (Locke, 1952). Minimally, all societies spell out rules which stipulate by what means people may legitimately lay claim to possession of particular valued goods. Societies also necessarily establish other rules with respect to the legitimate transfer of these goods between people. Societies may indicate that some roles, statuses, and properties may not be transferred except to other designated individuals within common lineage or status group. They may indicate particular transfers that ought to take place, such as dowries or bride-prices, to mark changes in kinship statuses. They usually establish specific rules with respect to transfer of goods from one generation to the next. Hence, in various ways societies establish rules to govern both the claims to valued goods and their transfers. Societies also establish normative standards to indicate how especially difficult and risky burdens ought to be distributed.

As a moral universal this principle of social allocation makes two stipulations: namely, that a given set of rules of the game applies to all members within specific communities and that by these rules members should gain access, use and enjoyment of the goods and the obligation to shoulder the burdens that they are due. Almost all societies assume that non members can legitimately be treated differently. This assumption is very significant because often the status of membership is only accorded to a small portion of the people living within particular societies. Full membership status is usually not extended to foreigners, slaves, and criminals and extended in part only to other groups of people who by virtue of age, gender, and lack of property have been viewed as being less than full members (Walzer, 1983).

This principle has especially been subject different interpretations correlated with different culturally validated criteria for determining what is due to whom. Principles of justice represent one of several competing criteria. Cultures influenced by Hinduism and to some degree Buddhism beliefs about dharma and karmic worth have often been invoked to address this question. In many settings the possession of charismatic attributes based either on birth or on proximity to believed sources of sacred power have been invoked to address this question. As

# MORAL UNIVERSALS AS CULTURAL REALITIES

Aristotle recognized when he argued that justice called for each person to receive his or her due, there are indeed many different views about what constitutes fair criteria of merit or due (Aristotle, 1953). In recent times there have been ongoing debates about the fitting understandings of justice between liberals, socialists, and conservatives, between utilitarians and communitarians, between feminists and non-feminists. Although they differ on particulars, all these parties concur in assuming that appropriate criteria for determining fitting allocations should be the same for all and include some notions of fairness, proportionality, and social merit. Criteria based on notions of dharma and charismatic attributes make no such assumptions.

### 5. People Should Not Steal

People ought not steal. Although interpretations of what constitutes stealing differ greatly, a broad consensus agrees in the basic import of this principle. People ought not seize and make use of any goods, material or otherwise, to which they do not possess legitimate claim.

These five principles all function to limit and control factors which, if not regulated, are likely to occasion conflicts and disputes. These principles variously channel some of the strongest and most influential human desires connected with erotic attachments, dependency, aggression, the pursuit of power, the protection of status, the acquisitions, and uses of possessions. These principles also function to define and reinforce the basic structures of the fundamental and universal human institutions of the family, adulthood, community and property. These principles facilitate social cooperation both, on the one hand, by reinforcing fundamental divisions within human communities and on the other fostering reciprocal relationships between individuals across these divisions. Thus, those standards which delineate the fitting claims to valued goods function to define and justify the division of social roles. Any division of social roles operates within a larger set of expectations which identify how those holding these roles are expected to act on behalf of others. For example, gender has often been used to identify distinct social roles as well as reciprocal obligations. The incest taboos at once define two different sets of basic divisions between parents and children and between an individual's own family and other families. Together with other standards regarding the fitting role of parents and children, this taboo fosters cooperative interactions of people across these divisions.

To the degree that particular versions of these principles are able to foster cooperative interactions, these principles themselves gain in respect and legitimacy. However, particular versions of these principles may have little effective influence

131

at reducing or limiting tensions and conflicts. People may violate kinship codes regarding marriage; adulthood may lose prestige as a moral status; parents may neglect their children; constant disputes may develop respecting the fitting allocations of valued goods; and individuals may attempt to right their wrongs by private acts of violence. These conflicts arise either because people ignore moral traditions, because they cannot achieve consensus with respect to competing moral ideas, or because existing moral traditions fail to provide adequate guidance in new and changing cultural settings. For whatever reasons, to the degree that they are unable to reduce conflicts and tension with respect to these matters, existing normative standards lose credibility and legitimacy. Men and women are more likely to believe, respect and trust normative standards that guide their interactions with others in ways that limit conflict and confusion. These five principles are universally acknowledged as authoritative by societies, albeit in culturally diverse formulations, not only because they function to foster cooperation but also because by fostering harmonious interactions, these principles indirectly reinforce and augment the credibility of the moral traditions which communicate them.

## VII. Evolutionary Moral Universals: Moral Principles That Make Moralities Worthy of Esteem

We can identify a number of moral universals that are now respected as normative but were not always either identified as moral principles or widely regarded as authoritative. These principles have been introduced at particular periods of history. They were not found or regarded as normative in primitive and archaic cultures. Sometime after these principles have been initially articulated, they have been accepted as normative not only within settings where they were first defended but in other settings as well. These principles have either been added to other moral systems or existing standards within the latter have then been reinterpreted in ways that accord with these historically introduced moral principles. Each of these evolutionary moral universals possesses an intrinsic credibility and compelling character such that the articulate ethicists of other moral systems have attempted either to incorporate these principles within their systems or discover them preformed in sayings and stipulations of their own moral traditions.

My argument regarding evolutionary moral universals parallels Parsons' case for evolutionary universals in social organization. Parsons defined evolutionary universals in society as "any organizational development sufficiently important to further [social] evolution . . . that is likely to be 'hit upon' by various systems operating under different conditions" (Parsons, 1964, p. 339). From Parsons' perspective, evolutionary universals possess the following traits. Thus, one, each of these developments in social organization facilitates the further developments within societies. They provide societies which adopt these organizational developments an adaptive advantage over other societies. Parsons recognized that the ideas with respect to these universals need not be spread by cultural diffusion. Rather, quite independently varied societies may bring about these organizational developments. Still, particular societies are likely to emulate each other in adopting these universals once they become known. Parsons identified six evolutionary universals. The first two, which he labelled as social stratification and cultural legitimation, emerged with transition from what he identified as primitive to archaic societies. The last four, which have emerged in societies no longer archaic, he referred to as bureaucratic organization, the money and market complex, generalized universal norms, and democratic associations (Parsons, 1977).

My formulation of evolutionary moral universals parallels yet diverges from Parson's model. Like Parsons, for example, I argue that these moral principles have been "discovered" quite independently by moral traditions with little or no contact between them. However, I also maintain that these principles have gained authoritative recognition not primarily because they seem to favour something as elusive or debatable as further moral evolution or even the more concrete capacity of humans to respond adaptively to their environment. Rather, these principles have gained authoritative recognition because they have in some fundamental sense seemed to be true and valid. These principles have been adopted because they have been judged to articulate truths that are intrinsically related to the nature and functions of morality.

We can identify at least four evolutionary moral universals, none of which have been generally regarded as normative in primitive and archaic cultures. The first two were initially introduced by the great religious and philosophical revivals associated with the beginnings of the great world religions--Buddhism, Brahmanic Hinduism, Confucianism, Christianity, Islam, and Rabbinic Judaism--and by Greek philosophy and Roman law. These principles set forth the following normative standards. One, people ought to be able to offer intelligible and coherent reasons for their moral choices and judgements. And, two, beyond assuming the ordinary responsibilities of adulthood, people can and ought to seek to develop further their own moral character.

# FREDERICK BIRD

## 1.  People Ought to Be Able to Offer Intelligible and Coherent Arguments for Their Moral Choices and Judgements

The principle that moral judgements and choices ought to be rationally defended has not always been assumed.  This principle was initially argued by Socrates and Plato in ways that subsequently modified not only Greek moral thought but also all those moral systems like Christianity, Judaism, and Islam influenced by Greek moral thought.  This principle has been variously defined: moral ideas ought to be rational, or in keeping with reason, or at least allowable by reason.  By these statements, it might be assumed that moral standards which originally derived from traditions and inspiration ought to be excluded as being not rational.  However, such conclusions are unfounded.  More broadly defined, this principle requires that particular moral judgements, evaluations, and decisions be justified in discourse that is reasonable, that is, intelligible, coherent, consistent and principled.  By this principle, it is not sufficient to defend decision by citing conventional formulae: it is necessary to argue why these formulae and not others are being cited.

Confucius and Mencius, for example, introduced this principle into Chinese moral thought.  Confucius in many ways defended what was traditional: but he developed a self-conscious attitude toward the tradition that was new and discursively articulated (Confucius, 1939; Weber, 1951).  Within Judaism, Maimonides' Mishnah *Torah* stands as an eloquent example of an articulation of ostensibly traditional moral teachings in a way that is preeminently rational.  Maimonides does not explicitly argue that these teachings are in keeping with reason.  He does, however, present these teachings as being consistent, coherent, practically useful, and well conceived.  He provides a rational defense not as in his *Guide for the Perplexed* by making a systematic philosophical argument but by arranging these traditional teachings into an organized set of teachings and articulating them in an easily intelligible explanatory discourse (Maimon, 1972).

This principle that moral decisions ought to be rationally defended is derived from an assumption that whatever is morally justified is also necessarily reasonable.  In light of this assumption many moral philosophers have argued that a close, intrinsic relationship exists between morality and reason.  Many, like Plato, Kant, Gert, Gewirth, and Habermas have attempted to identify the interrelationships between the principles of morality and principles of reason.  Primarily this principle requires that moral sentiments, claims, judgements and standards be communicated to others in ways that are intelligible, that are addressed in generic terms to any people similarly situated, and that are consistent (Habermas, 1984, Chapters 1, 3; Habermas, 1990; Kuhn, 1962, Chapters 5, 12; Winch, 1972, Chapter 3).  The imperative that moral justifications be rationally articulated thus expresses the correlative imperative that moral reasons be articulated in publicly defensible arguments comprehensible to anyone interested. It is instructive to examine the impact of this principle upon traditional moralities. Whenever this principle has been seriously considered and adopted, the discursive justification of moral standards and judgements has assumed far greater influence. Moral traditions no longer are defended either as an expression of common sense or inviolable revelations. Rather, these traditions are defended because they can be reasonably justified as being valid, practical, and/or sensible. This principle embodies what Weber described as substantive rather than instrumental or intellectual views of rationality (Weber, 1951, Conclusion; Weber, 1930, Introduction; Weber, 1978, Part I, Chapter 1). Correspondingly, these various arguments presuppose the correlative argument that men and women may wilfully decide not to adhere to particular traditions unless they can be intelligibly persuaded that they ought to. A moral argument is rational when, as Plato observed in The *Gorgias*, it is reasonably articulated in ways that are persuasive and coherent to the thoughtful reflections of another (Plato, 1960b, pp. 61, 76, 77).

## 2. Beyond Assuming the Ordinary Responsibilities of Adulthood, People Ought to Seek to Develop Their Own Moral Character

Each person is morally responsible for cultivating and developing his or her own moral character. Individuals can and ought to strive to achieve higher stages of moral excellence beyond that expected of ordinary adults. Although only a few people ever attain truly exemplary, saintlike states of moral excellence, each person is responsible for developing his or her own moral qualities as far as possible. Extrinsic and intrinsic rewards lay in wait for those who earnestly work at their own moral self-development. By means of thorough dedication individuals can achieve ends which transcend ordinary life experiences variously described as enlightenment, peace of mind, salvation, eternal life, or justification. Correspondingly individuals ought be held accountable for failures to work and realize these highly valued objectives. Primitive and archaic moralities only expected people to fulfil the expected roles of ordinary adults. Individuals were held accountable for complying or not complying with group norms. This moral universal expects more of people.

These ideas regarding individual moral responsibility have been quite variously expressed. Buddhism, for example, articulated the notion that suffering or personal well-being of each individual resulted from their ways of living and thinking. The *Dhammapada* counsels: "All that we are is the result of what we have thought . . . . If a man speaks or acts with an evil thought, pain follows him, as the wheel follows the foot of the ox that draws the wagon" (Dhammapada, 1936, Verse 1). The Buddha counselled each person to develop his or her own qualities of purity, earnestness, compassion through disciplined efforts. The Christian gospel urges individuals to work out their individual salvation with fear and trembling. They are advised not merely to follow traditional moral wisdom but to seek to be perfect like God: to excel not merely in what they do but in their motivations to act. Similar assumptions are articulated in less explicitly religious terms by Plato, Aristotle, and by Stoic and Epicurean philosophers. Aristotle, for example, argued that each person ought to strive to achieve the highest degree of happiness possible because this is natural and ultimately rewarding. This end is to be achieved, Aristotle argued, by diligently cultivating one's moral virtues (Rawls, 1970, Chapter 7; Donagon, 1977, pp. 23-5). Kant, following Rousseau, argued that each person as a moral actor ought to become an autonomous, self-governing individual, author of the rational, universalizable principles by which he or she acts.

The principle that individuals ought to work at developing their own moral excellence has influenced moral thought in several ways. The adoption of this principle makes the cultivation of excellence in moral character an intrinsically valued objective which supplements the more traditional objective of simply complying with existing social norms. Additionally, the adoption of this principle has everywhere resulted in the intensification of the notions of individual moral accountability. Beliefs about fault, culpability, and responsibility gain greater prominence because individuals are regarded as being both capable and obliged to develop and perfect their own moral character. At the same time the well-being which individuals experience or do not experience is more closely connected with their own efforts and dispositions, either current or former, and less upon factors beyond their influencing, such as bad luck, happenstance, or black magic (Ricouer, 1967; Weber, 1945).

This principle makes a fundamental assumption not presumed by historically earlier or more primitive moral systems and yet universally assumed today: namely moral standards are expected to play instrumental roles in enhancing and improving upon human well being. In archaic and primitive cultures moral standards are regarded as means of establishing and protecting the social order. They are assumed to play a conservative function. They are expected to help protect humans and their communities from impulses and actions that threaten their being. They are not expected to help bring into being as yet unrealized potentialities. However, the principle about self-development makes a different assumption. We are called upon to honour moral standards in order to realize new possibilities both for ourselves individually and by extension for our communities. This assumption in turn has been extended to popular assumptions about the role of other moral principles as well. Even Kant, who rigorously resisted utilitarian views about ethics, argued that it was reasonable for moral actors who acted on the basis of their duties to assume that such action would result in enhancing their happiness (Kant, 1952). The next evolutionary moral universal was introduced in early modern times in conjunction with the creation of self-governing cities and nations.

### 3. Political Communities Ought to Recognize That All Men and Women Possess Certain Irrevocable Human Rights

Three, political communities ought to recognize that all men and women possess certain irrevocable human rights. A human right is a claim by an individual to possess certain goods which other individuals ought to recognize. Rights do not exist in a vacuum. They always express claims by someone against others. Human rights have been defined in relation to three distinctive kinds of claims. Some rights have been defined in relation to claims by individuals not to be interfered with by others. Rights thereby define prerogatives of individuals to act with individual discretion without being controlled or bothered by others. The rights to liberty and the freedom of opinion, are usually defined in these terms. The rights to freedom from unwarranted arrest, to privacy, and the freedom from slavery are similarly defined. These rights protect the autonomy of individuals as members of communities. Other rights are defined in relation to claims which individuals make to the exercise of certain powers as members of communities. These include the right to unrestricted public speech, the right to negotiate contracts, and the right to form associations. Also included as rights which express claims to powers are the right to vote, to transfer properties, and to work for equal pay. Many rights at once express both claims to non-interference as well as claims to exercise specific powers, such as, for example, the rights to personal property, the right to free choice of spouses, the right to divorce, and the right to strike. Many rights in addition express the claim that political communities ought in specified ways provide particular benefits for their members. Accordingly, individuals should be able to make claims that an adequate education be provided for children, that roads be developed to facilitate travel, that the poor be provided welfare and that police protection be established. These rights guarantee individuals fair shares of social benefits identified as common goods.

Alan Gewirth has argued recently that it is reasonable for all individuals to demand the basic human right to sufficient amounts of freedom and well being in order to act voluntarily and with purpose (Gewirth, 1978, Chapter 1, 2). Most people today would concur with his judgement that this right is fundamental and entailed by the very nature of human action. Hence, it may be thought that this right is not new but basic to human life. However, while this basic intuition may not be new, the conception that humans possess rights that ought to be recognized and be protected by political communities is relatively new. Traditional moralities did not conceive of these issues in terms of a series of claims which individuals could justifiably seek to have honoured by others and insured by governments.

These ideas were clearly and formatively articulated initially by advocates of representative, legally bound governments beginning in the seventeenth century (Marshall, 1964; Bendix, 1964; Bendix, 1978). Moral discussions with respect to rights were not initially conceived in terms of human rights as such. Rather, rights of individuals were initially discussed in terms of the fitting claims which they could make as members of political communities; that is, as *citizens*. To be sure, Hobbes, Locke, Rousseau, the American Bill of Rights and The French Declaration of the Rights of Man and Citizen all refer to certain natural rights. But these various statements regarding natural rights were articulated in order to define explicitly the way in which governments ought to act in relation to individual citizens. Because humans possess, in Locke's terms, the natural right to life, liberty and the protection of property, then governments ought to act to protect the lives, liberties and properties of their citizens. Locke proceeded to discuss how governments ought not to interfere with the prerogatives of individuals with respect to property they rightfully claimed and how they ought to extend the franchise to qualified citizens (Locke, 1952).

As a result of observable historical developments, the governments of various modern nation states have recognized a series of rights of citizens. These include, first, civil rights, which defend the liberties of individuals to personal property, freedom of speech, freedom of religious adherence, freedom of association, and nondiscrimination over against the arbitrary interference especially of the government itself as well as other individuals. They identified as well a series of political rights, including the right to vote and the right to jury trials. Finally, governments have recognized in addition a series of social rights, which include especially the right to education and the right to various social welfare benefits. Over time, other social rights have been added such as the rights to pregnancy leaves, the right to child care and the rights to unemployment insurance if unemployed (Marshall, 1964, Chapter 6; Weber, 1961, Chapter 28; Bendix, 1964; Friedrich, 1964, Chapter 5).

These rights variously spell out the claims which, it is thought, individuals can legitimately make upon others. Rights cannot be acted upon unless others recognize these specific claims as legitimate. In most cases, people have expected that governments would guarantee that these claims were recognized and provide the means through legal adjudication to settle any disputes which might arise with respect to these claims.

# MORAL UNIVERSALS AS CULTURAL REALITIES

These assumptions respecting human rights have developed historically. As this principle has gained authoritative recognition by various societies, it has markedly influenced traditional patterns of conduct and traditional moral thought in several notable ways. Thus, in a way that has been decisive, governments have been defined as being accountable to the people they govern, even if they remain autocratic in form (Bendix, 1978). Moreover, the practice of slavery has been morally rejected and practically discontinued. Since all humans possess certain civic rights, then it becomes untenable to treat other individuals as property. Slowly and with considerable resistance, these collections of civic rights have been extended to women. Since women do not differ in their basic humanity from men, it has been argued, then these same liberties, rights, and benefits ought to be guaranteed for them as well. Finally, certain social rights, such as the claims to adequate health care, food, and economic security, have increasingly been regarded as basic and not optional. In time, the assumptions regarding human rights have been extended to larger populations and the range of rights have been enlarged.

The notion that men and women possess basic rights as human beings remains morally ambiguous for two reasons. First, it is impossible to think of rights as being the properties of isolated individuals. Particular rights exist as moral realities only where they are publicly recognized and enforced by institutional means. In practice, the honouring of these rights, then, is tied to political and legal activities of particular communities. Hence, human rights only gain practical recognition as prerogatives of individuals as members of particular political jurisdictions. They might thus best be described not as human rights but as citizenship rights. This universal might then be rephrased in these words: all human communities ought to recognize that their members possess certain fundamental rights to non-interference from others, to exercise their own powers, and to fair distribution of benefits designated as communal goods. Stated in these terms the notion of human rights is necessarily connected with assumptions regarding human communities as responsible for and to the individuals who produce and reproduce them by their consents and actions (Selznick, 1987).

Second, when groups of individuals too ardently pursue their rights as members of particular communities, they may occasion situations in which communal good will becomes exhausted. Quite independently of the legitimacy of any particular claims, communities are able to recognize and honour new rights only to the degree that historical preconditions allow. It is easier to honour rights that protect against abusive interference by others and rights that recognize the powers of individuals to enter into contracts, to vote, and to hold property than it is to honour those rights which call for the fair distribution of communal goods. Whether these goods are defined as tax dollars to be used for education, health services, or day care programs, or as empty lands for settlement, or natural resources to be utilized, they are limited. These limits are set by the resources and good will of the community. As a result, the claims to honour particular rights, such as tax benefits for homeowners, may conflict with claims with respect to other rights such as the right to decent health care services. As these claims and counter claims mount, the notion of human right becomes increasingly politicized. It loses its status as a moral universal and becomes merely a contentious assertion of particular wants and desires.

In very recent years, an additional principle has gained status as a moral universal as people everywhere have become increasingly aware of their often harmful impact upon natural environments. To be sure people differ considerably in their recognition that environmental problems may exist and in their judgements about the actions they think ought to be taken to address these related concerns. They debate over what issues are particularly critical. Is it global warming or the threats to bio-diversity? Which concerns are most important: excessive pollution, the exhaustion of non-renewal natural resources, or the destruction of forests and green spaces? Is the core problem lack of development or too much development? Although companies make excuses for not being more zealous and governments and corporations temporize and delay  actions, it is impressive to what degree people either feel these are legitimate concerns or feel the need to justify not doing more.

### 4.   People Ought to Respect Their Natural Environments and Conserve the Resources They Draw from Them

People ought respect their natural environments and conserve the resources they draw from them. This principle summarizes the core set of assumptions which almost everyone has now come to recognize.

The four principles discussed in the preceding paragraphs share the characteristic that they have over time gained recognition as features basic to all moral systems.  Together they have functioned to modify the fundamental assumptions with respect to the nature and functioning of morality in society.  It is typically presumed as self-evident that moral ideas ought to be rationally justified, that acting in keeping with moral standards ought to help bring about enhanced well being, that individuals ought to be held morally responsible for developing their own moral character, that moral systems ought to define basic rights which all humans possess as members of political communities, and that they ought to act with respect towards their natural environments. These assumptions have been absent, only partially accepted, or at least not clearly conceived by traditional moral systems. Moreover, traditional moralities subsequently have been re-conceived in

140

order to take these principles into account. This process of adoption is most clearly evident with respect to the assumptions with respect to human rights. In recent times, proponents of various traditional moralities have reinterpreted their own moral heritages either in order to adopt these ideas as welcome additions or in order to discern in their traditional teachings elementary expressions of these principles. As these principles have been recognized as authoritative these principles in turn have added prestige and esteem to particular moral traditions. Thinking about moral ideas in these terms fosters increased respect for morality. Or to state this observation in another way, individuals who have learned to recognize these principles as authoritative have correspondingly tended to discredit and to criticize traditional formulations of moral ideas that failed to take these principles into account.

## VIII. Conclusion: Moral Diversity, Moral Universals, and Ethics as Good Deliberation

It is possible to identify a number of moral principles which have in fact been universally regarded as normative. These principles are cultural artifacts. They are empirically observable not imagined realities. They stipulate expectations about significant matters. However, they exist not in one but many different cultural specific versions as they are articulated in keeping with local discourse and differing beliefs about moral goods and defended with different moral logics. Yet it is still possible to identify single principles of considerable moral weight in these different versions. Because of these cultural differences, it is often not simple and easy to occasion the recognition of these principles by people from different cultures. Used to interpreting these principles in terms of their own logics, beliefs, and discourse and in terms of the particular social norms which these principles often serve to justify, they may well resist alternative formulations that seek to identify these principles apart from these other encompassing accouterments. Through give and take discussions, people holding different moral beliefs may well be able to recognize a number of principles which they commonly regard as normative. As a further consequence of these discussions and recognitions, they may find ways of reaching agreements about contentious matters. This recognition facilitates agreements not because people then defer to these principles as newly discovered higher ethical standards but because they can see more clearly the way in which particular understandings of existing local standards are equivalent to the differently formulated standards in moral cultures of others. Rather than overcoming moral diversity, the recognition of moral universals can help us to discover pathways through these differences that connect and cross and thereby facilitate the making of normative agreements among people from different backgrounds.

The role which the recognition of moral universals can play in addressing the problems of moral diversity differs with the different types of principles which we have just examined. The first set, those which I described as making normative agreements, and thereby moralities, possible, play a direct and immediate role. These principles, which call for respect for those with whom we are interacting and negotiating, promise keeping, honest communication and reciprocity, are immediately and directly relevant to situations in which people from different moral cultures bargain and seek to reach agreements. These principles together constitute the core of what we can describe as a universally recognized ethic for acceptable transactions. Unlike many of the other principles I have discussed, these four assume practically the same basic form in all cultures. To be sure, there are significantly different rhetorics and rituals that accompany promise making in different moral cultures. But the basic form and understandings are the same in the ways that does not hold for culturally different conceptions of justice, for example. The fundamental meaning of these principles does not greatly change as a result of the different conceptions people hold regarding moral goods. In fact, these principles assume practically the same meaning no matter by what moral logics they are justified or in relation to what moral goods they are defended. While people may quite differently articulate their understandings of the moral grounds for acceptable transactions, they typically invoke strikingly similar expressions of these principles as a basic core of their positions. The particular moral good, that of arriving as defensible, voluntarily achieved normative agreements, remains similar in different cultures and is applicable for both symmetrical and asymmetrical relationships. As a result we can comparatively easily find through discernment and translation ethically equivalent but culturally different formulations of these principles. These principles can correspondingly fairly naturally and easily be invoked as normative guidelines for how transactions ought to be pursued and agreements reached.

We cannot make the equivalent claims about the second set of moral universals, which I described, as principles that make moral systems credible. These principles all function to define and promote social cooperation more broadly not at the level of direct transactions but in relation to the organization of social roles. These principles deal with subjects, like sexual pleasure, the uses of violence, and claims to material goods, which arouse strong feelings and intense differences. All focus on particular arenas of human endeavour and establish guidelines that restrict the access and direct the use and enjoyment of the corresponding valued phenomena. In some form these principles possess normative status in every human community. However, culturally specific versions of these principles are dramatically affected by how people identify and rank their moral goods and by the forms of moral reasoning they favour. As we identify these broad principles, we often more closely come to setting forth the parameters around on-going debates than distinguishing arenas of broad consensus. Yet we are doing both. People care very much about their particular versions of these principles and they likewise care very much about these principles.

In order to make these differences more manageable and to draw greater attention to common concerns, several complementary strategies can be followed. We can fairly easily ignore or tolerate the different versions of the principle regarding marital and sexual choices. Largely, aside from some mixed marriages, this principle only affects people who come from similar cultural backgrounds. Considerable variation between cultures is not particularly problematic although variations within cultures become more difficult. In modern times a convergence has emerged regarding the importance of allowing those involved their freedom of choice. Unlike the other principles I am now discussing, the principle respecting parental responsibilities is not subject to as many heated ideological and religious debates. A broad consensus exists, in spite of differing child rearing and educational practices, that children deserve good care and education. A broad consensus likewise holds with respect to the prohibition against stealing even though particular cultural understandings of what constitutes stealing differ markedly.

Arriving at consensus respecting the acceptable uses of violence and the fitting allocation of social goods and burdens is a much more difficult matter. In these cases especially differing notions of moral goods and different views about valid forms of reasoning greatly affect how these principles are interpreted. Walzer has made an instructive and helpful effort to identify a consensus with respect to the acceptable uses of violence (Walzer, 1978). In order to arrive at workable understandings with respect to these issues, it is often useful in the context of actual bargaining or ongoing interactions to begin by attempting to identify relevant valued goods or objectives which contending or competing parties can mutually agree upon. These may not be their highest goods. But they are mutually recognized valued states of being. Although this kind of exercise in utopian visualizing may seem highly idealistic, it serves the practical function of getting people, who are in situations where they are often aggressively criticizing and defending themselves against the criticisms of others, to become more fully aware of some real and valued areas of common concern and commitment (Weisbord, 1992).

The last set of moral universals can often be usefully invoked to help identify areas of common commitment. However, often people become more greatly exercised about the differing ways they express or interpret these principles, than what they hold in common. For example, the principle that people ought to give intelligible reasons for their moral choices and judgements serves as a catalyst compelling people to articulate the why's and wherefore's of their positions and thereby to allow or initiate discussions with others who may inquire about, challenge, or agree with their views. To offer reasons is to invite possible criticism. Offering reasons, therefore, creates the possibility through give and take discussions that people will persuade others or be persuaded in ways that allow for mutual adjustment. In principle, this universal is especially relevant to the task of managing moral diversity. However, in practice, contending parties often become more greatly concerned about the ways their arguments differ than that these different patterns of reasoning have brought them to similar positions.

Both the principles about human rights and environmental respect identify broad areas of universally felt concern. Problems arise here whenever we demand too strict and similar interpretations of these principles. In relation to their variable visions and different cultural traditions, people are likely to rank human rights in different orders and think of environmental issues with different time tables and different senses of urgency. Again, recognizing these principles serves not the immediate task of naming higher, more compelling standards to which they should directly subordinate their concerns. Rather recognizing these principles functions to identify similarly valued areas of concern about whose meaning and significance people will still continue to debate. These principles operate much like the rules that distinguish one sport or one game from another. Identifying such rules does not eliminate competition: In fact, it invites contests and competitions but sets the parameters in relation to which they will proceed.

The principle that people ought to seek to develop further their own moral character at first seems not likely to offer much assistance in addressing the problems of moral diversity. This principle has frequently been interpreted in keeping with the ways specific religious and ideological traditions define self-development. Quite different patterns of life follow from whether people seek development as Buddhist monks or as what Jung refers to as individuated selves, as hard working, worldly Calvinist saints, or free-spirited renaissance men and women. Moral systems hold up quite different views of the ultimate good in terms of self-development. Ironically, however, certain common themes have emerged out of current discussions of self-development. A number of people have with modestly favourable responses applied them to the problems of moral diversity. The basic theme here is that even though social rules and reasons differ, people involved in intercultural settings as politicians, business men and women, or diplomats ought to act with integrity (Srivastva, 1988). While this counsel does not directly resolve conflicts over specific rules, it tends to re-position the debate so that people feel freer to explore relevant alternatives using their imagination together with their sense of integrity.

The recognition of moral universals, conceived as I have done so in this essay, does not solve or overcome the problems associated with moral diversity. Nonetheless, it can serve several roles as people address these concerns. Several of these principles can be directly invoked to argue about the fundamental assumptions that ought to be respected as people enter into transacting interactions. Other principles can be invoked not as means of successfully ending debates on these matters but as parameters and guidelines in relation to which these debates should proceed. Even in the case of the principles about promise keeping and honest communication, rarely can these principles be directly invoked to resolve dispute or solve dilemmas. Rather, those people directly involved must do this by vocalizing their own arguments, attending to the concerns of others, and seeking to reach agreements, calling upon the recognition of these principles as potentially useful wisdom and mandates to which others are likely to feel compelled although in terms that are likely to differ.

**Endnote**

1    The research for this essay was made possible in part by a strategic research grant from the Social Sciences and Humanities Research Council of Canada to study how corporations manage moral issues. Earlier versions of this essay were presented to the Canadian Society for the Study of Religion, meeting at Calgary University in June 1994 and at a workshop of SEEP at Brigham Young University in March 1995. An earlier and shorter version of this essay appeared in the *Journal for Religious Pluralism* (1993), edited by A. Sharma. I am especially grateful for critical comments by Manny Velasquez of Santa Clara University, William Westley of McGill University, and Travis Kroeker of McMasters University. I am grateful to my colleagues in the Department of Religion for comments on an earlier and even shorter version.

# FREDERICK BIRD

## References

ARISTOTLE: *The Nichomacian Ethics*, translated by J.A.K. Thomson, Middlesex (Penguin Books) 1953, 1955.

BENDIX, REINHARD: *Nation Building and Citizenship*, New York (Wiley) 1964.

BENDIX, REINHARD: *Kings or People*, Berkeley (University of California Press) 1978.

BENNIS, WARREN; PARIKH, JAGDISH; and LESSEM, RONNIE: Beyond Leadership: Balancing Economics, Ethics, and Ecology, Oxford (Blackwell Ltd.) 1994.

BIRD, FREDERICK B.: "Good Conversations: A Practical Role for Ethics in Business" , in GEORGE ARAGON (Ed.): *The Role of "Good Conversation" in Business Ethics*, Boston (Boston College), 1991, pp. 13-95.

BIRD, FREDERICK B.: *The Muted Conscience: Moral Silence and the Practice of Ethics in Business*, Greenwich (Quorum Books) 1996.

BOK, SISELA: Lying, Cambridge (Harvard University Press) 1978.

BONHOEFFER, DIETRICH: *Ethics*, ed. by Eberhard Bethge, trans. by Neville Horton Smith, New York (Macmillan) 1955.

CONFUCIUS: *The Analects of Confucius*, trans. by Arthur Waley, New York (Vintage Books) 1939.

DE GEORGE, RICHARD T.: "Ethical Universals, Justice, and International Business", in this volume, 1996.

*The Dhammapada*, trans. by Irving Babbitt, New York (New Direction Books) 1936.

DONAGAN, ALAN: *The Theory of Morality*, Chicago (The University of Chicago Press) 1977.

DONALDSON, THOMAS: "A Hypernorm For Global Business: The Principle of Economic Civility", in this volume, 1996.

DUMONT, HENRI: *Homo Heirachus*, London (Paladin) 1972.

DUMONT, HENRI: *From Mandeville To Marx; The Genesis and Triumph of Economic Ideology*, Chicago (University of Chicago Press) 1977.

EDEL, MAY and EDEL, ABRAHAM: *Anthropology and Ethics: The Quest For Moral Understanding*, Cleveland (Press of Case Western Reserve University) Revised Edition, 1968.

ERIKSON, ERIK: *Toys and Reason*, New York (Norton) 1975.

FRIEDRICH, CARL: *Transcendent Justice*, Durham (Duke University Press) 1964.

GEERTZ, CLIFFORD: *The Interpretation of Cultures*, New York (Basic Books) 1973.

GEERTZ, CLIFFORD: *Local Knowledge*, New York (Basic Books) 1983.

GERT, BERNARD: *The Moral Rules: A New Rational Foundation For Morality*, New York (Harper Torchbooks) 1966, 1967, 1970.

GEWIRTH, ALAN: *Reason and Morality*, Chicago (University of Chicago Press) 1978.

GILLESPIE, KARE: "Middle East Response to the U.S. Foreign Corrupt Practices Act", *California Management Review*, Vol XXIX, No.4 (Summer 1987) pp. 9-30.

GOULDNER, ALVIN: "The Norm of Reciprocity ", *American Sociological Review*, Vol. 24, No. 2 (April 1956) pp. 161-178.

# MORAL UNIVERSALS AS CULTURAL REALITIES

GOULDNER, ALVIN: "The Importance of Something For Nothing", *For Sociology*, Middlesex (Penguin Books) 1973 , Chapter 9.

HABERMAS, JURGEN: *Theory of Communicative Action*, Vols 1 and 2 , trans. by Thomas McCarthy, Boston (Beacon Press), 1984, 1987.

HABERMAS, JURGEN: *Moral Consciousness and Communicative Action*, trans. by Christian Lenhardt and Shierry Weber Nicholson, Cambridge (MIT Press) 1990.

HEGEL, GEORGE FRIEDRICH: *The Philosophy of Right*, trans. by T.M. Knox, London (Osford University Press) 1952, 1967.

HEGEL, GEORGE FRIEDRICH: *The Philosophy of History*, trans. by J. Sibree, New York (Dover) 1956.

HOBBES, THOMAS: *Leviathan*, New York (Liberal Arts Press) 1958.

HUME, DAVID: "Enquiry Concerning the Principles of Morality", in David Hume, *Enquiries*, edited by Selby-Bigges, Oxford (The Clarendon Press) Third Edition, 1975.

ILTING, K. H.: "The Structure of Hegel's Philosophy of Right", *Hegel's Political Philosophy*, ed. by Z. A. Pelczynski, Cambridge (The University Press) 1971.

JONSEN, ALBERT and TOULMIN, STEPHEN: *The Abuses of Casuistry: A History of Moral Reasoning*, Berkeley (University of California Press) 1988.

KANT, IMMANUEL: *Fundamental Principles of the Metaphysics of Morals*, trans. by Thomas K. Abbott, New York (Liberal Arts Press) 1949.

KANT, IMMANUEL: *Critique of Practical Reason*, trans. by Lewis White Beck, Indianapolis (Bobbs-Merrill) 1956.

KING, WINSTON L.: *In Hope of Nibbana*, LaSalle (Open Court) 1964.

KLITGAARD, ROBERT: *Controlling Corruption*, Berkeley (University of California Press) 1988.

KLUCKHOLM, CLYDE: "Ethical Relativity: Sic et Non", in RICHARD KLUCKHOLM (Ed.): *Culture and Behavior*, Glencoe (The Free Press) 1964.

KOESTER, HELMUT: "Nomos Physios: The Concept of Natural Law in Greek Thought", in JACOB NEUSNER (Ed.): *Religion in Antiquity*, Leiden (Brill) 1968, pp. 521-541.

KOHLBERG, LAURENCE: *The Psychology of Moral Development*, San Francisco (Harper and Row ) 1984.

KUHN, THOMAS: *The Structure of Scientific Revolutions*, Chicago (University of Chicago Press) 1962.

LOCKE, JOHN: *The Second Treatise of Government*, New York (The Liberal Arts Press) 1952.

MACINTYRE, ALASDAIR: *After Virtue, Notre Dame* (University of Notre Dame Press) 1981.

MAIMON, MOSEN BEN: *A Maimonides Reader*, ed. by Isadsore Twersky, New York (Behrman House, Inc.) 1972 .

MAIANE, HENRY SUMNER: *Ancient Law*, New York (Henry Holt and Co.) 1879.

MARSHALL, T. M.: *Class, Citizenship and Social Development*, New York (Anchor Books) 1964.

NOZICK, ROBERT: *Anarchy, State, and Utopia*, New York (Basic Books) 1974.

NOZICK, ROBERT: *Philosophical Explanations*, Cambridge (Harvard University Press) 1981.

# FREDERICK BIRD

NUSSBAUM, MARGARET: *The Fragility of Goodness*, Princeton (Princeton University Press) 1985.

PARIKH, JAGDISH: *Managing Your Self*, Oxford (Blackwell) 1992.

PARIKH, JAGDISH: *Intuition*, Oxford (Blackwell) 1994.

PARSONS, TALCOTT: "Evolutionary Universals in Society", *American Sociological Review*, Vol. 29, No.3 , 1964, pp. 339-357.

PARSONS, TALCOTT: *The Evolution of Societies*, ed. by Jackson Toby, Englewood Cliffs (Prentice-Hall) 1977.

PLATO: *The Protagoras and the Meno*, trans. by W. K. C. Guthrie, Middlesex (Penguin Books) 1956.

PLATO (1960a): *The Republic and Other Works*, trans. by B. Jowett, Garden City (Anchor Books) 1960.

PLATO (1960b): *The Gorgias*, trans. by Walter Hamilton, Middlesex (Penguin Books) 1960.

RAPPAPORT, ROY A.: "Ritual, Sanctity and Cybernetics", in WILLIAM A LESSA and YVON Z. VOGT (Eds): *Reader in Comparative Religion*, New York (Harper and Row) Fourth Edition, 1979.

RAWLS, JOHN: *A Theory of Justice*, Cambridge (Harvard University Press) 1971.

RICOUER, PAUL: *Symbolism of Evil*, trans. by Emerson Buchanan, Boston (Beacon Press) 1967.

SEARLE, JOHN: *Speech Acts: An Essay in the Philosophy of Language*, Cambridge (Cambridge University Press) 1969.

SELZNICK, PHILIP: *Law, Society, and Industrial Justice*, New York (Russel Sage Foundation) 1969 (with the collaboration of Phillippe Nonet and Howard Collmer).

SELZNICK, PHILIP: "The Demands of the Community", *The Center Magazine* (Jan./Feb. 1987) pp. 33-45.

SHARMA, I.: *Hindu Ethics*. New York (Harper and Row) 1965.

SPENSER, HERBERT: *The Principles of Ethics*, Vols 1 and 2, New York (D. Appleton and Co.) 1893.

SRIVASTVA, SURESH (Ed.): *Executive Integrity and the Search for High Human Values in Organizational Life*, San Francisco (Jossey-Bass), 1988.

STOUT, JEFFREY: *Ethics After Babel: The Languages of Morals And Their Disconents*, Boston (The Beacon Press) 1988.

TAYLOR, CHARLES: *Sources of the Self: The Making of Modern Identity*, Cambridge (Harvard University Press) 1989.

TOENNIES, FERDINAND: *Community and Society*, trans. by Charles Loomis, New York (Harper and Row) 1957.

TROELTSCH, ERNST: *The Social Teaching of the Christian Churches*, Vol. I and II, trans. by E. Wyon, New York (Harper and Row), 1960.

VELASQUEZ, MANUEL: "Ethical Relativism and the International Business Manager", in this volume, 1996.

WALZER, MICHAEL: *Just and Unjust Wars*, New York (Basic Books) 1977.

WALZER, MICHAEL: *Spheres of Justice: A Defense of Pluralism and Equality*, New York (Basic Books) 1983.

# MORAL UNIVERSALS AS CULTURAL REALITIES

WEBER, MAX: *The Protestant Ethic and the Spirit of Capitalism*, trans. by Talcott Parson, New York (Scribners) 1930.

WEBER, MAX: "Religious Rejections of the World", From *Max Weber: Essays in Sociology*, trans. by H.H. Gerth and C.Wright Mills, New York (Oxford University Press) 1945.

WEBER, MAX: *The Religion of China*, trans. by H.H. Gerth, New York (Macmillan) 1951.

WEBER, MAX: *The Religion of India*, trans. by Hans H. Gerth and Don Martindale, New York (The Free Press) 1958.

WEBER, MAX: *General Economic History*, trans. by Frank H. Knight, New York (Collier Books) 1961.

WEBER, MAX: *Economy and Society*, 2 Vols, ed. by Guenther Roth and Claus Wittich, Berkeley (University of Caliufornia Press) 1978.

WEISBORD et al: *Discovering Common Ground*, San Francisco (Berrett-Koehler) 1992. (And 35 International co-authors: *How Future Search Conferences Bring People Together to Achieve Breakthrough Innovation, Empowerment, Shared Vision, and Collaborative Action.*)

WERTHEIM, W. F.: *East-West Parallels: Sociological Approaches to Modern Asia*, The Hague (W. Van Hoeve Ltd.) 1964.

WILLIAMS, BERNARD: *Morality*, New York (Harper and Row) 1972.

WILLIAMS, BERNARD: *Ethics and the Limits of Philosophy*, Cambridge (Harvard University Press), 1985.

WILSON, PETER J.: *Man, The Promising Primate*, New Haven (Yale University Press) 1980.

WINCH, PETER: *Ethics and Action*, London (Routledge and Kegan Paul) 1972.

ZARTMAN, I. WILLIAM (Ed.): *The 50% Solution: How To Bargain Successfully with Hijackers, Strikers, Bosses, Oil Magnates, Arabs, Russians and Other Worldly Opponents in this Modern World*, Garden City ( Doubleday) 1976.

ZARTMAN, I. WILLIAM and BERMAN, MAUREEN R.: *The Practical Negotiator*, New Haven (Yale University Press) 1982.

149

Chapter 7

# The Ethical Significance of Corporate Culture in Large Multinational Enterprises

MARK CASSON, RAY LOVERIDGE, SATWINDER SINGH

## I. Introduction

This chapter takes an instrumental view of ethical values in international business. It suggests that certain values transcend national differences in culture because they are universally important in supporting economic activity. It argues that investment in value systems of this kind is increasingly undertaken by private firms, partly to compensate for a decline in commitment to these values in society at large. These values are embodied in corporate cultures which are instilled in employees through the human resource management (HRM) practices of the firm. The results of an empirical study of HRM practices in large multinational firms are reported. They show that many firms have systematically invested in corporate culture in recent years, particularly in response to increasing volatility in the business environment. Firms involved in large scale mergers and acquisitions are particularly interested in corporate culture as a vehicle for the cultural integration and homogenisation of their employees.

Corporate culture, it appears, is usually a mixture of traditional ethical values and a rather strident form of individualism designed to encourage entrepreneurship amongst newly 'empowered' employees. The evidence suggests that investments in corporate culture have generated, at best, rather mixed results. The onset of recession, and the highly-leveraged nature of many mergers and acquisitions, has created enormous pressure on top management for quick results. The top managers responsible for disseminating a new culture have often become discredited because the people they have empowered have quickly been made redundant through delayering. The hollowness of their rhetoric, as perceived by ordinary employees, is also attributable to the way that the culture is usually imported through consultants rather than grown organically from the traditions of the firm. Although corporate culture could, in principle, encapsulate universal values in the sense described above, the rather sad conclusion from the evidence is that many attempts to create a corporate culture have actually served to discredit these values instead. Even the most basic business values have been jeopardised in some cases: an employer who makes redundant someone who has only just been told that they are a 'key player in the team' does nothing to encourage respect for the truth. Entrepreneurial values have been compromised as well. Employees are ostensibly encouraged to be creative, whilst top management reveals, by the selective nature of redundancies, that only those who conform rigidly to the official value system have any future with the firm.

## II.  A Functional Basis for Ethical Universals

One approach to the possibility of ethical universals is to ground such universals in values that serve an economic function. Values of this kind may confer survival value on those who adopt them. A number of values - notably respect for truth - are common to most of the world's great religions, and it could be argued that these are the world's great religions because they have survived the longest, and that they have survived the longest because they share this great respect for truth. Truth can therefore be construed not merely as a transcendent value but as an immanent value too - immanent in the sense that telling the truth really works so far as economic survival is concerned.

Although an ethical individual operating in an unethical environment may be taken advantage of by others, and lose out as a result, the same problem does not necessarily arise with the group as a whole. Provided that members of the group can recognise each other, they can each benefit from the others' ethical behaviour. The survival principle therefore operates at the group level even if it does not operate at the individual one.

The economic success of a group hinges crucially on its ability to sustain a sophisticated division of labour. The division of labour facilitates economies of specialisation (through the development of individual expertise, for example) and also permits the exploitation of economies of scale. The resulting efficiency gains not only raise living standards, but also provide an economic surplus which can be used for military investments, enabling the group to conquer territory into which its expanding population can migrate.

In a modern economy the division of labour operates both between firms and within them. A division of labour between firms can only be sustained by trade. For example, industrial workers producing machinery can only be fed if they can purchase food from the farmers, and the farmers can only produce food effectively if they purchase machinery made by the industrial workers. Trade makes people vulnerable, though. Buyers may be cheated by low-quality suppliers, and suppliers may not get paid at all.

The law is usually quoted as the obvious remedy for cheating in trade, but the law is often expensive to use. Where small-value transactions are concerned, the cost of collecting evidence and presenting it to a judge may exceed any recompense that may be obtained. It is cheaper for people to sort out their problems through 'give and take', and even cheaper if they can trust each other not to cheat in the first place.[1] This is where respect for the truth comes in. Respect for the truth means that people will honour the promises they have made. Trade can therefore proceed without costly legal support, and a potentially serious impediment to the division of labour is removed.

The same principles apply to the division of labour within the firm. While the division of labour between firms is typically driven by specialisation in the handling of material flow, the division of labour within firms is more often driven by specialisation in the handling of information flow. It is fairly obvious that employees within a firm can take advantage of their employer by supplying mis-information. By overstating their budget requirements, for example, they can siphon off profits to fund managerial perks. The information-intensity of intra-firm specialisation means that respect for the truth is vital in sustaining the profitability of the firm. If the employer cannot trust his own employees then he will finish up having to process all the information himself. This will restrict his ability to delegate, and impair the growth of a potentially successful firm.[2]

The universal importance of respect for the truth suggests that any society that wishes to prosper would promote respect for the truth as a public good. This is true even though public provision may involve an element of coercion. For a start, the material advantage to any individual from telling the truth depends on the expectation that other people will tell the truth as well. Thus the presence of a significant minority of opportunistic liars can destabilise the social equilibrium. To avoid this, the moral majority may decide that everyone must be subjected to moral suasion in the interests of everyone else. Another consideration is that the promotion of moral values benefits from a division of labour too. The emergence of a leader, and a social elite to support them, is characteristic of most social groups. An important role for the leader is to personify and to articulate the values of the group, including respect for the truth. To support this division of labour, from which everyone benefits, everyone is required to contribute to the leader's expenses by paying taxes to the group.

Notwithstanding the superior efficiency of public morality, postwar Western societies have tended to privatise morality instead. Respect for the truth, and other functionally useful values, are no longer systematically inculcated by state education, whilst the moral influence of nonprofit institutions such as the churches is in decline. Employers can no longer free-ride on public morality in the way they once could. Moral pluralism is becoming as much a feature of the domestic business scene as it is of the international business scene.

The decline of public morality has stimulated many large firms to invest in corporate values of their own. These corporate values are particularly interesting from a functional point of view because they are tailored quite specifically to the needs of the profit-maximising firm. Moreover, because the firm is investing in the values for its own use, rather than for the use of other firms as well, it is quite likely that the value system will be tailored to the specific needs of the firm. Cultural adaptation may mean, for example, that respect for the truth may be particularly strong in a firm where production methods are hazardous, and safety is consequently a paramount consideration, but relatively weak in a firm promoting branded products of questionable legitimacy - such as tobacco, alcoholic spirits and the like.

Adaptation of any kind incurs certain costs, however. For many firms who lack an explicit set of corporate values, the simplest way to acquire one is to buy it in from consultants. The quickest and cheapest solution is to acquire the standardised culture offered to everyone else. The burgeoning demand for 'off the shelf' corporate culture has certainly elicited a ready supply response from consulting firms.

It is an interesting question, however, as to how far these newly-supplied corporate cultures contain intrinsic functional value and how far they are merely a superficial response to perceived business needs. Do these corporate value systems embody the same profound insights into human nature as those that can be found in the world's great religions, or are they no more profound than the normal kind of advice obtained from a consulting firm? Are these systems sensibly adapted to the operational needs of individual firms, or is there a standard package--a kind of privatised public morality--that is supplied to all firms irrespective of their individual requirements?

## III. Corporate Culture and Strategic Human Resource Management

The corporate cultures offered by consulting firms in the late 1980s and early 1990s were sold on the basis that they addressed a number of key problems that had become critical about that time. The progressive liberalisation of trade under successive GATT agreements had made wealthy markets such as the US increasingly accessible to producers in low-wage countries. Many firms faced intense import competition in domestic markets that they had previously dominated in conjunction with one or two local oligopolistic rivals. Political reforms in many low wage countries meant that they now welcomed, rather than rejected, technology transfer affected by foreign firms. A major impediment to economic development in low-wage countries was therefore removed. The newly industrialising countries - notably the Asian 'tigers' - took full advantage of this to strengthen their export-oriented manufacturing industries. First Japan, and then Korea and Taiwan, challenged for industrial leadership in targeted industries. Liberalisation of capital markets meant that they could readily obtain the capital they needed for expansion not only from plentiful domestic savings but from overseas sources too. As a result of all this, world markets became highly integrated, consumer demand was 'globalised' and new sources of supply came on stream. US and European multinationals realised that they could no longer compete unless they rethought many of their fundamental strategies. The increasing intensity of competition had eliminated the profits in domestic markets which they had relied on to cover their overhead administrative costs. Firms had become mentally locked in to Fordist and Taylorist production management strategies, overseen by rigid bureaucratic hierarchies, which were ill-adapted to needs of the fast-changing global market-place. Continuous volatility in the market environment resulting from regular incremental product improvements affected by a variety of new entrants meant that faster competitive responses were required.

This diagnosis led consulting firms to offer a distinctive kind of cure encapsulated in a new kind of corporate culture. The nature of the cure is set out most clearly in the literature on strategic human resource management. A review of this literature indicates seven major themes.

(1) *Many managerial hierarchies are 'top heavy' and need to be de-layered by reducing the number of different levels in the pyramid.* This is alleged to improve communication, and consequently to accelerate decision making[3]. It also has the advantage of reducing overhead expenditure on salaries. A small head office is the visible symptom of successful de-layering[4].

(2) *The empowerment of employees increases morale because employees are trusted to make a wider range of decisions.* Empowerment may be a consequence of de-layering. When a superior's job is eliminated, the responsibilities may be shared out amongst the subordinates. The subordinates have greater discretion because their boss is no longer there to override their decisions[5].

(3) *Managers should 'network' themselves to other colleagues* in order to consult them informally before key decisions are made. If newly empowered managers are no longer co-ordinated by a conventional authority, then some other co-ordination mechanism is required instead. Networking encourages a manager to consult selectively with various people according to the nature of the decision he or she is about to make[6].

(4) *Newly empowered employees need guidance from corporate culture.* Corporate culture is a system of shared values and beliefs promoted by top management. The switch from traditional authority relations to more flexible networking relations requires the re-engineering of corporate culture. The new culture requires active dissemination. It will emphasise the highly volatile nature of the modern competitive environment, and the consequent need for managers to respond creatively to the opportunities provided by empowerment. The culture also needs to be explicit: it will normally include a mission statement, and will often give guidance on ethical issues too.

(5) *The performance of empowered employees must be monitored and assessed in a reasonably sophisticated way.* Ideally each employee would become a profit centre in their own right, but such separability may be difficult to affect in practice. The divisionalisation of the firm should be pursued as far as possible though, down through strategic business units to cellular work groups, individual projects or particular customer accounts. Sophisticated management accounting is useful in measuring an individual's contribution to narrowly defined short-run financial goals, but more judgmental methods are required to assess their contribution to overall long-run objectives.

(6) *Information technology has an important role in facilitating strategic HRM.* The empowerment of managers is facilitated by giving them access on demand to a centralised relational database[7]. They can, in principle, obtain information around the clock just by dialling in. This liberates them from the office, allowing them to negotiate face-to-face with clients in different time zones around the world. A database management system can also record managerial decisions (contracts approved, for example) and calculate performance measures from these records. These performance measures can then be made available to top management on a confidential basis for appraisal purposes[8].

(7) *Investment in training is necessary to support empowered employees.* Employees need to acquire additional competencies in order to use database

management systems and to cope with the additional responsibilities of their former superior's job. But most of all, they need to develop their social skills. Firstly, they have to learn to 'network' with their colleagues. Secondly, those advancing to top management positions, in which the major responsibility is the motivation and appraisal of other management staff, need to acquire the 'soft skills' of 'people management'. They must also be trained to succeed the present top management in the techniques of engineering corporate culture.

## IV. The Survey

In most large firms the implementation of cultural change is the responsibility of the HRM Director based at headquarters. He is supported by Personnel Directors in affiliated companies (Personnel being the rather old-fashioned, but more accurate, name of the HRM function). The chairman or chief executive of the company, is, of course, the symbolic representative of corporate values, but he is so busy that most of the work on corporate culture is done by the HRM Director instead. HRM Directors are usually assisted by a Compensation and Benefits Manager (often female) who does much of the routine administrative work connected with 'pay and rations'. This gives HRM Directors the time to reflect on strategic issues and advise the chief executive on organisational design. Although most top executives in large companies are highly stressed, HRM Directors are, perhaps, less stressed than their colleagues in marketing, production and finance. Their role is more to advise and counsel - even where recruitment of staff is concerned - leaving others to take ultimate responsibility for 'making budget', filling senior posts, and taking operational decisions. To obtain empirical evidence on the dissemination of corporate culture through strategic HRM, a survey of HRM Directors in large multinational firms was carried out.

The investigation involved a mixture of interviews and questionnaires. The study focused on ten countries. The US, Japan, UK and Germany were chosen for their obvious importance as source and host countries for leading MNEs. Canada was chosen for its strengths in mining and insurance, and for comparison with the US. Sweden was chosen to represent Scandinavian countries, which are alleged to have a distinctive corporate culture, and for its importance in the engineering industry too. Switzerland was chosen for the importance of its pharmaceutical firms-- as well as its firms in food and engineering. Brazil and India were chosen as two large, but very different, newly industrialising countries. Taiwan was chosen as a smaller country affording an interesting comparison with Japan. Firms based in other countries were picked up incidentally as a result of mergers, acquisitions or joint ventures that occurred while the study was in progress or had happened shortly before it began.

All firms in the Fortune 500 for 1992 that were registered in these countries were identified. For each parent, one affiliate in each of the ten countries was also identified, where it could be found. Domestic affiliates were included in the study in order to act as a control on the foreign ones. The names and addresses of 427 parents and 1,618 affiliates were obtained from the International Directory of Corporate Affiliations. However, 423 of the addresses proved to be inaccurate or out-of-date; in addition, 101 firms refused to participate and 39 said that the questionnaire was inapplicable, or they were too small to give meaningful replies (typically they were sales and distribution affiliates).

Despite an encouraging response to a small pilot study, the response to the first full-scale mailing in April-June 1993 was disappointing. Two reminders were sent out in October-November 1993 and April-June 1994--the second of these being backed up by a preliminary telephone call to ensure that the questionnaire was personally addressed to the appropriate individual. At the finish, the response rate achieved was 16.5 per cent: 56 usable replies were received from the parents and exactly 200 from the affiliates. The absolute number of responses is perfectly adequate for statistical analysis, although response bias is a serious concern. Fortunately, a number of checks can be made, and these turn out to be quite reassuring.

Open-ended interviews with HRM managers were conducted in 47 firms. Seven of the ten countries were visited personally, and additional interviews were carried out by telephone, and with respondents from overseas who were on business trips to the UK. Most of the interviewees were selected because they had provided interesting or unusual responses to the questionnaires; statistically, they were 'outliers' rather than 'representative firms'. In a few cases we interviewed non-respondents to try to find more about them; but in most cases, not surprisingly, the attempt to get an interview failed.

The interviewee was either the HRM director or the compensation and benefits manager; in some cases another person, such as the head of the international division, or even the chief executive, attended as well, but this was rare. Managers were invited to identify the major issues they faced, and fortunately most (though not all) of these were ones that had been covered in the questionnaire. Their remarks were helpful in discerning patterns in the questionnaire responses which might otherwise have been missed. Thus, the interview and questionnaire results provide useful corroboration for each other.

The interviews were also useful in identifying several reasons for the poor response rate, all of which are borne out by the statistical results. Firstly, as a consequence of de-layering, most HRM managers are far too busy to deal with anything other than the immediate demands of their job. The levels of executive stress encountered during interviews were often very high - and this was amongst managers who felt they could spare the time to see us. Secondly, because of the world recession, many of the managers had only bad news to tell - of several rounds of redundancy so far with probably more to come, and in some cases imminent closure or divestment of a major plant as well. Finally, the HRM managers in smaller affiliates were often doing very routine jobs, and had limited education and professional training. So far as they were concerned, HRM was simply 'old wine in new bottles'; indeed in one case the interviewee did not even know what the acronym HRM meant. It is not surprising that such people, preoccupied with the mechanics of hiring and firing, felt unable to respond to the strategic issues raised in the questionnaire.

A statistical analysis of a sample of respondents and non-respondents indicates that, as might be expected, the respondents are primarily the larger firms. This is not really a problem, given that the initial sampling was truncated by size of firm: it simply means, broadly speaking, that the censoring by size, which applies to the parents, applies to the affiliates too. A positive aspect of this is the very high quality of the responses that we did receive; indeed, a number of interviewees in the larger firms complimented us on the questionnaire and indicated that, despite its length, it had proved very interesting, and that was why they had agreed to be interviewed as well.

**Table 1.** Responses to the Question 'What activities of the Personnel Director are of greatest significance to the company?'

| Activity | Affiliate | | Parent | |
|---|---|---|---|---|
| | Mean | St.devn. | Mean | St.devn. |
| Head-hunting | 2.61 | 1.24 | 2.57 | 1.21 |
| Psychometric testing | 1.70 | 0.95 | 1.68 | 0.88 |
| Industrial relations and wage bargaining | 3.24 | 1.42 | 3.27 | 1.18 |
| Counselling employees under stress | 2.89 | 1.11 | 2.71 | 1.06 |
| Organising training programmes | 3.52 | 0.97 | 3.57 | 1.11 |
| Planning career paths for management development | 3.57 | 1.17 | 4.02 | 0.88 |
| Job evaluation | 3.38 | 1.10 | 3.13 | 1.00 |
| Monitoring and assessing employee performance | 3.72 | 1.03 | 3.80 | 0.87 |
| Advising on organisational design | 3.82 | 1.12 | 3.85 | 1.06 |
| Ensuring compliance with equal opportunities legislation | 3.49 | 1.13 | 3.32 | 0.94 |

Scale 1 (not important) - 5 (very important)

## V. An Overview of the Evidence

Table 1 summarises how HRM directors rate the importance of different aspects of their job. When this is interpreted in the context of other results (not reported here), three points emerge. The first is that there is a broad consensus on what HRM is all about - namely planning career paths, monitoring and assessing employee performance, advising on organisational design, organising training programmes and, to some extent, job evaluation. There is also a strong resistance to psychometric testing - at least for recruitment to managerial positions. Secondly, some firms rate head-hunting as important and others rate it as of no importance at all. Those firms who head-hunt are typically involved in mergers and acquisitions on a regular basis and are looking for people with troubleshooting abilities - typically people who can cut costs drastically to restore profitability in highly competitive industries.

The third point is that in the manufacturing sector driving down costs often involves potential confrontation with trades unions. Although trade union influence has been on the decline politically in a number of countries--notably the UK--they are still a force to be reckoned with on the shop floor in some mature industries. When working practices have not changed for a long time, and workers' attitudes have been hardened by many years in the same job, industrial relations and wage bargaining may hold the key to improving the firm's financial performance. Some firms have solved industrial relations problems by out-sourcing production, but this only transfers the problems to someone else instead. Other firms have abolished distinctions between managerial and manual grades and turned as many production jobs as possible into 'white collar' ones. This usually requires substantial investment in new technology, however, which many firms in declining industries cannot afford. There are still firms committed to manufacturing who must reconcile union wage demands with competitive pressure on product price caused by excess capacity in their industry. Given these constraints, fear and intimidation may hold the key to making the necessary changes in shop-floor attitudes. Personnel directors who have been head-hunted to tackle such problems clearly regard industrial relations issues as absolutely crucial.

The degree of divergence between the national cultures encountered in international business is best assessed from the responses obtained from the affiliates - the view from headquarters, the study suggests, is often distorted by wishful thinking that the culture of the firm is more coherent than it really is.[9] To illustrate how international differences in corporate culture were analysed, Table 2 summarises the responses to a representative question. The question is 'When explaining the company ethos to a new recruit, would you emphasise full integration into company life, not only during normal hours, but after hours as well?'

**Table 2.** The Importance of Socialisation Between Employees, as Reported by Affiliate Companies, and Analysed by Industry, Parent Country and Host Country.

| Type of effect | Industry | Parent | Host |
|---|---|---|---|
| Positive | | Japan | |
| | | | Brazil |
| | | | India |
| | | | Japan |
| | | | Taiwan |
| | | | Germany |
| | | | Sweden |
| Negative | Chemicals | | Canada |

Mean response: 2.37      Scale: 1 - 5
Proportion of variance explained ($R^2$): 0.30
Number of observations: 166
*Note*: The level of significance used is 10 per cent.

It was noted above that corporate cultures might be adapted to the needs of particular industries. To control for industry effects, respondents were classified into eleven industries; electrical engineering (including aircraft), chemicals, oil (including coal), food and drink, mechanical engineering, motor vehicles, metals, nonmetals, office equipment, pharmaceuticals and paper (including related products). The residual category, other manufacturing, was used as a control - a benchmark against which to assess the other industries. Respondents were also classified according to the parent country (where the headquarters was based) and the host country (where the affiliate was based), using the US as the control country in both cases. The responses were analysed by statistical multiple regression analysis using dummy variables. The effect of each country or industry was estimated by ordinary least squares, and significance was assessed using t and F statistics. Only those results achieving a 10 per cent level of significance are reported in the table. To economise on the information presented, only the sign, and not the magnitude of the significant effects is shown.

The mean response of 2.37, reported at the foot of the table, indicates, on a scale from 1 to 5, that on average socialisation is a relatively unimportant element in corporate culture. When variation about this mean is examined, however, a number of significant effects emerge. Socialisation is relatively unimportant in the chemical industry--which is plausible given the capital-intensity of this industry and its use of continuous flow plant based in relatively isolated locations. As might be expected, socialisation is particularly important in Japanese-owned firms. Perhaps more surprising is that it is distinctly unimportant in Canadian-owned firms. One factor here may be the concentration of Canadian-owned firms in resource-based industries rather than manufacturing industries, although in principle this should show up as an industry effect. One reason why it may not show up in that way is that for statistical reasons the level of aggregation used in the classification of industries is very high.

It is also true that affiliates based in Japan emphasise socialisation even though they are foreign-owned. This suggests that national culture influences multinationals both through the parent country (the ownership route) and the host country (the location route) - a conclusion borne out by many other results of the study not reported here. Japan is not the only host country whose national culture is important though. National culture appears to be important in newly-industrialising countries such as Brazil, India and Taiwan, and in two European countries: Germany and Sweden.

Respondents were asked to rate other aspects of corporate culture too. Respectability (mean response 3.93) came out as the most important. Respectability requires that you exemplify corporate values in your everyday conduct so that, as you become more senior, you are a good role model for others. With its emphasis on acting out the corporate value system, respectability is very much a feature of new-style corporate culture, and is particularly emphasised by affiliates based in the US. Interestingly, it is strongly rejected by Canadian-owned affiliates, and also by affiliates based in Canada. This not only highlights cultural divergence in North America, but underlines the fact that the new-style corporate culture is very much a US cultural product, and one which near neighbours striving to retain their cultural identity may well resist.

Loyalty (mean response 3.40) is the second most important element of corporate culture. As might be expected, it is very strong in Japanese-owned affiliates but, interestingly enough, not so much in foreign affiliates operating in Japan. It is affiliates operating in the newly-industrialising countries for whom loyalty is a particularly important factor. It is considered very important in Italy too.

Ambition (mean response 3.15) and hard work (mean response 3.19) are both moderately important, but nowhere near as important as respectability. Ambition is defined as 'wanting to get to the top' whilst the work ethic implies that 'work carries priority over personal and social commitments'. The work ethic is much more popular in affiliates based in the US than in affiliates based in Canada, Italy

161

and the UK. It is strongly rejected by UK parents (relative to the US, at any rate). Lack of a work ethic does not imply tolerance of laziness because of the special way that the work ethic is defined, though its weakness in the UK might suggest an interpretation along these lines. Rejection of the work ethic, in this context, merely implies a commitment to a balanced set of goals, rather than to goals in which work carries priority over everything else.

Ambition is a fairly traditional value, particularly in a hierarchical system, where getting to the top is the main thing that counts. The fact that it is traditional, and hierarchically centred, may indeed explain why in the present business climate it receives only modest support. This may also explain why ambition is significantly strong in just one type of firm, namely the French-owned firm. Many French firms still adopt a fairly conservative approach to management (as defined below) and therefore their culture is likely to reflect conservative values. French industrial policy is much more geared to deterring foreign entry into Europe than to encouraging French firms to globalise through investment in the US and Japan. In addition, some leading French firms operate in sectors, such as cosmetics, where their position remains relatively strong, so the need to change is less. Finally, the usual French resistance to US cultural products--including the new-style corporate culture--must be taken into account.

The final value suggested to respondents was calculation--a willingness to submit to hardheaded objective appraisals and in due course administer such appraisals to subordinates. This earned a modest mean response of 2.87. Moreover national differences in this factor seem to be fairly weak - the only significant effect is the propensity to favour calculation in Taiwan.

Overall, these results suggest that national differences in culture remain a significant influence in international business. While the globalisation of markets may be reducing national differences, it has certainly not eliminated them. When supplemented by additional results not reported here, it becomes evident that cultural differences between neighbouring countries - such as the US and Canada, and the UK and France, are just as significant, if not more significant, than differences between countries a long distance apart. The pattern is too complicated to be summarised adequately in terms of Oriental culture *versus* Western culture, or in terms of a triadic distinction between the culture of the US, Europe and Japan.

If there is a distinction to be made, it is between the cultures of the newly-industrialising countries on the one hand - such as Brazil, India and Taiwan - and the mature industrialised countries on the other. Commitments to employee socialisation, and to the promotion of national interests as well as corporate interest, are much stronger in the former case. The values espoused in the corporate culture tend to be of a more conservative and traditional kind as well. In the light of what is said later, this may well be regarded as a potential source of economic strength.

Within the industrialised countries other general distinctions can be made, though these distinctions operate just as much at the level of the firm as at the level of the country as a whole. These distinctions become very clear from the interviews that were carried out. They are discussed at some length below.

## VI. The Dynamics of Cultural Change

This section summarises the principal findings on inter-firm differences in corporate culture obtained from the interviews. These findings are also corroborated by the statistical analysis. The most striking finding is that the dynamics of cultural change can be understood in terms of the interactions between three main types of firm.

*The enterprising traditionalist* has a longstanding record of steady if unexciting innovation. Its corporate culture affords managers a mixture of material and emotional motivations. The culture is often implicit rather than explicit. When it is formalised, it is concerned with business ethics rather than with corporate mission *per se*. It can usually be traced back to the 1930s, and sometimes even earlier--in the case of Japanese firms it may be closely identified with the founder of the firm. The firm tends to grow organically--it may make small acquisitions from time to time, but it does not seek to grow through large ones. Top management tends to be confident of the firm's good standing in the equity market - headquarters is not too bothered about the share price on a short-term basis. The main concern is with the company's reputation in general. It is proud of its record on employee training, product safety, paying taxes properly, and so on. It tends to perform well. Enterprising traditionalists can be found in most countries, but perhaps most particularly in Japan.

*The Post-modernist* seeks to acquire a corporate culture of this kind on the grounds that what has worked for the enterprising traditionalist can now begin to work for it as well. The necessity for acquiring a strong culture has often arisen in the aftermath of a merger or acquisition. The acquiring firm feels it needs some potent propaganda to alter conservative hierarchical attitudes in its latest acquisition - the larger the acquisition, the more strongly this is felt.

The typical Post-modernist is a product of the 1980s merger boom. Its propaganda therefore incorporates a redesigned logo which is applied to everything connected with the company. The propaganda emphasises the emotional rewards of belonging to the firm, but in practice many of the incentives are individualistic and competitive - certainly in the aftermath of a merger, a cheap form of short-term motivation is to play upon people's fears of losing their job. 'Short-termism' is apparent in top management too, particularly where the company is highly geared and creditors have to be convinced that improved performance is already on the way. Post-modern firms are based mostly in the US, though there are some in Sweden and the UK. Unfortunately for its shareholders, the typical Post-modern firm does not seem to be doing very well.

*The conservative firm* tends to favour a fairly conventional form of hierarchy. This does not mean that it is unitary rather than multidivisional, though. Many conservative MNEs have a classic matrix form; they are organised into product divisions, each having national subsidiaries in key countries, with functional departments inside each subsidiary. The conservative firm is unlikely to be heavily involved in joint ventures because its managers prefer its boundaries to be clearly defined. The conservative firm free-rides passively on the culture of its parent country. Although it is not particularly entrepreneurial, it possesses a durable advantage such as numerous patents, good industrial relations or 'national champion' status. In some cases it may also enjoy a measure of protection; its products may be difficult to trade and its domestic market may be regulated. It performs reasonably well, and has so far had no reason to incur the substantial costs of cultural change. The conservative firm is becoming very rare in the UK and US, but seems to be still quite common in France, Germany and Japan.

The relation between these three types of firm is illustrated in Table 3. The table shows that the enterprising traditionalist has evolved a culture which has enabled it to survive in a volatile environment for a considerable time[10]. The Post-modernist wishes to imitate the enterprising traditionalist because its own environment has ceased to be stable (or it has just realised, almost when it is too late, that it never really was). The Post-modernist feels handicapped by its own conservative traditions and needs to acquire new attitudes very quickly. By contrast, the conservative firm is quite content with its attitudes; it has no need to question them because it is surviving quite nicely in its stable environment.

**Table 3.  A Cultural Typology of Firms**

| Present environment | Previous environment | |
|---|---|---|
| | Volatile | Stable |
| Volatile | Enterprising traditionalist | Post-modern |
| Stable | | Conservative |

Using this approach, it is not difficult to see why Post-modern firms may not be doing very well.  Firstly, the firms were not very good to begin with - they have normally been acquired because they were slow to recognise for themselves that their environment had changed.  Secondly, their new culture comes without any tradition, and therefore lacks credibility with employees.  So far as the ordinary employee is concerned, there is no positive evidence that the new attitudes will work - only the negative evidence that the old attitudes appear to have been wrong.  Unlike the enterprising traditionalist, there is no history of success that employees can refer to for reassurance on this point.  Thirdly, credibility is actively undermined by the pressure for quick results, which leads top managers to act at variance with their stated values, as explained in more detail below.

Furthermore, there is the problem facing any imitator - of copying the bad as well as the good, and the superficial as well as the fundamental.  Finally, there is the risk that the circumstances of the firm they are copying are not so similar to their own as they believe, and that the culture needs to be modified in ways that they do not understand if it is to be implemented successfully.

Unfortunately, this attitude of uninformed imitation is the very attitude encouraged by the research methodology of management 'gurus' and the consultants that follow them, who identify successful firms and urge other firms to follow them.  The fact that the success of these firms is often ascribed to their charismatic leaders reinforces the urge to indiscriminate imitation by exploiting the universal social instinct to follow successful people.  What is really required is informed imitation based upon a proper understanding of entrepreneurial traditions.  This in turn requires that managers are guided by a proper economic analysis of culture of the kind that was summarised in section 2.

## VII.  The Impact of Recession

The recent world recession has undoubtedly thrown many firms' plans for cultural change off course.  Part of the failure of many Post-modern firms can be ascribed to their special vulnerability in this respect.

The need for de-layering was recognised before the onset of the recession.  It was obvious to Western managers that in the new competitive environment created by trade liberalisation and the challenge from Japan, established firms would have to reduce their managerial overheads, and that greater exploitation of new information technology was the natural way to do this.  Until the end of the 1980s, however, the  business outlook was basically optimistic, and it was assumed that, after some organisational renewal, growth would be resumed.  De-layering of management could therefore be effected in a civilised way that preserved the firm's reputation with its employees.  While some people would, of course, be hurt by losing their jobs, it would be a once-for-all exercise that would sooner or later be forgotten by those who remained with the firm.  Indeed, those that remained would be happier because they would be 'empowered' by the leaner structure and the flatter hierarchy.

In practice, one round of job losses has been followed by another, compulsory redundancy with minimal compensation has replaced voluntary severance with generous compensation, and empowerment has come to mean doing other people's jobs as well as one's own.  In the short run, this has increased the workload of the personnel department.  In a recession, employees are reluctant to quit because of the difficulty of finding another job, and this means that candidates for redundancy needed to be identified, and the financial entitlement of alternative candidates costed out.  In cases where new jobs are generated that are too specialised to be filled by existing employees, the recruits will normally be offered only fixed-term contracts instead of the ordinary contracts that used to be offered before.  Because of their short-term nature, these contracts need to be regularly reviewed.

In many firms, adjustment to recession used to be affected by early retirement.  Nowadays job losses are often targeted on young managers who were appointed in the 1980s at what now seem to be inflated salaries.  Their forced departure can be acrimonious, which increases the stress on the personnel department.  Stress is also increased by the fact that the personnel department itself is likely to be de-layered; for despite the short-term increase in work, the long-term scenario is that a reduced workforce calls for a smaller department.

The recession also means that HRM directors are faced with resolving the confusion caused by the excessive pace of de-layering.  As the recession has become protracted, the short-term imperative to reduce overheads has come to the fore, and the long-term objectives of de-layering have been pushed into the background. As its competitors de-layer, each firm feels obliged to de-layer even further in order to retain its competitive edge. For top managers anxious to impress the financial markets, scaling down the number of managers seems to have become an end in itself.

The rapid disappearance of management jobs has created numerous 'holes' in the hierarchy. A majority of the parent firms in this study entered the de-layering process with the legacy of a matrix management structure. In this structure, there was already some ambiguity between the competing claims of straight line reporting to one superior and dotted line reporting to another. As senior posts disappear, the ambiguity increases. Employees may be told to 'network' themselves to others simply because no one in the organisation is quite sure any longer who the employee should really be reporting to. If this ambiguity is not resolved, then the efficiency of the organisation may be impaired. 'Flattening the hierarchy' improves communications only if people know who it is that they are supposed to be talking to. The personnel department not only has short-term problems, therefore, but the longer term problem of reconstituting the organisation in a coherent way at an acceptable cost.

## VIII. The Long-term Outlook

Although the original aim of cultural change through empowerment was clearly to improve morale, in practice morale in many companies has been seriously damaged by the changes of the last few years. Terms such as 'empowerment' and 'networking' have become discredited because they do not mean what they say. In this sense, they now have the same standing, in many companies, that the corporate mission statement does. A few interviewees claimed that the situation was better than this, and in one or two cases they may be right. The majority accepted, however, that compulsory redundancies seriously damage morale because they break the implicit contract regarding a lifetime career with the company. Needless to say, Japanese firms considered this a very serious issue--though some of the Japanese affiliates in the West were more reconciled to compulsory redundancies than were their parents in Japan. It was suggested by one interviewee that European firms had been more seriously affected by loss of morale than US firms, partly because the US firms entered the recession in a leaner state and so had fewer adjustments to make, and partly because their culture placed more emphasis on hard work rewarded by high pay than on building a lifetime career with a single firm.

Indeed, the move to flatter structures means, as many commentators have noted, that the traditional concept of a management career may be coming to an end. It was always an illusion, of course, for many young managers to believe that they had a realistic chance of attaining the top job; but climbing the pyramid was still an exciting game. A clear pecking order existed, and once the middle ranks were reached there were always a good number of subordinates around to offer deference.

It is the middle managers who have the most to lose as well as the most to gain from de-layering. Their status relative to their colleagues is now more ambiguous. This is reflected in the way that many firms are reorganising managerial pay scales into a few broad (and usually overlapping) bands, allowing individual managers to renegotiate their salary without changing their level in the hierarchy. While the chief executive still knows that he is at the top of the hierarchy, and the raw recruit still knows that he is at the bottom, the middle manager cannot quite be sure of where he or she stands anymore.

The resulting insecurity is heightened by the increasing use of fixed-term contracts, and the way that issues of in-sourcing versus out-sourcing are kept regularly under review. Managers are not really sure whether they belong to the company or not. 'The company has my loyalty for as long as they pay my monthly salary', as one Compensation and Benefits Manager remarked.

With little job security offered, and little loyalty offered in return, it is not surprising that investment in training is also kept under careful review. Most large firms appear to charge training to the profit centre in which the trainee works, so that in this case divisional management rather than the personnel department determines how much training each manager receives. In addition, the personnel department will normally have a small budget of its own to provide general training of relevance to a wide range of employees.

Although training is carefully budgeted, many HRM directors indicated that it now carries higher priority than it used to. In the UK certainly, expenditure on training appears to have been maintained better in the present recession than in the previous ones. This is one positive legacy of the rise of strategic HRM. Over the next few years, many firms face a major job in rebuilding the morale of their employees.[11] Fear is an effective motivator in the short-run, but morale is vital in the long run. In light of this, it is interesting to note that when asked, 'What motivates people?', none of our interviewees--however high-ranking--was able to give a straight answer. After some evasion, several opted for 'interesting work'. An interesting job, it appears, is one that is varied, and that poses new challenges which require the development of new competencies. To fully benefit from such work, the manager must be able to 'grow with the job'. The responsibilities of the job should be clearly defined and success should be publicly acknowledged. Professional accreditation can be an important boost for the manager's confidence, whilst a sympathetic boss can also give valuable support.

This response, entirely unprompted, accords with the theoretical framework used in this study. It is based upon a far more holistic view of human motivation than that which underpins the cultural engineering approach of the Post-modern firm. It is not just the vision of a successful firm - 'becoming number one', for example - that inspires the employee, but the interest and variety involved in working towards this goal. This view is most clearly aligned with that of the enterprising traditionalist firm, whose managers pursue a series of innovative projects in the course of a conventional career. The enterprising traditionalist, it seems, is based upon a better implicit model of human motivation than the Post-modern firm. This is, perhaps, the fundamental reason behind its superior economic performance. Both theory and evidence therefore suggest that its advantage in performance is likely to persist in the future.

## IX. Summary and Conclusions

In conclusion, it needs to be emphasised again that investing in a new corporate culture is an expensive business. Cultures tend to emerge over a long time as a collective interpretation of shared experience. They are transmitted from generation to generation through education and socialisation. Attempts to accelerate this process are likely to be costly. The greater the discrepancy between the corporate culture and the culture of the society from which the employees are drawn, the greater these costs are likely to be. This is particularly relevant in an international business context, where many different national cultures are already represented within the firm, and especially true at a time when national culture in the parent country may have become pluralistic, and in some cases 'relativistic' too. Diversity, relativism, and even downright cynicism do not constitute a congenial environment in which to plant a culture based on a commitment to corporate goals.

The second point is that the need for a new corporate culture does not necessarily arise from the fact that the old corporate culture was wrong, but rather from the fact that times have changed, and that what was once appropriate is now no longer so. Some of the 'high priests' of the new corporate culture appear to argue that previously the culture was all wrong. This is particularly true when they are analysing how the Japanese were able to out compete US firms. It is especially noticeable in their stylised account of competition between national cultures in the motor industry. Some of their recommendations amount to little more than a prescription to do the opposite of whatever it was that was done before.

It is not the case, however, that previous cultures were intrinsically flawed. Hierarchy, for example, is a nearly universal principle in nature and society, and has recently evolved as an efficient solution to communication problems in computer networks as well. De-layering the hierarchy, busting the bureaucracy, and thriving on chaos (to name just a few of the current clichés) are not universal principles for efficient organisation. They only make sense as indicators of the direction in which organisations need to adapt in response to recent changes in the business environment.

When a firm operates in a mature industry that affords a stable environment, a conservative culture that regards a conventional hierarchy as the only legitimate form of organisation may not be a problem. Indeed, it may be beneficial in helping to legitimate central authority. There is no advantage in promoting internal entrepreneurship when opportunities for innovation are few.

If, however, opportunities for innovation increase, and the industry ceases to be mature, then organisational change may be required. In this case the conservative culture may prove an obstacle. If top management is slow to recognise the problem, then the 'market for management control' may be activated. With sufficient liquidity and an optimistic outlook in the financial markets, a takeover may occur. The management of the acquiring firm will attempt to 'turn around' the firm, not only by installing new technology but also by changing the organisational structure. There will be 'hard' changes in reporting and accounting procedures, and 'soft' changes in culture too.

This raises the problem that, following an acquisition, cultural change tends to be affected 'top down', whilst to be fully effective it also needs to take place 'bottom up'. The need to change culture at all levels of the organisation gives strategic HRM a crucial role to play in reaching out to the new employees that have been acquired, identifying the potential entrepreneurs among them, and integrating them into key roles in the enlarged organisation. The issue which then needs to be resolved - and on which theory can provide only limited guidance - is whether current strategic HRM practices are equal to this task or not.

Unfortunately, current strategic HRM practices have, by and large, proved unequal to the task. Some companies have made two successive attempts at cultural change, hoping to have learnt the lesson, the second time around, from their initial failure. The most important lesson of all seems to have eluded many companies, however. It is that corporate values cannot be faked by bringing in consultants to promote values in which senior management evidently does not believe itself. Recent 'scandals' over top executive pay are only the tip of the iceberg in this respect. The cynicism and relativism of current Western society cannot be tackled simply by creating entrepreneurial units where people believe in things while at work which they do not believe in at home. A corporate culture only has credibility if those who espouse it evidently live by it, and if significant elements of the culture resonate with the traditions of the firm and the values of the society in which it is embedded. The implication is that corporate culture will not become really effective until it ceases to be regarded as a 'quick fix' for the problems of individual companies and becomes part of a more comprehensive agenda of social reform.

**Endnotes**

1    M.C. CASSON *The Economics of Business Culture: Game Theory, Transaction Costs and Economic Performance*, Oxford (Clarendon Press) 1991; A. ETZIONI: *The Moral Dimension*, New York (Free Press) 1988; I.R. MACNEIL: "Exchange Revisited: Individual Utility and Social Solidarity", *Ethics*, 96 (1986), pp. 567-593; D.W. GREISINGER: "The Human Side of Economic Organization", *Academy of Management Review*, 15 (199), pp. 478-499.

2    M.C. CASSON: *Entrepreneurship and Business Culture*, Aldershot (Edward Elgar) 1995; M.C. CASSON: *The Organization of International Business*, Aldershot (Edward Elgar) 1995.

3    G.B. ADAMS and V.H. INGERSOLL "Painting Over Old Works", in: B.A. TURNER (Ed.): *Organizational Symbolism*, Berlin (de Gruyter) 1990; J.P. KOTTER and J.L. HESKETT: *Corporate Culture and Performance*, New York (Free Press) 1992; P. BLYTON and P. TURNBULL (Eds.): *Reassessing Human Resource Management*, London (Sage) 1992; H. DRUMMOND and E. CHELL: "Should Organizations Pay for Quality?", *Personnel Review*, 21, No. 4 (1992), pp. 3-11.

4    H. LEVINE: "The Squeeze on Middle Management", *Personnel*, 63, No. 1 (1986) pp. 62-69; V. Smith: "Restructuring Management and Management Restructuring", *Research in Politics and Society*, 3 (1988), pp. 221-239; S. DOPSON and R. STEWART: "What is Happening to Middle Management?", *British Journal of Management*, 1 (1990), pp. 3-161.

5    A. FREEDMAN: *The New Look in Wage Policy and Employee Relations*, New York (Conference Board) 1985; J.A. KLEIN: "The Changing Role of First Line Supervision and Middle Managers", *Report No. 26*, Washington D.C. (AndS. Department of Labor) 1988.

MARK CASSON, RAY LOVERIDGE, SATWINDER SINGH

6   S. Hill: "How Do You Manage the 'Flexible Firm'? The Total Quality Model", *Work Employment and Society*, 5, No. 3 (1991), pp. 397-415; A. Williamson, P. Allen and E. Snape: "TQM and the Management of Labour", *Employee Relations*, 13, No. 1 (1991), pp. 24-31.
7   P. Osterman: "The Impact of Computers on the Employment of Clerks and Managers", *Industrial and Labor Relations Review*, 39 (1986), pp. 175-186; N. Oliver and B. Wilkinson: *The Japanization of British Industry*, Oxford (Blackwell) 1988; J. Child and R. Loveridge (on behalf of the MESS team): *Information Technology in European Services*, Oxford (Blackwell) 1990.
8   S. Zuboff: *In the Age of the Smart Machine*, New York (Heinemann) 1988; R. Broderick and J.W. Boudreau"Human Resource Management, Information Technology, and the Competitive Edge", *The Executive*, 6, No. 2 (May 1992), pp. 7-17; G.M. Hoffman: *The Technology Pay-off*, Brassridge (Richard D. Irwin) 1994.
9   B. Partridge: "The Problem of Supervision", in: K. Sisson (Ed.): *Personnel Management in Britain*, Oxford (Blackwell) 1989; R. Scase and R. Goffee: *Reluctant Managers*, London (Unwin Hyman) 1989.
10  P. Cappelli: "Examining Managerial Displacement", *Academy of Management Journal*, 35, No. 1 (1992), pp. 203-217; A. Wilkinson, P. Allen, and E. Snape: "TQM and the Management of Labor", *Employee Relations*, 13, No. 1 (1992), pp. 24-31.
11  P. Cappelli: "Examining Managerial Displacement", *Academy of Management Journal*, 35, No. 1 (1992), pp. 203-217; A. Wilkinson, P. Allen, and E. Snape: "TQM and the Management of Labor", *Employee Relations*, 13, No. 1 (1992), pp. 24-31.

Chapter 8

# The German Historical School and the Belief in Ethical Progress

BERTRAM SCHEFOLD

## I. Introduction

Where do our ethical rules come from? Are they immutable or historically relative? If historically relative: what engenders their change? But is it at all useful to know? Would it not be better to pretend that they are immutable so as not to question the rules for our conduct?

There seems to be a way of accepting historical relativism in ethics without subverting the standards of action. If one believes not only in evolution but in progress, if this progress is not only material but also immaterial, if it includes a refinement of moral standards and of behaviour, then we may trust that it is worthwhile to conform to emerging new mores and laws - or to enforce them - because they improve the social order. However, there is a risk of living with this premise. If some social catastrophe destroys the hopes for progress, the system of values collapses.

The rise and fall of the German Historical School were accompanied by such hopes and disillusionment. Drawing on earlier works [NÖRR, SCHEFOLD, TENBRUCK(eds.) 1994; SCHEFOLD 1994; SCHEFOLD 1994a], I want to show how this belief was formed and how it dissolved under the twin influences of the methodological shift towardss the concept of a value-free science on the one hand and of the intellectual crisis that began before the First World War and was dramatically aggravated by it on the other. The psychological impact did not change the lives of the members of the German Historical School very much in appearance, in that they continued their work. The value of their researches actually improved as they were freed from teleological connotations but they lost part of their political impact, and at least some of the attempts to claim political relevance through decisionist reorientation were ill-fated. After the Second World War, the school petered out and a new generation of economists with a positivist methodology took over. They were more sophisticated analytically but also more optimistic in their belief to be able to control the economy than later events warranted. A new paradigm of progress, devoid of explicit ethical concerns, was established.


## II. The Historical School and its Origins


We can point to the roots of the historical school only summarily. 'Political Justice, says ARISTOTLE [1968, p. 295][1], is of two kinds, one natural, the other conventional (nomikón)'. And as formal laws may change, so what is regarded as virtuous. Aristotle's relativism recedes, however, when he elaborates on the virtues to be held by the citizens of the polis. Some of the virtues discussed by him have economic connotations, like the virtues of liberality and magnanimity. It turns out, for example, that he recognises the theory of generations: dynasties may rise through accumulation and decline through spending. However, whereas the moralists of the 18th century take side with the parsimonious parents, Aristotle speaks out in favour of the magnanimous descendants. For the administration of the city of classical Athens was dependent on voluntary co-operation; the so-called liturgies represented donations by wealthy citizens to the state for religious, cultural and military aims. The magnanimous therefore was expected to spend rather than to save. Liberality was also necessary for the political intercourse of the free citizens who met in assemblies and communal feasts where generosity was called for [SCHEFOLD 1994b].

Aristotle's theory of just exchange is similarly concerned with norms for trade that allow to maintain the free community of citizens. It would be best to be self-sufficient in the production of the means adequate for a life of contemplation or of politics, but some status-preserving exchange between independent households is recognised as necessary and acceptable. Relations of dependence like labouring for wages, by contrast, are criticised, and the violation of the rules for the

---

1    1134 b 19.

good life is worse if an excessive concentration on wealth-getting such as usury leads to a confusion of means and ends because wealth - which is only a mean to the good life - becomes an end in itself.

Throughout most of antiquity and the Middle Ages, the Aristotelian ethics were associated with the prevailing social order; he bequeathed the idea that commerce is dangerous for the morality of society. Out of innumerable examples, we mention that of SALLUSTIUS [1985, p. 336][2]. He implored Caesar to fight monetary greed because of its corruptive influence on public life: 'nam ubi cupido divitiarium invasit, neque disciplina neque artes bonae neque ingenium ullum satis pollet, quin animus magis aut minus mature postremo tamen succumbat'. Sallustius did not mean to abolish money or wealth - he was very rich himself, partly on account of his rapacious behaviour as proconsul in Africa - but he asked himself by which means the citizens could lead a dignified life and the social order would be maintained. Hence also the emphasis on honesty and respectability that we find in Cicero, another rich patrician.

The role of ethics for business begins to change in the Mercantilist period. Serra, to take one example, retained the Aristotelian framework. Justice is devoid of certain truths; what is just cannot be proved but only be shown by means of rhetorical and topical arguments [SCHEFOLD 1994c, p. 14]. For him, the art of government has satisfactorily been treated by the ancients (deve bastare quanto si è scritto da gli antichi) [Serra 1994 {1613}, p. 6], positive law is found in Justinian, and some control of traditional and defined standards of conduct is necessary. But the critique of the drive for profits has disappeared, economic growth has become an aim in itself, with accumulation accelerating because of desirable cumulative effects.

Mercantilism is the period in which a new order for commerce is created spontaneously. As examples, I may mention the standardisation of commodities (which were classed according to origin, style, the qualities of the materials employed), the institutions for the payment of debts created by the merchants, like bills and their clearing, or the genesis of banks that issued notes. The self-organisation of the merchants included a conscious activity to describe and teach their activities by means of manuals and to induce the state to pass legislation that would stabilise the new order. Savary was the outstanding example of a merchant who was successful in business, who wrote a treatise on commercial practices (which became a standard textbook for a century) and who helped to create commercial law in France [SAVARY 1993 {1675}]. Yet, Savary's moral standards were conventional; his book is a treatise on how to become an honest merchant: '.

---

2    Epistula II VII 4.

.. tout mon but n'a esté en entreprenant cet ouvrage que de conduire les jeunes gens pendant le cours de leur Négociation par les voyes justes, & raisonnables . . . ' (cited in: SCHEFOLD 1993, p. 20). Savary's conservatism with regard to standards of conduct may in part be explained by the desire on the part of the merchants to demonstrate their probity, contrasting it with the less reliable and luxurious behaviour of the nobility. It is in striking contrast with his revolutionary drive to create new instruments for trade and commerce and his admiration for the Italians whom he regards as most advanced in this regard but whose cunning in business transactions appears to him sometimes to be perilously close to dishonesty. A more theoretical minded Mercantilist like PETTY [1992 {1690}] is decidedly less scrupulous in his writings, and not for nothing legal charges were brought against him.

A different perspective emerges when it is asked which forms of government are favourable to trade and to the growth of industry. Authors like Serra and Petty are impressed by the republicanism of the Dutch. James STEUART [1993 {1767}] (who held a wider perspective) had absorbed the teaching of German Cameralism and arrived at a more relativist conclusion. The republics were favourable to trade but the kingdoms had more means to stimulate domestic demand [SCHEFOLD 1993a, p. 16]. Steuart's outlook was paternalistic. He conceived of an ideal states- man who was often introduced only as a device to illustrate what good policy would mean in certain situations, but there are also expressions of his belief that there can be actual good statesmanship. In Steuart we find the origin of the concept of the spirit of a people which, through Hegel, should later become important for the German Historical School: 'the spirit of a people is formed upon a set of received opinions relative to three objects; morals, government, and manners: these once generally adopted by any society, confirmed by law and constant habit, and never called in question, form the basis of all laws, regulate the form of every govern- ment, and determine what is commonly called the custom of a country.' (cited in [SCHEFOLD 1993a] p. 6-7). He regarded the spirit of a people not only as characteristic for nations in the age of rivalry but he also had an interest in eco- nomic evolution that he expressed in the form of a theory of stages.

The invocation of the importance of customs and good statesmanship, in governing the economy, looks suspicious to the liberal; the assertion that they change is a threat to the forces of tradition. Hence, ethical relativism began to become a serious problem in economic thought. Aristotle's relativism had been tempered by his belief in a natural core of political justice and by the precedence he gave to the institutions of the city state. Roman traditions and Christian beliefs had solidified ethical standards. Enlightenment, the critical turn of philosophy and the growth of knowledge about the diversity of human and, in particular, economic institutions now posed the problem of relativism with a radicalism unknown since the time of the Sophists.

In consequence, people themselves were thought to be different according to the form of the economy or state. 'The member of a republic, and the subject of a monarchy, must differ, because they have different parts assigned to them by the forms of their country-- the one destined to live with equals, or to contend by his personal talents and character for preeminence; the other, born to a determined station, where any pretence to equality creates a confusion, and where nought but precedence is studied.' [FERGUSON 1793, p. 319]. The richest treasure of such characterisations is encountered in Montesquieu.

The solution was found by perceiving or at least assuming a direction of evolution. It is one thing to be aware of a correspondence between economic or political forms and morals or laws, and another to be able to explain how changing forms change the rules of conduct. 'Whenever commerce is introduced into any country, probity and punctuality always accompany it. These virtues in a root and barbarous country are almost unknown. . . . This is not at all to be imputed to national character, as some pretend. . . . . It is far more reducible to self-interest that general principle that regulates the actions of every man, and which leads man to act in a certain manner from views of advantage. . . . . ' [SMITH 1978, p. 538]. In his 'Lectures on Jurisprudence' (Report dated 1766) Smith expressed the conviction that commerce so to speak brings the morals required to support it with it. Commerce may well dissolve traditional morals in a country but it is now supposed to establish a new order spontaneously and, as it were, effortlessly. This hypothesis, qualified by Smith because of disadvantages of the consequences of the commercial spirit such as the monotony of work in an advanced stage of division of labour, is further qualified by the recognition that virtue is not directly to be derived from utility, as he stresses in 'The Theory of Moral Sentiments' [SMITH 1979 {1759} p. 188]. But the implicit optimism is most striking in 'The Wealth of Nations'. The famous observation that it is not from the benevolence of the butcher or baker that we expect our dinner but from their self-interest has been commented upon as follows: 'Smith fairly bubbles over here with the excitement about the possibility of discarding moral discourse and exhortation, thanks to the discovery of a social mechanism that, if properly unshackled, is far less demanding of human nature and therefore infinitely more reliable' [HIRSCHMAN 1981, p. 296].

We do not really know how Smith would ultimately have reconciled the economic determinism of 'The Wealth of Nations' with the more cautious formulations of the theory of 'Moral Sentiments'. But it is certain that the German Historical School, though it shared Smith's enthusiasm for progress, was less optimistic that morals and legislation would follow the spread of commerce. Rather,

177

the growth of morals was the expression of a much broader social development and a precondition of economic development.

Authors of the German enlightenment in the 18th century had stressed the roles of religion and of education for the improvement of morals. Lessing had coined the idea of an 'education of mankind'. Successive prophets and religious movements had improved the forms of communal life, according to God's will, and ultimately, the time would come when man will do good for its own sake and not for hope of recompense [LESSING 1780]. A more secularised idea of the task of education permeates the writings of the poets and philosophers of the German classic period like Schiller.

On the other hand, laws and other institutions like infrastructure favourable for the development of a liberal economic system were to be created from above, claimed List and his school. List's point was not so much to increase national income but national productive forces, and this required initially some protection, good administration, improvement of skills and good regulation.

## III. The Older Historical School

An analytical theory of the formation of institutions was not available - the classical authors possessed an analytical theory of value but their observations on the evolution of society contained few theoretical connections. The historical school used intuition to evoke coherent and consistent representations of stages of development, characterised by certain basic traits, and they brought a vast historical knowledge and their reading of the sources to fruition by using analogies. Less reliable information was available about non-European cultures in the first half of the 19th century than in the second. This may be one of the reasons why the older historical school relied more on comparisons between the different phases of European development than the younger which had richer anthropological materials at its disposal.

ROSCHER [1994 {1861}; SCHEFOLD 1994d] in particular found the most astonishing parallels of modern developments in the works of the Greek and Roman writers, even with regard to questions that seem only to concern modernity like the practice of socialism or monetary influences on the business cycle. The contemplation of growth and decline of the ancient world, stretching over more than a millennium, offered ample opportunity for the discussion of the relation between moral and material progress. He attempted to overcome the facile opposition of 'primitive' and 'modern' institutions by trying to isolate the meaning of the norms and values, of customs and legal institutions for the continuity of the economy of the Polis. He insisted on complementarities like that of the existence of slavery and of certain forms of luxury production or on the correspondence between the readiness of citizens to provide for public gifts and the quality of cultural development. Roscher's belief in progress was tempered by his respect for cultural achievements of the past and his religious convictions that led him to regard our knowledge of human destiny with scepticism. The limitations of Roscher have been criticised repeatedly [EISERMANN 1956; PRIDDAT 1995], but a more favourable judgement was expressed by STREISSLER [1994].

The clearest interpretation of historical development in terms of a determined evolution towards higher forms of culture is to be found in HILDEBRAND [1922 {1848}]. Hildebrand's main book, published 1848, i.e., eight years after List, is a reaction against the romantic and socialist criticisms of the new industrial system. It contained a criticism of ENGELS [1845] which was of particular importance. Hildebrand disproved the conclusions Engels drew from his statistics very effectively. He did not deny that the workers often lived in abject conditions but he showed that these were better than prior to the industrial revolution, by means of a comparison with backward rural areas in Germany. He thought that morality was improving - his proofs were that the rates of crime were falling (taking proper account of population movements) and that the system of credit was based on mutual trust, in Great Britain more than in any other country in Europe. He thought that it was one of the advantages of the factory system to lay bare the maladjustment between capital and labour power. Poverty had existed before and actually been worse; now one could think of how to reduce it [HILDEBRAND 1922 {1848}, p. 184]. In phrases of similar rhythm and dramatic force as those employed by Marx and Engels in the 'Communist Manifesto', but of the opposite tendency, he wrote of the advantages of the division of labour and of the growth of industry:

> 'Sie haben die Armut der unteren Schichten der Gesellschaft nicht geschaffen oder vergrößert, sondern nur ans Tageslicht gebracht. Sie haben das Elend und das Laster ebenso wie den Reichtum, die Bildung und die sittliche und geistige Kraft des Menschen konzentriert und dadurch den vorhandenen Gegensatz zu einer sichtbaren und unleugbaren Tatsache erhoben. Sie haben die Hände des Arbeiters durch den gleichmäßigen Takt der Maschine an angestrengte regelmäßige Tätigkeit, Ausdauer und gewissenhafte Zeitbenutzung gewöhnt und in ihm Tatkraft und Energie des Willens großgezogen. Sie haben die Arbeiter aus einem Geschäftszweige in den anderen gedrängt und durch diese Nöte zum Gewerbewechsel ihren Blick erweitert und ihnen eine gewisse Beweglichkeit des Geistes und Selbstvertrauen verliehen. Sie haben die

einzelnen isolierten Berufsgenossen in große Gemeinschaften vereinigt und dadurch in ihnen zum ersten Male Selbstbewußtsein, gesellschaftliche Ansprüche und einen Trieb nach Vervollkommnung geschaffen. Selbst alle kommunistischen und sozialistischen Bestrebungen der neueren Zeit, soweit sie einen Boden in den Herzen der neuen Arbeiterwelt haben, was sind sie anderes als ein phantastischer Ausdruck jenes an der modernen Industrie erwachten Selbstbewußtseins der Arbeiter?' [HILDEBRAND 1922 {1848}, p. 184-185]³.

Hildebrand concludes: 'The machines lead humanity slowly towards a future in which a much wider range of intellectual culture will be available to each individual, with an easier satisfaction of all physiological needs' [HILDEBRAND 1922 {1848}, p. 186, my translation].

In consequence, unemployment is addressed as a necessary price of progress. Hildebrand, himself a liberal who had to emigrate after the failure of 1848 because of his convictions, hoped that the freedom of expression would help to overcome the disadvantages of the factory system. The growth of productivity would ultimately allow most workers again to leave the factories and to seek different employment - these passages sound a little like an anticipation of Fourastié: *Le grand espoir du XXe siècle*, but it turns out that Hildebrand thinks more of a return to agriculture than of a migration to a new service sector.

He then praises property which he regards as a lever of the human spirit. It allows the realisation of individual ideas and fortunately, he observes, property becomes more and more widespread. Commerce, too, is a lever of culture, as the

---

3    My translation: 'They have neither created nor enhanced the poverty of the lower strata of society, but they have only brought it to light. They have concentrated misery and vice as much as riches, intellectual culture and the moral and spiritual power of man, and hence they have transformed the corresponding opposition into a visible and undeniable fact. They have adapted the hands of the worker through the even rhythm of machines to hard, regular work, to perseverance and conscientious use of time, and they educated his energy and will. They have driven the workers from one sector to the other and have enlarged their views and given them some agility of mind and self-assurance by forcing them to change their jobs. They have united the single isolated professional companions into large unions and have created self-consciousness, social aspirations and a drive to perfection in them for the first time. Even all communist and socialist activities of recent times - to the extent that they are rooted in the hearts of the new world of workers - what else are they if not a fantastic expression of that new self-consciousness of the worker, aroused by modern industry?'

extension of credit shows. He regards the money economy analysed by Smith only as an intermediate stage, after barter, while the future belongs to extended systems of credit - this theory of stages was to become famous and the object of a celebrated article by HILDEBRAND [1922 {1864}].

Yet, despite this optimism, Hildebrand does not believe that commercial morals are a unilateral consequence of commercial progress. He lacks theoretical criteria to distinguish speculative activities from fraudulent ones and seems inclined to regard speculation generally as immoral. If this behaviour does not predominate, he concludes that the 'moral forces of peoples' are more powerful than the 'theoretical principles of the Smithian school', in particular in a country like Great Britain where, Hildebrand believes, the state and public life are an ethical school of the population [HILDEBRAND 1922 {1848}, p. 229].

Hildebrand's economics is, in his own view, primarily an ethical system. No natural laws operate in the economy. The possibility of theorising on the basis of abstract hypotheses is not considered by him--hence his conclusion that economics is either naturalistic and deterministic or ethical and normative, where it is not simply descriptive. Moral forces are the main condition of development, and these moral forces can neither be created by government nor through economic institutions. They are the 'spiritual capital' of the people which is acquired through long, hard work, as a slowly ripening fruit of history, of national culture and of a well ordered and free public life [HILDEBRAND 1922 {1863}].

He thus arrives at the following conclusion for his theory of stages which culminates in the system of credit:

'Wenn es gelungen sein sollte, den Leser zu überzeugen, daß das wirtschaftliche Leben der Völker einer gesetzlichen Entwicklung zu immer höherer Kultur unterworfen ist, so wird derselbe auch einverstanden sein, wenn zum Schluß noch der Satz ausgesprochen und behauptet wird, daß nicht nur das Leben der einzelnen Völker, sondern auch die Wirtschaft der ganzen Menschheit einen gesetzlichen Verlauf zu immer höherer Vervollkommnung nimmt, und daß der Lessingsche Gedanke einer Erziehung des Menschengeschlechts nicht nur auf die Religionen und die ihr verwandten Gebiete der geistigen Kultur, sondern auch auf das nationalökonomische Leben des Menschengeschlechts seine Anwendung findet.' [HILDEBRAND 1922 {1864}, p. 357][4].

---

4    My translation: 'If it should have been possible to convince the reader that the economic life of peoples is subject to a regular development to ever higher forms of culture, the same will also agree if at last the proposition is expressed and if it is asserted that not

This is an explicit formulation of the secularisation of Lessing's idea of the education of mankind, transferred from the sphere of religion and culture to that of morals and economics.

# IV. The Younger Historical School

The historical school, especially the younger, was a complex phenomenon; we consider it here in a special perspective - ethical progress - on the basis of a small number of examples. With the rekindling of interest in the historical school, a literature has arisen which considers other aspects such as the relationship to classical and neoclassical economic theory or its methodology (see e.g. HÄUSER [1983]; KOSLOWSKI [1985]). Before we turn to the main exponent of the younger historical school, Gustav Schmoller, it may be interesting to consider the first substantial work of another member of the younger generation who was, like Hildebrand, on the liberal and left wing of the school, Karl Bücher. He approached the social question, one of the main influences on the ethical thinking of the historical school, through a book on the slave revolts in antiquity. It provides a stark example of the method of seeking an orientation by means of historical analogies. Of course, Bücher was interested in the historical question also for its own sake; he had studied ancient languages and established facts with care. But an analogy provided not only a motive to study a certain historical question - as it may do for a modern historian - but it carried a message as well.

Bücher regarded the slave revolts which we associate with their main leader, Spartacus, as the first 'international labour movement'. It caused an important setback to the system of 'capitalist slavery' which the Romans had taken over when they conquered Sicily and Carthago, Greece and the Hellenistic monarchies. These slave revolts seemed to Bücher to mark the culminating point of a 'capitalist' penetration of all areas of life in antiquity when no 'consolation' seemed possible anymore because the inequality of property and income increased progressively,

---

only the life of the individual peoples but also the economy of all mankind takes a regular course to higher and higher forms of perfection, and that Lessing's idea of an education of mankind may be applied not only the religions and the kindred areas of spiritual culture, but also to the economic life of mankind.'

with the slow disappearance of the middle layer of society. The proletarian movement of that period seemed to Bücher like a 'lightening of socialism', comparable to the modern phenomenon [BÜCHER 1874, p. 115].

Labour thus became the basis for an entitlement to the economic product, in direct opposition to the conception of citizenship which the Greeks had developed, a citizen who regarded it as below his dignity to work if he could avoid it, and whose participation in the political life of the state was based on his ownership of property. Religious ethical systems now were necessary to overcome the contradiction between the poverty of terrestrial life and the aspiration of happiness and moral values. Hence the socialist communities which, according to Bücher, were able to maintain a certain degree of egalitarianism, like the first Christians, as long as religious enthusiasm remained strong. The implied message was that, by analogy, revolution was possible and even religious socialism, if nothing was done to relieve the social question.

This was the form a radical pamphlet could take when the spirit of the historical school was alive. Bücher, a man of a wide range of interests within economics, later turned to quite different questions - medieval economic history, an analysis of the division of labour, statistical matters, a theory of stages and, a curious and very successful book, an analysis of the rhythm of worksongs [SCHEFOLD 1988]. Analogies later were used with more reservations; history does not teach us to be clever next time but to be wise forever, said Burckhardt. At the methodological level, it came to be regarded as questionable to speak of 'capitalism' or 'socialism' in antiquity [SALIN 1967], when the youngest historical school, after Schmoller, attempted to understand each social and economic formation within its own context.

Schmoller himself was as much a historian as he was an economist. He felt himself to be a heir of German classical culture with its idea of a universal education of the individual. Classical culture aimed at the creation of an ideal life which would enhance the understanding and the value of the individual [DILTHEY 1961, p. 11]. According to Schmoller, Schiller and Goethe were: '. . . not only the poets but also the teachers and educators of their time. It was not circumstantial that one was at the same time philosopher and historian, the other equally remarkable as statesman, psychologist and scientist. They were aware of the great tasks of their time.' [SCHMOLLER 1888, p. 26, my translation]. But, Schmoller felt, Schiller had given undue prominence to the pursuit of the beautiful. Schmoller accepted the moral value of aesthetic education, but it was not the only element of culture; religion and morals, political institutions and the sciences were also indispensable to it. Accordingly, Schmoller was proud that his generation had reacted by turning to 'realistic action', culminating in the creation of Germany's political unity, long after the same had been obtained by the Western nations. This was regarded as a cultural achievement, not simply as a matter of national power politics, let alone of imperialist rivalry. The pressing need to relieve the social tensions accompanying this development became the main concern. The ideals of the classical period were to be maintained, Schmoller had asserted, but in fact waned as the economy grew and tensions between the social classes increased. However, this was denounced only by Nietzsche, and later by keen observers of the generation that followed on Schmoller.

His endeavour was to integrate the divergent tendencies and disciplines. Historical individuality and the logic of the pursuit of self-interest were brought together in his book through three convergent approaches: (1) There was the description of the forms of economic and political life in different periods, still interpreted as economic stages although Schmoller had in reality long begun to interpret them in terms of the notions which were developed subsequently under the heading of economic systems and economic styles. (2) He used an intricate psychological analysis in order to demonstrate how the different motives interacted and, finally, (3) the consideration of ethics. There is a tension between individual and social norms which must be balanced in different ways according to the positions of people in society; Schmoller came close to identifying his ethical approach with sociology. This empiricist turn did not imply a total denial of universal values but represented something of a retreat in comparison with the stronger views held by members of the older historical school (for a comparison of their ethics see [PRIDDAT 1995a, in particular p. 135]).

We here have to investigate the second and the third of the three approaches, beginning with his psychology. We assume that we know what the 'spirit of acquisition' is. Schmoller insists that it is not the only economic virtue. There are also diligence and efficiency and the propensity to save which are necessary in different degrees in different circumstances (in the life of the primitive, of the household in antiquity or for the modern middle classes). There is further the entrepreneurial spirit which grows with the extent of the market, accompanied by the talent for organisation and combination, the propensity to risk and relentlessness. These qualities are useful though not necessarily the highest from an ethical point of view.

Schmoller was not a utilitarian and saw a growing contrast between morals and manners on the one hand, the useful on the other. His theory of the growth of moral sentiment seems to be based on that of Adam Smith. We observe third persons doing good actions and are happy to see that the good is done so that, conversely, we learn to judge our own action in the mirror of what others feel about ourselves. Schmoller then introduces the image of the impartial spectator and of the conflict between the immediate impulse and the conscience. These general forms of moral sentiment are universal – Schmoller cites the authors of antiquity, not Smith, – but the concrete contents are surprisingly different in different societies and can be understood only if 'the entire representations of causality and religious ideas of a tribe or a people' are taken into account [SCHMOLLER 1978, p. 43]. Schmoller dedicates a number of pages to what would nowadays be called the sociology of religion. Religion is responsible for that abstract sentiment of a duty which is a mighty impulse against the lower instincts [SCHMOLLER 1978, p. 47]. Norms and customs precede the legal enactment of moral standards and were previously rightly regarded as more fundamental than formal law. 'Moribus plus quam legibus stat res Romana' [quoted by SCHMOLLER 1978, p. 52].

In his perusal of different religious systems, he also touches Calvinism. He perceives the importance of the ascetic lifestyle for economic success, as long as customs and law are adapted to the needs of people and the circumstances in which they live; an excessive rigidity, by contrast, is dangerous for development. Conservatives and the exponents of tradition are in fear of a dissolution of morality while ingenious reformers transform morality and the cultural world. He does not suggest that the reversal of values would have to be preceded by a reorganisation of the economic system.

He then traces the separation of formal law from moral tradition. He notes that the Islam does not know an independent secular system of morals and insists that the system of morality and the legal system remain complementary. Their differentiation is an indicator of progress. He therefore regards the theory of a natural order – i.e., the Smithian theory – as old-fashioned. The system of liberty is too simple because it is based only on the interplay of the motive of self-interest among people, ignoring all the others, while the socialists are wrong because they believe that everything must be regulated by law. In a phrase reminiscent of Lowe's theory of 'spontaneous conformity' [LOWE 1988], he emphasises that the extent and the severity of the legal system can be reduced where the informal moral system grows stronger.

Society needs education towards the collaboration in institutions. Each institution depends on habits, morals and law; its personal representation is called its 'organ'. Marriage is an institution and the family the corresponding organ. The mercantilists believed to be able to create institutions at will while the liberals wanted to reduce their number. The point, however, is to create them according to the views of the society, and these are discovered in an evolutionary process. Schmoller recognises that there is some truth to a Darwinian interpretation of social evolution – the decline of the least successful strata is the price of progress. But Darwinism underestimates the potential of conscious creation.

These considerations are part of the introductory chapters of Schmoller's treatise. We are here not concerned with the central parts on technology and production, markets, money, the forms of firms and economic policy, but we now turn

185

to the end of the book where progress is evaluated. The economic aspects of progress are only its outward appearance [SCHMOLLER 1978, p. 748]. This is not only because power and wealth are regularly accompanied by a flowering of other aspects of culture. Rather, his point is that economic progress is a reflection of the growth of the potential of men, in particular of the economic abilities of humans, and of better economic institutions and their organs.

Schmoller distinguishes between mechanical and teleological theories of development. The former contain the materialist explanations, based on climate, race, anthropology, technology, the division of labour or the forms of economic intercourse. Marx e.g. stresses the material forces of production, Durkheim the division of labour, Hildebrand, with his stages, the forms of economic communication. The teleological theories contain the religious interpretations like that of Lessing, the dominance of ideas (as in Hegel), the forms of political rule (as in Plato), and certain more modern constructions. Schmoller was quite ambivalent in the reception of these doctrines. The results of historical research suggested a generalisation of the theory of development, taking account of the cultural factors as determining influences. As an example, Schmoller mentions a typology by the historian Lamprecht, in which the spiritual culture is characterised in terms such as 'animism, symbolism, typism, conventionalism, individualism, subjectivism', and to these correspond different levels of material development and of economic organisation. This attempt to connect the manifestations of culture with economic phases was very ambitious; Schmoller declined such high aspirations, but the subsequent generation was to work precisely in this field.

Schmoller's own theory of stages was based on the economic constitution. It is excellent as a contribution towards the understanding of mercantilism but perhaps less interesting in other respects; at any rate, it cannot be said that his theory of stages was definitely superior to others like that of Hildebrand or Bücher. Especially the latter had more insight with regard to primitive economies and antiquity. But it is to be noted that a number of key concepts which later became prominent in the work of Max Weber and Sombart are already to be found in Schmoller like the distinction between 'Bedarfsdeckungswirtschaft' and 'Erwerbswirtschaft', the true roots of which go back, of course, to Aristotle.

All theories of development are, at the same time, theories of growth and decline. Schmoller sees the latter ultimately as caused by a weakening of moral forces. He regarded the big nation states, but also Great Britain with its Empire, as stable, and the Ottoman Empire and China as potentially prone to dissolution. Schmoller has been accused of nationalism but national cohesion in the sense of ethnical homogeneity was here clearly not his main criterion.

On the whole, the forces of development prevail, and hence the ultimate optimistic conclusion that economic and moral growth will continue to be associated. 'The time will come when all well and normally developed humans will be able to combine a descent spirit of acquisition and the desire to develop individuality, self-assertion and the acceptance of their own selves with perfect justice and the highest public spirit. It is to be hoped that the road to get there will not be as long as that which led from the brutality of the physically strong man to the modern cultural human being' [SCHMOLLER 1978, p. 775, my translation].

This optimism sounds astonishing a century later. It was based to a not negligible extent on ignorance about the moral achievements of primitive cultures. But Schmoller's identification of economic and cultural progress was characteristic for his time. As an other example, one might discuss Wagner's 'Common Needs' which were supposed to grow with the evolution of society. They resemble public goods, and Wagner held the 'law' that, on their account, the share of the expenditure of the state must grow in any 'progressive cultured people' [WAGNER 1991 {1876} chapter 4].

## V. The Youngest Historical School

The experience of the First World War, of the unfavourable peace, of the social revolution that followed and of the great inflation which occurred only five years after the defeat shattered all previously held convictions and, in particular, the belief in ethical progress in Germany. Schmoller's notion of progress now came under attack [RAAB 1934]. But opposition against the valuations of the Historical School had started in the 1890ies. A separation of scientific analysis from policy recommendation was clearly necessary, and it implied restraint with a regard to evaluations that are to some extent inevitable in a science such as economics which, if it is treated as a moral or historical science, cannot exist without some value judgements and must contain a few even in its analytical form because of the choice of assumptions and the orientation of questions. In the new historical situation, confronted also with new economic problems such as runaway inflation, the economists reoriented themselves, and interest in analytical economics and quantitative empirical work grew.

The concerns of the Historical School were transformed under the influence of Max Weber and Werner Sombart. There arose a 'Verstehende Nationalökonomie' as a branch of economics aimed at the 'understanding' of different economic forms. The concept of 'economic style' was developed for which Sombart also used the term 'economic system', but he meant much the same as an economic style. One felt that it was now the task of German economics to relate theory and

187

history by uncovering the inner logic of different economic styles or systems, and to reconcile the understanding of the individuality of different economic periods with an analysis of the laws which pertained perhaps to one case but not to the other [SALIN 1963 {1927}]. In its attempts to relate analytical concepts with historical observations, the theory was to be intuitive ('anschaulich').

Spiethoff, a pupil of Schmoller's, tried to assemble a catalogue of characteristics of economic styles, starting with the economic spirit, the variations of which had played such an important role in Schmoller's psychology and his sociology of religion. Further characteristics obviously are natural endowments and technology, but also the economic and social constitution (this is again reminiscent of Schmoller) and the economic dynamism. The latter point was a contribution of Spiethoff himself who was preeminent for his analytical and historical research in business cycles. A neoclassical theorist would regard the cyclical character of the movement of an economy as a result of other data of the system, and a Keynesian economist might emphasise the 'animal spirits' of entrepreneurs as a determinant of the dynamism of an economy, but Spiethoff thought that the static character of many traditional societies and the degree to which modern economies are capable of expansion were to be regarded as separate characteristic elements of the style. The elements were not thought to be independent but, in their special form, mutually reinforcing each other.

I have discussed economic styles at some length elsewhere [SCHEFOLD 1994e; SCHEFOLD 1995]. In order to provide at least one example, I take up the 'Economic Style of the Late Middle Ages' by Bechtel [BECHTEL 1930; see also SCHEFOLD 1994f]. Bechtel tries to show that the period from the last third of the $14^{th}$ to the beginning of the $16^{th}$ century in Germany represented an economic formation of a particular character which could also be demarcated geographically. He did not analyse it in its entirety but only the city economy. Polemicizing against Bücher, he distinguished between small cities of a few hundred and larger cities of a few thousand inhabitants; he considered only the latter as the really dynamic element. One knows that this era starts with the crisis following upon the spreading of the plague and that it ends with the repercussions of the discovery of the new world and the consequent change of the roads of economic communication in central Europe. It is a period in which corporations strengthened and trade grew.

The distinguishing feature of Bechtel's work consists in the use of works of art not only for the purposes of illustration but of explanation. We here encounter representations of architecture, of painting and of graphics which are analysed by means of the methods of the historian of art in order to provide evidence of a new feeling of social adhesion and of individuality. The so-called 'Hallenkirche', a church in the form of a hall, regarded as characteristic for late German gothic, is for Bechtel not only the expression but also the mean to develop the consciousness of a church community which attempts to gain independence with respect to nobility and clergy. Who visits the church daily will not only feel the desire to see the aspiration of the community expressed in an adequate form of architecture, but the individual consciousness will also be influenced by such architecture, in the same way as painting and graphics influenced the new understanding of the individual.

This new individuality does not only correspond to the more active role of the personality of entrepreneurs as merchants but the artists help to create this consciousness – Bechtel is intent to demonstrate the sequence historically. To this change in mentality, there corresponds an economic and social development of the corporations and their constitutions, a geographical extension of the domain of activity of merchants, a changing relationship between artisan and customer and other developments which we cannot summarise here. It is precisely this mutual influence of economic and cultural characteristics which Schmoller had noted but, in the end, not incorporated into his historical account because he felt that these relationships were too tenuous to explain economic facts such as the changes in the organisation of firms. Max Weber in his 'Protestant Ethic' had been careful to avoid assertions about causality. The growth of rationalisation corresponded to the cultural meaning of Calvinism but Weber never asserted that capitalism was engendered by this religious orientation. He wanted to find out in how far religious influences co-determined the qualitative form and the quantitative expansion of the capitalist spirit across the world and which concrete aspects of a culture based on capitalism could be explained in their terms [SCHEFOLD 1992a, p. 10]. Bechtel, who was bolder but less important, had fewer followers.

Not all the work of the youngest historical school was quite as esoteric, but its method was attacked as lacking instrumental value. Some economists tried to show that analytical economics and the 'Verstehende Nationalökonomie' were not mutually exclusive in principle but that only *theory* provided the conceptual tools required for economic policy, because only theory establishes causal links.

It was also asked whether the historical approach was not in need of theory to explain past developments. Ludwig von Mises [MISES 1933] defended the conceptual unity of Austrian theory with its emphasis on utility maximisation as the unique form of rationality against the differentiation of several distinct forms of rationality in Max Weber. In fact, Mises's attempt to demonstrate that even traditional forms of rationality could be interpreted in terms of rational action was formally successful but it threatened to empty economics of its descriptive content, and the logical consequences of integrating traditional forms of rationality into economic theory, e.g., by assuming that there is a preference for the use of traditional methods of production, were not worked out. But SCHUMPETER [1954, p. 236] proposed to combine the historical understanding of a personality like

Sombart with the theoretical acumen of an Edgeworth - a program which, he hoped, the future would fulfil.

As the power of the historical theory in explaining past developments increased, it lost its normative potential. Sombart himself would compare the approach of the youngest historical school to an aristocratic luxury – he regarded the free growth of science, supported by the community, as an aristocratic trait of bourgeois culture. But he let loose his former reservations when the National Socialists came to power and wrote an ill-famed book, entitled German Socialism [SOMBART 1934] in which he argued for a nationalist approach to economic policy, trying to show that German traditions would favour such an approach. His concrete measures were in part quite sensible. They included, prior to Keynes, Keynesian methods to reduce unemployment and the proposal to control technological development where it threatened to be harmful to nature. But it contained too many concessions to the new rulers, and Sombart was lucky in that the National Socialists declared not to be in need of his professorial advice. National Socialism thus did not mean that the historical school prospered while theory was oppressed; rather, economists of all orientations had to suffer if they did not support the new system, and many were forced to emigrate.

## VI. The Final End of the Historical School

The publication of EUCKEN's [1940] 'Grundlagen der Nationalökonomie' was the most memorable contribution of German economics in the period of the Second World War. Eucken's work has often been regarded as the end of the historical school but it can also be interpreted as one of its crowning achievements in that it clarified the method for combining theory and history. He attempted to provide a theoretical framework in order to distinguish different economic systems as ideal types by distinguishing between different forms of allocation, different forms of markets and of the monetary system. The real economy then is interpreted as a superposition of the ideal types. It is to be determined by first considering the economic order in vigour, and then by considering the economic process. All of Eucken's examples were historical, stretching from the economy of the ancients via the Middle ages to the nineteenth century, but he omitted his own time, undoubtedly for political reasons. Eucken's programme to provide a complete account of the elementary forms which were to be combined as ideal types proved utopian; the growth of economic theory has multiplied the possibilities, but he contributed much to show the way in which the 'antinomy' between theory and history may be overcome.

Eucken's stress of the economic order as the main determining factor had important consequences after the war when the legal and institutional framework for the reconstruction of the German economy had to be erected. The so-called German 'Ordoliberalismus' now proposed, distinguishing itself from classical liberalism, that the state was responsible for a stable economic order and also for the maintenance of competitive conditions in the face of tendencies towardss concentration, but that it should abstain from interfering with the day-to-day process of economic activity. Of course, this distinction proved often difficult to sustain. The question never was quite resolved when anticyclical policies would be acceptable. The idea, however, was clear: to base the legitimacy of economic intervention on its conformity with the principles of the economic system.

After the war, German economists primarily felt the need to get acquainted with the new developments in economic theory during the 1930ies and -40ies, from which they had been cut off. This, together with the dynamism of reconstruction, left little room for what remained of the historical school. At the end of the 1950ies, two famous debates took place. One, on concentration in the economy [NEUMARK 1961] started from the observation that the control of competitive conditions was not as easy as perhaps had been imagined, and it was also doubtful to what extent it was really necessary, since the theory of imperfect competition had given way to an analysis of the effects of competition as a process, and here it turned out that even monopolistic competition could be functional. Salin now argued, using not only economic but also sociological and political considerations, therefore donning the armoury of the historical school, that concentration was inevitable and even desirable, especially in view of the process of European economic integration. He aroused the theorists and shocked the ordoliberals, but it was really the last time that the historical school scored some points.

A subsequent meeting of the Verein für Socialpolitik (the German Economic Association) was concerned with economic methodology [GIERSCH and BORCHARDT 1962]. Now it was a debate between German Keynesians, educated in econometric techniques, on the one hand, and members of the historical school on the other. The latter were sceptical with regard to formal theory and doubtful whether the econometric techniques could serve as reliable instruments of forecasting. They remembered the years of the great depression with its many specific and individual aspects which seemed to defy a simple representation, e.g., in the form of the multiplier-accelerator model. They now were utterly defeated but several of the defenders of Keynesianism of 1960 had become monetarists by the 1970ies when Keynesian policies, put to the test, did not produce the desired results. Both discussions proved that ethical considerations were dominated by considerations of efficiency.

The great questions of the historical school, regarding the relationship between economy and culture, in the meantime had receded into the background. There was, for instance, still the work of Weippert who produced refined essays on such subjects, but his success was limited. A domain in which the historical school should have excelled was the comparison of economic systems, but that discussion was now dominated by the question of whether the Eastern or the Western method of allocation, the plan or the market, would produce more growth in the long run, and thus it was turned into a rather technical problematic.

However, there were some authors who saw the rivalry between East and West in a wider historical perspective, linking state socialism with traditions of oriental despotism and with the economic theories that have been invoked to explain it. They opposed to it the tradition of Western values of democracy which are linked to market liberalism. RÜSTOW's [1950-57] analysis of the rise of totalitarianism was particularly impressive. This discussion contained an important moral element in that Rüstow and Röpke [RÖPKE 1944; 1951] criticised 'capitalism' from a 'liberal' point of view because of its tendencies towards concentration and proletarianisation. They proposed the idea of a 'Vitalpolitik' against the trend, a policy for raising the vitality of people, through decentralisation of production, improvement of agrarian conditions, the raising of the standards of living of the workers, and, in particular, through the creation not of employment in general but of opportunities for *productive* work in particular. And it is remarkable that this particular postulate was endorsed by the minister of economics, Ludwig Erhard. He angrily rejected suggestions that he should feel responsible for culture when reconstruction went on at a fast pace with little regard for the beauty of cities and the environment, as some felt – the economy perhaps was a mundane subject but he could not help it. Nevertheless, he did recognise that the problem of work could not be reduced to a problem of employment; the work process and the quality of the product and the consequent satisfaction of the worker also mattered. Fast growth and full employment soon made these considerations redundant and the corresponding discussions grew silent.

So it happened that the concerns of the historical school, in particular their ethical concerns, were forgotten by about 1960, after they had been weakened considerably in the first half of the century, and economics ceased to be a 'moral science' in Germany for about one generation. Progress in economic research and teaching was still made, perhaps more than ever before, but in other domains.

# THE GERMAN HISTORICAL SCHOOL

## References

ARISTOTLE: *The Nichomachian Ethics*, with an English translation ed. by H. Rackham. Harvard (University Press) 1968 [1934, 1926].

BECHTEL, H.: *Wirtschaftsstil des deutschen Spätmittelalters. Der Ausdruck der Lebensform in Wirtschaft, Gesellschaftsaufbau und Kunst von 1350 bis um 1500*, München und Leipzig (Duncker &Humblot) 1930.

BOCK, M., H. HOMAN and P. SCHIERA (Eds.): *Gustav Schmoller heute*, Berlin (Duncker & Humblot) 1989.

BÜCHER, K.: *Die Aufstände der unfreien Arbeiter 143 bis 129 v. Chr*, Frankfurt am Main (Sauerländer) 1874.

DILTHEY, W. : *Die Philosophie des Lebens*, Eine Auswahl aus seinen Schriften. Stuttgart (Teubner) 1961.

EISERMANN, G.: *Die Grundlagen des Historismus in der deutschen Nationalökonomie*, Stuttgart (Enke) 1956.

ENGELS, F.:"Die Lage der arbeitenden Klasse in England", in: K. MARX und F. ENGELS: *Werke Band 2*, Berlin (Dietz) 1974 [1845] pp. 225-506.

EUCKEN, W.: *Grundlagen der Nationalökonomie*, Jena (G. Fischer) 1940.

FERGUSON, A.: *An Essay on the History of Civil Society*, London (Cadell) 1793 [1767].

FOURASTIÉ, J.: *Le grand espoir du XXe siècle*, Paris (Gallimard) 1989 [1950].

GIERSCH H. and K. BORCHARDT (Eds.): *Diagnose und Prognose als wirtschaftswissenschaftliche Methodenprobleme*, Berlin (Duncker & Humblot) 1962 (= Schriften des Vereins für Socialpolitik NF.25, Verhandlungen auf der Arbeitstagung des Vereins für Socialpolitik in Garmisch-Partenkirchen).

HÄUSER, K.: "Gründe des Niedergangs. Überlebendes und Überlebenswertes", in: BOCK et al.., 1989, pp. 31-61.

HILDEBRAND, B.: *Nationalökonomie der Gegenwart und Zukunft und andere gesammelte Schriften*, Hrsg. und eingeleitet von H. Gehrig. Jena (G. Fischer), 1922 [1848].

HILDEBRAND, B.: "Die gegenwärtige Aufgabe der Wissenschaft der Nationalökonomie", repr. in: Hildebrand: *Nationalökonomie der Gegenwart und Zukunft und andere gesammelte Schriften*, Hrsg. und eingeleitet von H. Gehrig. Jena (G. Fischer), 1922 [1863] pp. 268-309.

HILDEBRAND, B.: "Natural-, Geld- und Kreditwirtschaft", repr. in: Hildebrand: *Nationalökonomie der Gegenwart und Zukunft und andere gesammelte Schriften*, Hrsg. und eingeleitet von H. Gehrig. Jena (G. Fischer), 1922 [1864] pp. 325-357.

HIRSCHMAN, A.O.: *Essays in Trespassing*, Cambridge (University Press) 1981.

KOSLOWSKI, P.:"Der ökonomische Zwischenbau, Volkswirtschaftslehre als ethische und kulturelle Ökonomie", in: BOCK et al., 1989, pp. 185-222.

KOSLOWSKI, P. (Ed.): "The Theory of Ethical Economy in the Historical School", Heidelberg (Springer) 1995 (= Studies in Economic Ethics and Philosophy).

# BERTRAM SCHEFOLD

LESSING, G.: *Sämtliche Werke in 6 Bänden*, Berlin (Knaur) o.J. [1780], vol. VI, 1780, pp. 413-434.

LOWE, A.: *Has Freedom a Future?* New York (Praeger) 1988.

MISES, L. von: *Grundprobleme der Nationalökonomie. Untersuchungen über Verfahren, Aufgaben und Inhalt der Wirtschafts- und Gesellschaftslehre*, Jena (Fischer) 1933.

NEUMARK, F. (ed.): *Die Konzentration der Wirtschaft*, Berlin (Duncker & Humblot) 1961 (= Schriften des Vereins für Socialpolitik NF 22, Verhandlungen auf der Tagung in Bad Kissingen).

NÖRR, K.W., B. SCHEFOLD and F. TENBRUCK (Eds.): *Deutsche Geisteswissenschaften zwischen Kaiserreich und Republik. Zur Entwicklung von Nationalökonomie, Rechtswissenschaft und Sozialwissenschaft im 20. Jahrhundert*, Stuttgart (Steiner), 1994, 452 pp.

PETTY, W.: *Political Arithmetick*, Düsseldorf (Verlag Wirtschaft und Finanzen) 1992 [1690].

PRIDDAT, B.P.: "Intention and Failure of W. Roscher's Historical Method of National Economics", in: KOSLOWSKI (ed.) 1995, pp. 15-34.

PRIDDAT, B.P.: *Die andere Ökonomie*, Marburg (Metropolis) 1995a.

RAAB, F.: *Die Fortschrittsidee bei Gustav Schmoller*, Freiburg (Kehrer) 1934.

RÖPKE, W.: *Civitas Humana. Grundfragen der Gesellschafts- und Wirtschaftsreform*, Zürich (Rentsch) 1944.

RÖPKE, W.: *Die Lehre von der Wirtschaft*, Zürich (Rentsch) 1951.

ROSCHER, W.: *Ansichten der Volkswirthschaft aus dem geschichtlichen Standpunkte*, Düsseldorf (Verlag Wirtschaft und Finanzen) 1994 [1861].

RÜSTOW, A.: *Ortsbestimmung der Gegenwart. Eine universalgeschichtliche Kulturkritik.* Bd. I-III, Erlenbach/Zürich (Rentsch) 1950-57.

SALIN, E.: "Hochkapitalismus. Eine Studie über W. Sombart, die deutsche Volkswirtschaftslehre und das Wirtschaftssystem der Gegenwart", repr. in: E. Salin: *Lynkeus*, Tübingen (Mohr) 1963 [1927]: pp. 182-212.

SALIN, E.: *Politische Ökonomie. Geschichte der wirtschaftspolitischen Ideen von Platon bis zur Gegenwart*, Tübingen (Mohr) 1967 [1923].

SALLUST: *Werke*, Lat. und dt. von W. Eisenhut und J. Lindauer. Zürich (Artemis), 1985

SAVARY, J.: *Le parfait négociant*, Düsseldorf (Verlag Wirtschaft und Finanzen) 1993 [1675].

SCHEFOLD, B.: "Karl Bücher und der Historismus in der Deutschen Nationalökonomie", in: *Deutsche Geschichtswissenschaft um 1900*, ed. by N. Hammerstein. Stuttgart (Steiner) 1988, pp. 239-267.

SCHEFOLD, B. 1989: "Normative Integration der Einzeldisziplinen in gesellschaftswissenschaftlichen Fragestellungen", in: BOCK et al., 1989, pp. 251-269.

SCHEFOLD, B.: "Einleitung zur "Political Arithmetick" von William Petty", in: *Kommentarband ("Vademecum") zur Faksimileausgabe von Sir William Pettys "Political Arithmetick"*, Düsseldorf (Verlag Wirtschaft und Finanzen), 1992, pp. 5-36 (= Klassiker der Nationalökonomie).

SCHEFOLD, B.: "Max Webers Werk als Hinterfragung der Ökonomie. Einleitung zum Neudruck der 'Protestantischen Ethik' in ihrer ersten Fassung", in: *Kommentarband*

# THE GERMAN HISTORICAL SCHOOL

*("Vademecum") zur Faksimileausgabe von Max Webers "Die Protestantische Ethik und der 'Geist' des Kapitalismus"*, Düsseldorf (Verlag Wirtschaft und Finanzen), 1992a, pp. 5 -31 (= Klassiker der Nationalökonomie).

SCHEFOLD, B.: "Savarys 'Parfait négociant': Die Ordnung der Märkte durch Händler und Staat", in: *Kommentarband ("Vademecum") zur Faksimileausgabe des Neudruck von Jacques Savarys 'Parfait Négociant' in seiner ersten Fassung*, Düsseldorf (Verlag Wirtschaft und Finanzen) 1993, pp. 15-48 (= Klassiker der Nationalökonomie).

SCHEFOLD, B.: "Die Verbindung von Theorie, Geschichte und Politik bei James Steuart. Einleitung zur Neuausgabe von Steuarts 'Political Oeconomy'", *Kommentarband ("Vademecum") zur Faksimileausgabe des Neudrucks seines Werkes "An Inquiry into the Principles of Political Oeconomy"*, Düsseldorf (Verlag Wirtschaft und Finanzen) 1993a, pp. 5-16 (= Klassiker der Nationalökonomie).

SCHEFOLD, B.: *Wirtschaftsstile Bd. 1: Studien zum Verhältnis von Ökonomie und Kultur*, Frankfurt am Main (Fischer Taschenbuch Verlag) 1994 (= Fischer Wissenschaft 12243).

SCHEFOLD, B.: "Der Nachklang der historischen Schule in Deutschland zwischen dem Ende des zweiten Weltkriegs und dem Anfang der sechziger Jahre", Referat zur Tagung der Fritz Thyssen-Stiftung in Frankfurt am Main vom 8. bis 11. September 1994a, 35 p. + 1 p. engl. Summary (to be published in:) Kontinuitäten und Diskontinuitäten in den Geisteswissenschaften zwischen den zwanziger und fünfziger Jahren.

SCHEFOLD, B.: "Spontaneous Conformity", Contribution to the Festschrift for Adolph Lowe, ed. by H. Hagemann and H.D. Kurz. Aldershot (Edward Elgar) 1994b (to be published).

SCHEFOLD, B.: "Antonia Serra: der Stifter der Wirtschaftslehre?" *Kommentarband ("Vademecum") zur Faksimileausgabe seines Werkes*, Düsseldorf (Verlag Wirtschaft und Finanzen) 1994c, pp. 5-27 (= Klassiker der Nationalökonomie).

SCHEFOLD, B.: "Einleitung zu Wilhelm Roschers 'Ansichten der Volkswirthschaft aus dem geschichtlichen Standpunkte'", *Kommentarband ("Vademecum") zur Faksimileausgabe von Wilhelm Roschers "Ansichten der Volkswirthschaft aus dem geschichtlichen Standpunkte"*, Düsseldorf (Verlag Wirtschaft und Finanzen) 1994d, pp. 5-23 (= Klassiker der Nationalökonomie).

SCHEFOLD, B.: "Classical Athens: Stage, System, Style or What? An Interpretation in the Tradition of German Research on the Ancient Economy", Paper presented at the Conference "Economic Thought and Economic Reality in Ancient Greece", Delphi, 22.-26.9.1994e, 38 pp (to be published).

SCHEFOLD, B.: "Nationalökonomie und Kulturwissenschaften: Das Konzept des Wirtschaftsstils", in: *Deutsche Geisteswissenschaften zwischen Kaiserreich und Republik. Zur Entwicklung von Nationalökonomie, Rechtswissenschaft und Sozialwissenschaft im 20. Jahrhundert*, hrsg. von K.W. NÖRR, B. SCHEFOLD u. F. TENBRUCK. Stuttgart (Steiner) 1994f, pp. 215-242.

SCHEFOLD, B.: "Theoretical approaches to a comparison of economic systems from a historical perspective", in: KOSLOWSKI (ed.) 1995, pp. 221-247.

SCHMOLLER, G.: *Grundriß der allgemeinen Volkswirtschaftslehre*, Berlin (Duncker & Humblot) 1978 [1900, 1919].

# BERTRAM SCHEFOLD

SCHMOLLER, G.: *Zur Litteraturgeschichte der Staats- und Sozialwissenschaften*, Leipzig (Duncker & Humblot) 1888.

SCHUMPETER, J.: "Sombarts Dritter Band", in: Schumpeter: Dogmenhistorische und biographische Aufsätze, Tübingen (Mohr) 1954, pp. 220-240.

SERRA, A.: *Breve Trattato delle cause, che possono far abbondare li regni d'oro, & argento*, Düsseldorf (Verlag Wirtschaft und Finanzen) 1994 [1613].

SMITH, A.: *Lectures on Jurisprudence*, Oxford (Clarendon Press) 1978 (Glasgow Edition of the Works and Correspondence of Adam Smith V).

SMITH, A.: *The Theory of Moral Sentiments*, Oxford (Clarendon Press) 1979 [1759] (Glasgow Edition of the Works and Correspondence of Adam Smith I).

SOMBART, W.: *Deutscher Sozialismus*, Berlin (Buchholz & Weisswange) 1934.

STEUART, J.: *An Inquiry into the Principles of Political Oeconomy*, Düsseldorf (Verlag Wirtschaft und Finanzen) 1993 [1767]: .

STREISSLER, E.W.: "Wilhelm Roscher als führender Wirtschaftstheoretiker". *Kommentarband ("Vademecum") zur Faksimileausgabe von Wilhelm Roschers "Ansichten der Volkswirthschaft aus dem geschichtlichen Standpunkte"*, Düsseldorf (Verlag Wirtschaft und Finanzen) 1994, pp. 37-121 (= Klassiker der Nationalökonomie).

WAGNER, A.: *Allgemeine oder theoretische Volkswirtschaftslehre. Erster Teil: Grundlegung*, Düsseldorf (Verlag Wirtschaft und Finanzen) 1991 [1876].

WEIPPERT, G.: *Wirtschaftslehre als Kulturtheorie*, Göttingen (Vandenhoeck & Rupprecht) 1967.

Chapter 9

# Deriving Ethical Principles from Theories of the Firm

## Philip L. Cochran

Theories of the firm describe the relationship between the firm and its various constituencies. At their core theories of the firm describe and define the rationale for the very existence of the firm. A rich variety of theories of the firm exist. These include but are not limited to: neoclassical (investor owner), worker owner, consumer owner (also known as the consumer cooperative), societal owned (public) firms. These theories of the firm all focus on a single, homogeneous groups of principals and posit that the firm is or should be managed in the sole interests of those principals.

Aoki (1984: 7) underlines this point when he states that orthodox theories of the firm have in common the assumption that the firm is being managed ". . . in the sole interests of a particular group of its participants, identified as either shareholders, managers, or workers. They try to capture the essence of the firm by focusing their analytical attentions on the utility maximization of a dominant class of participants. . . ."

If one carefully examines a particular theory of the firm it should be possible to derive certain ethical principals from it. Theories of the firm, by their very

197

nature, suggest different obligations to various constituency groups of the firm. Some of these obligations can, in turn, have ethical overtones.

Theories of the firm can usefully be divided into two broad categories: naive and sophisticated. The naive theories look at only a single connection between the firm and its owners. In the interest of parsimony the primary interest of the major group of principals is the only interest recognized by the theory. The sophisticated theories recognize that a firm's principals may be impacted by a firm's activities along a number of dimensions.

# I. Naive Theories of the Firm

### 1. Naive Neoclassical Theory

The naive neoclassical theory of the firm implicitly assumes that the firm is owned by a group of investors whose only links with the firm are financial. These investors join together voluntarily and pool their resources in order to achieve certain ends, i.e., increasing their wealth. The one and only goal of the firm is to engage in those activities that most increases the value of the owners' shares (Brealey and Myers, 1981, p. 21).

Given this premise, one is led logically to the conclusion that firms have no ethical obligations beyond those to their shareholders. It is for this reason that Milton Friedman argued that "there is one and only one social responsibility of business -- to use its resources and engage in activities designed to increase its profits so long as it stays within the rules of the game" (Friedman, 1962, p. 133). Neoconservatives, such as Friedman, contend that it is the role of government to write the "rules of the game" and that business should adhere narrowly to its prescribed role, namely maximizing corporate profits.

However, even Neoconservatives such as Friedman recognize that management should engage in certain activities (such as selling a safer product or providing a less hazardous workplace) to the extent that such activities increase profits by reducing legal expenses, increasing goodwill, increasing sales, and so on. Note, however, that the only justification for engaging in any activities that others might call "socially responsible" is return to shareholders. If these activities do not translate directly to the "bottom line" then they should not be conducted.

Thus, if increased investment in worker safety programs increases shareholder wealth by reducing the chances of expensive future lawsuits or by increasing worker loyalty then this activity should be supported. If, however, such activities

198

can be clearly shown to decrease shareholder wealth then they should not be undertaken.

Likewise, if it can be shown that customers will pay a premium for safer products then safer products should be produced. For example, a number of firms such as Johnson and Johnson have learned that a reputation for safe products can be a positive marketing tool. Some analysts attribute Tylenol's rapid return to its pre-poisoning market share to Johnson and Johnson's positive public image. People did not blame the company for the poisonings nor did they see the poisonings as evidence of poor quality control. Johnson and Johnson's quick and very public reaction to the poisonings was to immediately recall all the Tylenol on store shelves and to offer to buy back any Tylenol that consumers had already purchased. This reaction was applauded in many circles as being "socially responsible." However, a neoconservative could easily argue that this quick reaction strategy lead to a much better effect on the "bottom line" than would a policy of legalistic responses and slow reaction.

What are the ethical responsibilities of such a firm? Clearly, under this scenario the principle, perhaps only, direct responsibility of such a firm is to its investors or stockholders. What responsibilities does such a firm have for worker or customer safety? Generally the only direct ethical responsibilities of such firms will be to invest resources into worker or customer safety to the extent to which such investments increase the firm's profits (thus increasing the return to shareholders.) That is, continue investing until the marginal cost of investments in safety equals the marginal cost of bad publicity, lawsuits, etc.

## 2. Naive Worker-Owner Theory of the Firm

A worker owned firm is a firm in which the workers and only the workers hold residual property rights to the firm. That is, all the profits go to the workers. There are a few such firms in the U.S. and in other countries.

However, this was the national model in the ex-Yugoslavia. In 1958 Benjamin Ward published a now classic paper in the *American Economic Review* entitled "The Firm in Illyria: Market Syndicalism" in which he demonstrated that the objective function of a worker owned firm would not be the same as that of an investor owned firm. Whereas in an investor owned firm the objective function would be profit maximization, in a worker owned firm the objective function would be profit maximization per worker. This would occur because every time a new worker was hired that he or she would have a claim on the total residual profits of the firm. An implication of this finding is that worker owned firms would be more capital intensive than investor owned firms.

PHILIP L. COCHRAN

Under this model a worker owned firm would have motivations similar to that of an investor owned firm with respect to product safety. That is, it would continue to invest in product safety until the marginal cost of the additional investment equals the marginal returns of the additional investment.

With respect to worker related issues, such as worker safety, the naive model would yield a result similar to that of the investor owned firm. Though this is clearly flawed, it is nonetheless a logical extension of the theory.

### 3. Naive Customer Owner Theory of the Firm

A customer owned firm is a firm in which the customers and only the customers receive the residual profits. Consumer cooperatives are one category of employee owned firms. Consumer cooperatives are organizations established to purchase and distribute goods and services to their members. The distinguishing characteristic of the consumer cooperative is that the customers are in most cases members of the organization. Though not widespread in the United States some consumer cooperatives have become reasonably large. For example, Recreational Equipment Incorporated, the largest consumer cooperative in the U.S., had 1993 gross sales of over $100 million.

Though there are a number of ways that consumer cooperatives are organized, the most common plan is known as the Rochdale Plan. The Rochdale Plan calls for open membership with each member receiving one vote. Sales are made only to members. Membership requires a nominal capital investment. Goods are priced at market levels and dividends (patronage refunds) are paid in proportion to members' purchases.

The naive objective function of a consumer owned firm is minimization of the cost to the consumer. Thus with respect to any ethical obligations to workers the consumer owned firm would look similar to and investor owned firm. Even with respect to consumer issues if the only link between the consumer and the firm is a financial link then issues such as truth in advertising, product safety, and so on should be no more relevant for a consumer owned firm than for an investor owned firm.

See Table 1 for an explication of the naive theories of the firm. The obvious weaknesses that are imposed by the core assumption of these theories (that the only relationship between the firm and its principle constituency group is financial) lead to what I have termed the sophisticated theories of the firm.

**Table 1: Naive Theories of the Firm**

|  | Obligations to Investors | Obligations to Workers | Obligations to Customers | Obligations to Society |
|---|---|---|---|---|
| Investor Owner | Maximize profits | None | None | None |
| Worker Owner | Not applicable | Max. profits per worker | None | None |
| Customer Owner | Not applicable | None | Minimum prices | None |
| Society Owner | Not applicable | Possible | Possible | Maximize social return |

# II. Sophisticated Theories of the Firm

## 1. Sophisticated Neoclassical Theory

Even before we relax the simplifying assumption that the only link between the firm and its shareholders is financial it is important to recognize that not all shareholders necessarily have the same financial goals. Depending on an individual's risk preferences he or she might prefer higher or lower risk investments. Depending on an individual's tax bracket she or he might prefer a different mix of dividends and appreciation. Depending on an individual's age he or she may be more or less inclined toward stability of future earnings. Thus even under a naive neoclassical model management must still attempt to balance the interests of various constituents within the shareholder group.

Similar arguments could also apply to worker and consumer owned firms. For example, in a worker owned firm there might be some workers (say younger workers) who would prefer that the firm invest more heavily into research and development that might show significant returns in a decade or two. On the other hand, an older worker might be more interested in earnings stability and thus might opt for an investment strategy that emphasized mature markets.

When one drops the simplifying assumption made in the naive neoclassical model that the only link between the investors and the firms is a financial link then one can build a more sophisticated and realistic -- but still neoclassical -- model. For example, imagine that the owners of a factory have homes built on the same river as the factory but downstream from the factory. Assume that the owners and their families use this river for recreation including swimming. Assume that they draw their drinking water from the river.

It would seem intuitively obvious that these owners would be interested in more the just the profits flowing from the firm. They would also be concerned about the pollutants potentially flowing into the river. Thus, there is a set of links between the firm and the investor owners. Clearly one of the links is financial. But just as clearly, another is through the effects that the firm has on the environment. If some of the owners also work at the firm then there is yet another link.

## 2. Sophisticated Worker Owner Theory of the Firm

If we extend Ward's logic one step further--management of an employee owned firm has a stronger obligation to provide a safe workplace for its workers than does management of a similar, but investor owned, firm. If management of a worker owned firm had the choice of adopting a set of work rules that increased the probability of worker injuries but also increased profits (and thus financial return to the workers) it would have a difficult tradeoff. The workers might be willing to accept greater risk for higher returns. Certainly management would have an obligation to fully inform workers regarding the nature of any such tradeoff.

On the other hand, in an investor owned firm (operated according to neo-classical economic principles) the primary responsibility of management is to its investors. Under these circumstances management might engage in some sort of cost/benefit calculus weighing the additional revenues from such new work rules against the increased probability of lawsuits, bad publicity, decreased worker morale, and so on resulting from the higher probability of worker injuries. It would be less inclined to fully disclose the potential dangers to its workers. In sum, though the decisions reached by such firms may be similar and in some cases identical, the decision making calculus is different because the constraints are different.

In numerous but fewer dramatic situations, such as worker training and job enrichment programs, the management of an employee owned firm would in all likelihood choose solutions different than would the management of a pure investor owned firm. For example, job enrichment can be justified in an investor owned firm if and only if it has a positive impact on the bottom line. However, in a worker owned firm job enrichment might be seen as an end itself. Increasing worker utility is a firm objective.

### 3. Sophisticated Consumer Owner Theory of the Firm

Some of the early literature on consumer cooperatives contended that they were superior to investor owned firms in a number of dimensions including "the elimination of many competitive practices, such as misleading advertising or 'high pressure' selling . . ., the elimination of many of the motives for fraud . . ., the elimination of accounting inaccuracies" and so on (Warne, 1923, pp. 4-5).

In a more recent context, the emphasis is more likely to be on product quality and safety. For example, REI maintains a staff of quality control engineers in order to adequately evaluate merchandise prior to offering it for sale to its members. This staff is maintained as a duty to REI's customer/members. Its existence is not predicated upon any assumptions regarding the profitability of this unit. In a similar, but investor owned firm, such a staff would have to be justified on the basis of return to stockholders.

The pure customer owned firm's primary obligation is to its customers. If such a firm had a choice between making a substantial profit (after legal expenses, bad public relations costs, and so on) by selling a product that would injure some of its customers or making only a marginal profit by selling a safer product it would clearly be obligated to do the former. In this case (provided that the firm is within the law) there is no separate class of investors who have claims that conflict with those of the customers, no case can be made for the latter alternative. That is, the firm would have no *direct* obligations. See Table 2 for a summary of the sophisticated theories of the firm.

### Table 2: Sophisticated Theories of the Firm

|  | Obligations to Investors | Obligations to Workers | Obligations to Customers | Obligations to Society |
|---|---|---|---|---|
| Investor Owner | Max. owner utility | None | None | None |
| Worker Owner | Not applicable | Max. worker utility | None | None |
| Customer Owner | Not applicable | None | Max. customer utility | None |
| Society Owner | Not applicable |  |  | Max. societal utility |

## III. Combined Theories of the Firm

What happens when you begin to combine these uni-owner theories of the firm? Aoki proposed a so called "J Model" firm. He argued that such a firm closely mirrors the model of the Japanese firm. In such a firm the objective is a joint function of investor and worker interests.

Aoki states that "in the neoclassical theory, only the shareholders (entrepreneurs) are explicitly recognized as rational maximizers." He goes on to point out that missing is an explicit treatment of interactions among shareholders, managers and employees and it is difficult to maintain that firm-specific resources are endowed in a single, monolithic agent such as the entrepreneur (as a proxy for the body of shareholders). The firm must be viewed as a sort of coalition of financial as well as human resource-holders.

In a recent work that has received wide publicity, Kotter and Heskett (1992) argue that "firms with cultures that emphasized all key managerial constituencies (customers, stockholders, and employees) . . . outperformed firms that did not have these cultural traits by a huge margin" (p. 11). Though their study investigated the effects of corporate culture and though they used the term "constituencies" and not "stakeholders" their results are consistent with the growing literature on stakeholders. One could view Kotter and Heskett's work as a model for a firm that tried to maximize the returns to three constituencies: customers, stockholders, and employees. Aoki suggested that his "J-model," which sought to balance owner and employee interests, "is perhaps fated to be subsumed under the yet to be developed general theory of the firm . . . ." See Table 3 for a summary of the combined models.

**Table 3A: The Coalition (J Model) Theory of the Firm**

|  | Obligations to Investors | Obligations to Workers | Obligations to Customers | Obligations to Society |
|---|---|---|---|---|
| Investor Owner | Maximize returns to shareholders and to workers. | | None | No Direct |

**Table: 3B The TriPartite (Kotter and Heskitt) Theory of the Firm**

|  | Obligations to Investors | Obligations to Workers | Obligations to Customers | Obligation to Society |
|---|---|---|---|---|
| Investor Owner | Maximize returns to shareholders, workers, and customers. | | | No Direct |

# IV. Actual Ownership Patterns

In 1976 Peter Drucker published a controversial new book, *The Unseen Revolution: How Pension Fund Socialism Came to America*. In this work he presented the then startling argument that American workers were rapidly becoming the real owners of corporate America. He based his thesis on the fact that in 1975 pension funds owned 25% of the equity capital of American business. In 1976 Drucker predicted that the percentage of stock owned by pension funds would soar to 50% by 1985 and to more than 66% by 1995 (1976, p. 1).

By 1985 fully 49% of the stock of the *Fortune* 500 firms for which data was available was owned by institutional investors. Since the beneficial owners of such pension funds are American workers and their families they are, in fact, the real owners of American industry. Drucker's prediction has proven be uncannily accurate.

# V. Toward a Stakeholder Theory of the Firm

Most theories of the firm have a basic shortcoming---a failure to fully incorporate the diverse interests and values of all their principal stakeholders. Fama (1980) puts it this way . . . ownership of capital should not be confused with ownership of the firm. Each factor in a firm is owned by somebody. The firm is just the set of contracts covering the way inputs are joined to create outputs and the way receipts from outputs are shared among inputs. In this nexus of contracts' perspective, ownership of the firm is an irrelevant concept.

# PHILIP L. COCHRAN

If ownership is irrelevant and the "nexus of contracts" is a better model then we seem to inevitably be lead to a stakeholder model in which the firm is part of a web of obligations among a wide range of constituencies. The first authors to explicitly discuss a stakeholder theory of the firm were Evan and Freeman (1988) in their article "A Stakeholder Theory of the Modern Corporation: Kantian Capitalism." In this work Evan and Freeman propose "the bare bones of an alternative theory, a stakeholder theory of the modern corporation" (Evan and Freeman, 1988: 97). In this theory the authors suggest that the neoclassical concept that the sole responsibility of managers should be to the firm's stockholders should be replaced by a broader theory that managers should be responsible to a wide range of stakeholders.

Evan and Freeman argue that firms are already, in effect, managed in the interests of a wide range of constituents beyond just the firm's stockholders. They note that laws have seriously constrained the ability of managers to manage the affairs of the firm solely in the interests of the stockholders. They contend that externalities, moral hazards, and monopoly power has led to still further constraints on the freedom of managers. They then go on to propose two stakeholder management principles:

> P1: The corporation should be managed for the benefit of its stakeholders: its customer, suppliers, owners, employees, and local communities. The rights of these groups must be ensured, and, further, the groups must participate, in some sense, in decisions that substantially affect their welfare.

> P2: Management bears a fiduciary relationship to stakeholders and to the corporation as an abstract entity. It must act in the interest of the stakeholders as their agent, and it must act in the interests of the corporation to ensure the survival of the firm, safeguarding the long-term stakes of each group. (Evan and Freeman, 1988: 103)

In his 1991 article Goodpaster attacked the idea that managers have a fiduciary responsibility to non-stockholder stakeholders (though he did not refer to the Evan and Freeman article.) Goodpaster contends that any theory that management has any fiduciary responsibilities to non-stockholder stakeholders (in his terminology "multi-fiduciary stakeholder" approach) is fundamentally flawed. He asserted that:

# ETHICAL PRINCIPLES FROM THEORIES OF THE FIRM

> The relationship between management and stockholders is ethically different in kind from the relationship between management and other parties (like employees, suppliers, customers, etc.), a fact that seems to go unnoticed by the multi-fiduciary approach. If it were not, the corporation would cease to be a private sector institution -- and what is now called business ethics would become a more radical critique of our economic system than is typically thought. On this point, Milton Friedman must be given a fair and serious hearing. (Goodpaster, 1991: 69)

This is an important, but fundamentally unsatisfying, thesis. It is often difficult, if not impossible, to separate fiduciary from non-fiduciary responsibilities. In today's world most stakeholders are also stockholders -- if not directly then certainly indirectly. The average American has a pension fund or funds that hold portfolios of common stock that tend to mirror the stockmarket. As a result virtually all workers of any given major firm are either primary or secondary stockholders in that firm. That is they either own actual shares or the rights to shares of their firm (often acquired through employee stock ownership plans), or they hold the stock indirectly through the company's pension fund, private IRAs, or other mutual fund investments. The same argument holds for consumers -- the majority of consumers of the products of the major firms also own stock (directly or indirectly) in the firms that make the products which they buy -- as well as virtually any other stakeholder group.

It is unrealistic to assume that firms can produce different products for stockholder consumers than for non-stockholder consumers. Likewise it is impractical for firms to create different working conditions for stockholder-employees than for non-stockholder employees. The same argument could obviously be made with respect to any other stakeholder groups. Thus this implicit assumption of the neoclassical theory (that only financial links exist between the shareholders and the firm) is incorrect. Thus, on occasion, those legal and moral obligations of the firm to one or more stakeholders might supersede the financial claims of stockholders.

This lead in 1992 to Brenner and Cochran's paper in which they called for a more complete stakeholder theory of the firm. In 1995 the *Academy of Management Review* published an important set of articles in this area including articles by Clarkson, Donaldson and Preston, as well as by Quinn and Jones. See Table 4 for a preliminary summary of how a stakeholder theory of the firm might inform the field of business ethics.

**Table 4: A Generalized Stakeholder Theory of the Firm**

|  | Obligations to Investors | Obligations to Workers | Obligations to Customers | Obligations to society |
|---|---|---|---|---|
| Dispersed Ownership | Satisfactory Profit | Safety, Job Satisfaction | Safety, Value, Honesty | Environmental Obligations |

The stakeholder theory of the firm as discussed in this paper is an attempt to better explain firms in the modern world. These firms are discovering that they are subject to the demands of various stakeholders playing out their values in a myriad of interactions. Where the limits of this stakeholder concept end is difficult to determine.

One well-known example of a firm which placed obligations to stakeholders above those to shareholders is the Merck Co. At a cost of over $10 million Merck developed a drug to combat a viscous tropical disease, River Blindness. River Blindness afflicts millions of people every year. If not treated, it eventually leads to total blindness.

However, a simple and effective drug developed by Merck cures the disease and prevents its recurrence. After Merck developed the drug it tried to find some agency to purchase and distribute the drug. Unable to find any agency to do so Merck vowed to do so itself. At a cost in excess of $10 million per year it distributes the drug.

Merck has no expectation whatsoever of recouping either their original investment or their ongoing distribution costs. This is clearly a case of a firm recognizing obligations to tertiary stakeholders that exceed those to their stockholders.

**References**

ABBOTT, WALTER F. and MONSEN, R. JOSEPH: "On the Measurement of Corporate Social Responsibility: Self Report Disclosure as a Method of Measuring Social Involvement", *Academy of Management Journal*, 22, No. 3 (1979), pp. 501-515.

AOKI, M.: *The Co-Operative Game Theory of the Firm*, New York (Oxford University Press) 1984.

# ETHICAL PRINCIPLES FROM THEORIES OF THE FIRM

AOKI, M.: "The Japanese Firm in Transition", in: K. YAMAMURA and Y. YASUBA: *The Political Economy of Japan*, Stanford (Stanford University Press) 1987 (Vol. 1).

AOKI, M.: "Toward an Economic Model of the Japanese Firm", *Journal of Economic Literature*, XXVII, 1-27, 1990.

BARNEA, AMIR, HAUGEN, ROBERT and SENBET, LEMMA: "Market Imperfections, Agency Problems, and Capital Structure: A Review", *Financial Management*, Summer 1981, pp. 7-22.

BREALEY, RICHARD and SENBET, MYERS: *Principals of Corporate Finance*, New York (McGraw-Hill Book Company) 1981.

BRENNER, STEVEN and COCHRAN, PHILIP L.: "The Stakeholder Theory of the Firm: Implications for Business and Society Theory and Research", *Contemporary Issues in Business and Society*, ed. by Dean Ludwig and Karen Paul (Mellon Publishing) June 1992.

CLARKSON, MAX B.E.: "A Stakeholder Framework for Analyzing and Evaluating Corporate Social Performance", *Academy of Management Review*, January 1995, pp. 92-117.

COCHRAN, PHILIP L. and WOOD, ROBERT A.: "Corporate Social Responsibility and Financial Performance", *Academy of Management Journal*, March 1984, pp. 42-56.

DE GEORGE, RICHARD D.: *Business Ethics*, New York (Macmillan Publishing Co.) 1982.

DONALDSON, THOMAS: *Corporations and Morality*, Englewood Cliffs, NJ, 1982.

DONALDSON, THOMAS and PRRESTON, LEE: "The Stakeholder Model of the Corporation: Concepts, Evidence, and Implications", *Academy of Management Review*, January 1995, pp. 65-91.

DRUCKER, PETER: *The Unseen Revolution: How Pension Fund Socialism Came to America*, New York (Harper and Row) 1976.

EVAN, W. M. and FREEMAN, R. E.: "A Stakeholder Theory of the Modern Corporation: Kantian Capitalism", in: T.L. Beaucamp and N.E. Bowie: *Ethical Theory and Business*, Engelwood Cliffs (Prentice Hall) 1988.

FREEMAN, R. EDWARD: *Strategic Management: A Stakeholder Approach*, Marshfield, Massachusetts (Pitman Publishing Inc.) 1984.

FRIEDMAN, MILTON: *Capitalism and Freedom*, Chicago (University of Chicago Press) 1962.

GATEWOOD, ELIZABETH and CARROLL, ARCHIE B.: "The Anatomy of Corporate Social Response: The Rely, Firestone 500, and Pinto Cases", *Business Horizons*, 24 (September/October, 1981), pp. 9- 16.

GOODPASTER, K. E.: "Business Ethics and Stakeholder Analysis", *Business Ethics Quarterly*, 1, (1991), pp. 53-73.

HILL, CHARLES W. L. and JONES, THOMAS M.: "Stakeholder-Agency Theory", *Journal of Management Studies*, 29, No. 2 (1992), pp. 131-154.

PALMER, JAAMES L.: "Can Consumer Cooperation Correct Important Defects in Marketing?", *The Journal of Marketing*, April 1937, p. 390.

QUINN, DENNIS P. and JONES, THOMAS M.: "An Agent Morality View of Business Policy", *Academy of Management Review*, January 1995, pp. 22-42.

STRAND, R.: "A Systems Paradigm of Organizational Adaptions to the Social Environment", *Academy of Management Review*, 1 (1983), pp. 90-96.

# PHILIP L. COCHRAN

WARD, BENJAMIN: "The Firm in Illyria: Market Syndicalism", *American Economic Review*, 66, No. 4 (1958), pp. 373-386.
WARNE, COLSTON E.: *Consumer's Cooperative Movement in Illinois*, Chicago (University of Chicago Press) 1923.

Chapter 10

# The Moral Boundary of International Business: A Postmodern Vision of Contemporary Neo-Confucianism

SHUI-CHUEN LEE

I.   The Philosophical Underpinning of Postmodernization
II.  The Problem of Morality and Efficiency in Production
III. Moral Community and Ethical Civil Society
IV.  The Postmodern Condition of International Business

In talking about international business, the objects concerned are usually those multinational corporations, which are products of the modernization of the western world of the last three hundred years. International business is certainly something carried out by this kind of corporation. Ethical universals, if any such things exist, [1]will be something that will bind upon such corporations. It is easier to manage and more fruitful to present my case by focusing on the moral boundary of corporations than to tackle the problem in the more elusive term of international business. In fact, corporations have occupied a most significant position in the analysis of modern society since its birth in history, and there have been abundant discussions and scholarly works on its nature and functions. [2] Thus, corporations will be the object of discussion in the following.

Throughout the process of modernization, free market is one of the most influencing powers in the establishment of civil society and has gained not only

---

1   For example, Hegel had taken seriously with corporations in his justly famous work of *Philosophy of Right*, Oxford (Oxford University Press) 1952, tran. by T.M.Knox. Cf. also PETER F. DRUCKER: *Post-Capitalist Society*, New York (HarperBusiness) 1993, esp. ch.2, pp.48-67.

SHUI-CHUEN LEE

independence from the state, but also independence from the control of society in the democratic nations. Business is left to the market and is to be done according to the rules of economics. The state should not interfere with the function of the market but should simply provide the space for the free competition of corporations. It culminates into the saying that 'the business of business is business', which means that business has nothing to do with anything other than the making of profits.[3] Though the tide seems to be turning against this amoral view of business,[4] the common practice of the insiders and the tacit assumptions of common folks toward business remains quite aloof in the demand of corporation social responsibility. There have been rigorous and lengthened arguments against and for the moral responsibility of firms or corporations in the last thirty years. It seems difficult to convince those so-called neoclassical economists like Milton Friedman that business has to shoulder not only economic but also social, that is, ethical responsibility. One of the forceful and commonly accepted arguments is the inevitable conflict of making profits and fulfilling ethical responsibility when the corporation is not in the position of pursuing any ethical goal other than making profits, which is fortified by the property right of corporation stockholders.

Though the rise of international business and corporations has its roots in the process of modernization, and the characteristics are being shaped in the process, the modern world has been evolving into the so-called postmodern world. Therefore, it would be more beneficial to situate the discussion squarely in the content of postmodernity or postmodernization. For some scholars are arguing that a new type of corporation, namely, the virtual corporation is rapidly forming and transforming the landscape of international business.[5] Furthermore, the post-modern critique of modernity brings home a radical critique of the modern corporation, especially upon its rational ground.

What makes the present problem more controversial and becomes a seemingly insurmountable task is that, as the western world moves into the postmodern phase of development, the ground for the primacy and authority of rationality is being rapidly eroded away. If anything goes and the morality of every action is left to individual judgement, the talk of ethical universals sounds glaringly out of place

---

2  A classic statement of this position is Milton Friedman. See his "The Social Responsibility of Business is to Increase its Profits", *The New York Times Magazine*, (September 13, 1970).

3  This is a term adopted from RICHARD T. DE GEORGE: *Business Ethics*, New York (Macmillan Publ. Co.) 1990.

4  Cf. WILLIAM H. DAVIDOW and MICHAEL S. MALONE: *The Virtual Corporation*, New York (HarperBusiness) 1992.

MORAL BOUNDARY OF INTERNATIONAL BUSINESS

with the postmodern development of the world in large and the business world in particular. In other words, we need to first clear the ground of a postmodern world for the discussion of ethical universals, and then argue how and why corporations and international business must observe some underlining ethical universals to fulfil their missions. Finally, what these ethical universals are will be explored.

## I. The Philosophical Underpinning of Postmodernization

Following Max Weber's diagnosis, the process of modernization is generally regarded as a process of rationalization. In Jurgen Habermas' terms, it is a process that the three aspects of rationality, namely, the instrumental, the practical moral and the practical aesthetic rationality[6] are penetrating and infiltrating into every corner of human endeavour, which results in the emerging of the modern society in the modern world. However, in the historical process the three aspects of rationality were not evenly developed or developed in the right order. The foremost is being the so-called instrumental rationality in the development of modern science and technology. It is upon its great success, especially in its application to the production line, that the West became disenchanted and the modern world is sometimes glorified as the scientific age. However, the leading principle of the operation of instrumental rationality is to choose the most efficient means to a certain aim. Its implication to business is to enhance the efficiency of the process of production that has greatly improved the culminating effect of the wealth of the West in the last three hundred years and led to the birth of modern corporations. Translating into the language of business, the principle of efficiency is the maximization of profits, which becomes the most important and sole responsibility of a modern corporation.

The central and prominent role of instrumental rationality leads to the one-sided development of western modernization, and eventually every social action is evaluated under the pressure of efficiency. This has led to some of the well-known problems of the modern world, of which environmental pollution is but one of the most concerned disasters. In fact, its overarching status results in what Weber characterized as the paradoxical development of the "iron cage" through the process of modernization. This is the so-called dark side of modernity. To remedy the one-

5    Cf. JURGEN HABERMAS: *The Theory of Communicative Action*, 1 & 2, Boston (Beacon Press) 1984, trans. by Thomas McCarthy.

213

sidedness of modernization, Habermas proposes to replace the primacy of instrumental rationality with the practical moral and aesthetic rationality, putting the former under the guidance and control of the latter. This is his way of completing the unfinished project of modernity.[7]

On the other hand, Jean-Francois Lyotard argues that the project of modernity has been liquidated and the world has entered into the postmodern era, in which the supremacy of rationality is no longer legitimate.[8] His objection to rationality is expressed in his rejection of any kind of grand narratives that were proposed to argue for the legitimacy of rationality in all human affairs. He has a good sense of the suppressive effect of rationality upon the individual. Released of the legitimating claim of rationality on everything, his postmodern world allows, so to say, greater freedom to the individuals.

Though Habermas and Lyotard are in conflict and argue hotly against each other, their ideas are in fact individually defective. However, they are complimenting in that rationality and individuality are both needed for the sake and health of the individual and for the society as well. I have argued that according to the Confucian conception of morality, any moral act is both rational and individual.[9] It is rational in that the value of a moral act is absolute and universal. It is, to use Kant's terminology, what will be done and approved by any rational being in the situation. On the other hand, any moral act is a creation of the agent and is thus uniquely his or hers. It bears the unique personality of the agent. In a similar vein, every creative act is both universal and personal. Hence, the realization of the creativity of the individual reveals both the rationality and the individuality of the individual. Philosophically speaking, rationality is recognized as the subjectivity of human being after Kant. It constitutes the worthiness of the person and commands respect from others. The controversy between Habermas and Lyotard is thus one between subjectivity and individuality. These two constitute the worthiness and authenticity of a human being. The neglect or suppression of the one or both could not but cause enormous harm to the individual as a human being.

---

6    Cf. his "Modernity - An Incomplete Project". It was originally delivered as a talk in 1980 and subsequently published in a number of anthologies on modernity and postmodernity. Cf. HAL FOSTER (Ed.): *Postmodern Culture*, London (Pluto Press) 1985, pp. 3-15, tran. by S. Ben- Habib.

7    Cf. his *The Postmodern Condition: A Report on Knowledge*, Manchester (Manchester University Press) 1984, trans. by Geoff Bennington & Brian Massumi.

8    Cf. my "On Modernity and Postmodernism: A Contemporary Neo-Confucian Reflection"(in Chinese), *The Philosophical Exploration of Contemporary Neo-Confucianism*, Taipei (Wen Ching Publ. Co.) 1993.

I have also adopted Charles Jenckes' double coding theory to form a basic framework for postmodern theory in general. Basically, this theory allows the juxtaposition and realization of two, or more, different systems of values or orientations together, with one of the codes always being that of the modern, the other code could be any other than modern.[10] The significance of this model is on the one hand to preserve the achievements of the project of modernity, and on the other to allow for the individual difference for a person, a society, a nation, a people, or diverse values and achievements of human beings through history. In other words, the rationality and the individuality of individuals, societies, and cultures could be accommodated within this model. In the following, it will be applied for the moral problem of the corporations.

## II. The Problem of Morality and Efficiency in Production

In the development of the modern society, the most significant result is the establishment of a civil society with the civilians and the market under its umbrella, which is independent of the state power. The independent and free market embodies the human right of property that is regarded as a basic right of the individual against the state, the large society and any other organization or individual of the society. Thus, the corporation is something that belongs to its owner or owners like any other property owned by a citizen. In a free market, a corporation is owned by its stockholders and its executives or managers, and workers are hired to carry out the will of its owners. As a corporation is set up primarily for the production of goods, and stockholders generally expect to harvest profits from it, it is natural that the managers of a corporation have a duty toward their employers to maximize the profits of the corporation. The rational way to achieve maximum profit is to maximize its economic efficiency--that means to have as little cost and as great profits as possible. The more input in respect of a fixed amount of output means lower efficiency and less profits. The first responsibility of the managers is to maximize the profits of the corporation. Since Adam Smith, the classic and neoclassic economists believe that as far as each businessperson takes care of his or her own business, that is to make as much profit

---

9    Cf. my "Contemporary Neo-Confucianism and Postmodern Theories" (in Chinese), monograph published in 1995 by the Institute of Chinese and Philosophy of the Sinica Academia of Taipei.

as possible, the invisible hand will take care of the total social responsibility such as, that the economic efficiency of the society will be the highest, yielding the largest amount of tax revenue for the operation of the state and providing the greatest number of jobs for everyone, and so on for all kinds of social goods. Thus, as employees of the stockholders, managers of a corporation have the primary duty to maximize the profits of their corporation and should not divert their trustees' money to anything other than the production line. Furthermore, the managers are not good at any such ethical or social welfare pursuance. They better leave such ethical or social responsibility to the public authorities, just as the latter better leaves economic matters to the market. Any social or ethical responsibility incurred inevitably increases the cost of production and thus lowers its profit and causes all the malaises of a malfunctioning market.

However, the amoral view of business has received heavy gunfire throughout the last thirty years. The increasing number of frauds of businesspeople, the enormous effects of the operation of corporations upon the population, and the serious social and natural pollution as a consequence of ruthless pursuance of profits have caused the increasing demand for social and ethical responsibility of the corporations. Besides the rapid development for the need of business ethics, more and more ethical regulations are being placed on the operation of business transactions, and more and more corporations and managers take seriously the social and ethical responsibilities as part and parcel of their daily duties.[11] The rigorous attack comes from a brand of socioeconomic scholars; they counter the neoclassic economists position and propose that the social responsibility of corporations is both economic and moral.[12] They first place the corporation rightly in the society where its business is carried out. The slogan of the neoclassical economists is replaced by 'the business of business is business in society', and emphasizes its close relationship with the wider community. They argue that what a corporation needs to consider is not just the stockholders, but all those stakeholders around it, namely, the employees, the suppliers, the communities concerned, even its competitors, and concerned environmental groups.[13] The

---

10  J.D.Feldman, H.Kelsay and H.E.Brown have made a survey of the articles published in *Harvard Business Review* from 1940 to 1980 and found a shift of managerial responsibility from a narrowly focused role to a more widely conceived moral role. Cf. their paper "Responsibility and Moral Reasoning: A Study in Business Ethics", *Journal of Business Ethics*, 5, pp. 93-117.

11  Cf. MAX B.E. CLARKSON: "The Moral Dimension of Corporate Social Responsibility", *Morality, Rationality, and Efficiency: New Perspectives on Socio-Economics*, ed. by Richard M. Coughlin, New York (M.E. Sharpe, Inc.) 1991, pp.185-196.

12  Ibid.

formerly utilitarian and for-my-own-interest is now replaced by the deontological 'we' as the centre of responsibility of corporations.[14]

The economic activity is an essential part of human life. It has a lot to do with the happiness and well being of human beings. However, as the Confucianists had understood long ago, doing business is but a means for the improvement or attainment of personal and social happiness. It has no end of itself. In the last analysis, the purpose of business, and also the function of free market, is for the betterment of the economic conditions of the society and ultimately for the betterment of human social life. The selfish personal gain over others' or societal loss is never justified. Notwithstanding their objection to moral or ethical responsibility of corporations, the neoclassical claim has to presume that what a person gains in business will ultimately contribute to the whole. The only difference seems that they think it is better for the corporations to achieve the social responsibility in an indirect way and we should leave them to do what is legitimate and what they and only they could achieve, namely, the most efficient economic performance.

However, as business is a kind of deliberated, calculated rational action, it has some sort of motives or aims to fulfil or satisfy. It involves and affects a large number of people and different communities; it could not be that it has nothing to do with morality. For example, in talking about costs, the cost contributed by the corporation has a close and interrelated interaction with the community. By simply dumping the wastes outside the factory, the corporation obviously paid little for the cost of treating them, however, the wastes will not evaporate into thin air. The pollution of the environment will have an adverse effect on the community as a whole, and ultimately the society has to pay for it--most of the time paying much more than if it were treated before spread around. The more corporations affect the daily lives of the community, with its relatively great economic power, the more responsibility it has to take into consideration.

The remaining problem is how much the moral responsibility will affect the economic performance of a corporation. In a study of the problem, Max B.E.Clarkson found that the taking of moral responsibility together with economic responsibility as part of the social responsibility of a corporation does not lower its economic performance. In fact, those that have taken an unbalanced concentration on the maximization of profits resulted in a lower ratio of profitability than their

---

13  The I/We paradigm is first raised by AMITAI ETZIONI: *The Moral Dimension: Toward a New Economics,* New York (Free Press) 1988.

competitors.[15] As the modern world moves toward the 21st Century, people on Earth realise more and more, with living in an interrelated community, the demand of moral and social responsibility of corporations becomes ever higher. Through the awareness of consumers' rights and the power of dollar-votes they have in fact imposed moral imperatives to corporations and thus tend to support those more morally concerned corporations. Toward the end of the 20th Century, it could be regarded as being established theoretically and practically that ethical or moral responsibility is more or less incorporated into the necessary cost of a corporation.

## III. Moral Community and Ethical Civil Society

Following Amitai Etzioni's idea of the I/We paradigm and invoking the support of the great social and ethical philosophies of Kant, John Rawls and Rousseau, Norman E. Bowie proposes boldly the conception of the firm as a moral community.[16] As in line with the view of the socioeconomic position, Bowie takes the firm as composed of stakeholders rather than just stockholders and he lists the following conditions for a firm to be a moral community:[17]

1. The firm should consider the interests of all stakeholders in any decision it makes.
2. That consideration should involve getting input from all the affected stakeholders.
3. It should not be the case that for all decisions, the interests of one stakeholder take priority.
4. Each business firm must establish procedures designed to insure that relations among the stakeholders are governed by principles of justice. These principles of justice are to be developed in accordance with conditions 1 through 3 and must receive the endorsement of representatives of all stakeholders.

---

14  Cf. his "Corporate Social Performance in Canada 1976-1986", *Research in Corporate Social Performance and Policy*, 10, pp.241-265. Quoted from his "The Moral Dimension of Corporate Social Responsibility", p.194.

15  Cf. his "The Firm as a Moral Community", in: RICHARD M. COUGHLIN (Ed.): *Morality, Rationality and Efficiency: New Perspectives on Socio-Economics*, pp.169-184.

16  Ibid., pp176-7.

And later he adds one more condition:

> 5. The firm should contribute to the development of the individual's autonomy and self-respect.

In general the first four conditions constitute a Rawlsian just society. It comes very close to a democratic one even though one-man-one-vote is not instituted into the conditions. The fifth one has more to do with Kant in that it referred to the intrinsic value of each person that makes him or her worth being respected. Being a moral community, the corporation will incorporate the moral dimension into its social responsibility and will thus underline the ethical universals for it.

However, this normative model of a moral community has overstepped on the one hand the limits of a production corporation, and on the other falls short of making the firm a really moral community. For there have to be some allowances for a corporation to steep more to the productive function and certain priority to the interest of the stockholders, otherwise it would degenerate into a communistic-like commune. In fact, the point of moral responsibility of corporations is not to replace economic responsibility in total. The moral bottom line is to guard against the making of profits upon the loss of the individuals or of the society. There should be plenty of free space for the managers to cope with the duty of an employee in charge of making profits for the employers. On the other hand, the five conditions together are still not able to make up a moral community in the sense that each could have certain kind of internal relationship with each other, other than just a working relation in terms of rights and duties. The conditions could constitute a fair and rational community, but it lacks the kind of closeness and friendliness like family members or close friends.

Furthermore, from the vision of postmodern society, such a just community could not lessen the kind of alienation that modern man faces in a fairly wealthy and democratic society. For, in such a society, the members are doubtless equal and fairly treated, but without appropriate attentions to individual particularities and personal relationship with each other is quite aloof. This kind of alienation originates from the tendency of externalization of personal relationships by treating everyone as objectively equals. With further loosening of familial ties and fewer personal interactions in the postmodern phase, the necessary affections that nourish our hearts, our feelings, and our sympathy would slowly dry up. This kind of alienation could not be remedied through more and further democratization of public life. Thus, Habermas' construction of a rational society could not achieve what he aims to solve. On the other hand, the Lyotardian way of cutting the individual aloof from his or her subjectivity or rationality is still farther away from the solidarity urge of the modern soul.

To soften and finally solve the malady of the modern society, we need to make our community more knitted like a family. According to the traditional wisdom of Confucianism, the society is a further extension of the familial tie. The close and born-with relationship within the family is called *lun li*, or Ethical. It is a kind of what I called internal relationship. The difference between internal and external human relationship could be explained in the difference in our treatment of our children or students in comparison with that of men of the street, especially when it involves some sort of immoral act, say stealing something. We usually give some kind of punishment to the child but will not take him or her to court.

The problem of modern society is that we could have a large number of external relationships but hardly any intimate close relation with anyone outside the family. The outside world becomes more and more indifferent and unconcerned and the individual more and more isolated and self-centred. The widespread of nuclear or broken families in the modern world could no longer provide the individual the desired solidarity and security. Organizations other than the family have to take care of this aspect of social needs and must be injected with some Ethical element over and combined with the elements of justice. Thus by double coding the modern development of a just democratic society with the oriental ethical one, we have the possibility of an ethical civil society. In this society, the family is on the side of a standard ethical union while the other organizations could be on various degrees of internal relationship, and finally with the political institutes on the other end as a typical just society. The individual is embedded in this ethical civil society so that both his or her freedom and affection find their proper nourishment and development. This constitutes the backdrop of the ethical universals of international business.

## IV. The Postmodern Condition of International Business

To define more definitely the ethical universals of a corporation in the postmodern world, we need to make a little more clearly what are the basic human conditions that relate to economic activities, which then lead to the reconsideration of the nature and function of business. Finally, the precise postmodern conditions for ethical universals for international business will provide us with some guideline for the setting up of the ethical universals.

In a sense, economic activities are those activities that pertain to man's survival. Thus as long as a man has to live on, there must be some kind of economic activity done to support his or her life. Though the Earth seems big enough, with plenty of resources, the resources for supporting human beings are not unlimited, especially in contrast with the infinite desires of man. In fact, the shortage of some living necessities in the not too far future becomes a glaring concern. The further we use them and the more we waste them, the faster we shall end up in some serious blunders. Thus, we could not afford ruthless exploitation and inefficient employment of economic resources. It is here that we need to further rationalize our practice in economic or business activities.

Though business and its free market system have contributed greatly to the modernization of the traditional society, the iron cage effect of its bias in the ruthless pursuance of efficiency and hence of profits poses as great problems and disasters as its services to the progress of humanity. It is time to relocate the proper role of business as to serve the society and humanity as its basic aims. On the other hand, we have to uphold the free and competitive market for the proper operation of business so that the efficiency of business and the reward for proper and creative economic contributions could work to generate a healthy and abundant material provision for the daily needs.

The postmodern challenge to rationality in general and morality in particular has been vehement and destructive. However, the underlining of minimum rationality in the forms of justice and morality is not only needed for any society, but is in particular necessary for business to achieve its moral mission. Zygmunt Bauman gives an interesting and enlightening analysis of postmodern ethics and rightly points out that morality is by all means personal and autonomous which remains valid in the postmodern world.[18] However, his rejection of moral rules and universalizability of morality is unfounded.

It should be pointed out that the moral law that we are talking about is a self-ascribed imperative in the Kantian sense, not the mores and norms of any particular society, nor the laws of the state. The latter might and should be a codified version of the moral command of the moral self and has to be endorsed by the moral self as a rational being before any act in accordance with rules could be claimed to be moral. The moral law is a self legislation of the moral agent and is thus personal and autonomous. However, it is regarded as valid by and for any rational being in the situation and thus universal for all. Some postmodernists seem to forget that what counts as moral is precisely that it rejects parochialism of oneself or of one particular community.

---

17   Cf. his *Postmodern Ethics*, Oxford (Blackwell Publ.) 1993, esp. chps. 1 and 2.

According to Confucianism, morality ultimately stems from the sympathetic feeling towards the suffering of other human being.[19] This is the foundation of the human world in which the postmodern world and the firm as moral community have to be rooted. By the normative analysis of a postmodern society, we have taken seriously the socioeconomists' wisdom of rectifying the business of business in *society*. The nature and function of a postmodern corporation should be understood from this perspective. With family as the most Ethical in the Confucian sense and the political party the least, the firm would be half way in this kind of Ethical relationship: it should provide the individual with a just and rewarding working community with a strong person-to-person relationship and discharge the production function of the society efficiently. The ethical civil background will provide some broad guidelines for its management and business transactions.

---

18  It is interesting to point out that not just Confucianists and Hume, Habermas and, to a lesser extend, even Lyotard have similar perceptions.

Chapter 11

# The Sodality of Good Character: "Fraternity" and "Sorority" as One Thing

DAVID KIRKWOOD HART

> As a model of solidarity [fraternity] is flawed and partial, celebrating the
> unity of men and exclusion of women. As a basis for future action it is
> increasingly anachronistic, ignoring major changes that have occurred in
> the composition of the labour force.[1]

The conduct of international business is severely complicated by the absence
of a mutually accepted set of moral values, by reference to which troublesome
intercultural problems might be resolved. The news media make much of such
problems, many of which are quite real: Muslim businessmen are troubled by the
presence of women executives in European firms with which they do business;
some American business leaders are troubled by the occasional "gifts" demanded
by key officials, as the price of doing business in their countries; and so on.
      Some of the problems are more mundane: a merger of firms in two countries
is jeopardized by seemingly irreconcilable cultural differences in what is considered
good management or good personnel policy within an international workforce; the
widely differing standards of workplace and environmental safety that must be met
in order to do business; and so on.

The instances cited above do not necessarily involve corruption, but they do concern fundamental differences in ways of viewing the world: what is objectionable in one country is considered essential to the religion of the other country; what is considered good, aggressive management in one culture is considered boorish bad manners in the other country. Such contradictions, along with a multitude of others, pose genuine problems in creating and maintaining an effective and humane global free market.

Most business scholars and practitioners would agree with that assertion, and many would argue that what is needed is a code of international business ethics that would guide all parties in the global marketplace. I agree, since I am an ardent advocate of codes of ethics. Nevertheless, we must face the hard reality that most codes of ethics--whether domestic or international--are not taken very seriously. Therefore, and prior to all else, we must ask why that should be so, especially when the intentions of the authors and the sponsoring companies are usually so good?

The reason is not that business people--whether national or international--are insensitive to ethics. To the contrary, most of the executives I have dealt with, both in consulting and in conferences, have been very concerned about acting ethically. Granted, there are some who see ethics as a hindrance, and others who treat the subject with contempt, but they are a minority. There are two, interrelated reasons why codes of ethics are in trouble. First, modern business people are usually well educated--while most codes of ethics usually consist of an assemblage of cliches. It is clear to them that an intelligent individual, knowledgeable in business, could write a code that would be soothing to the conscience in about an hour. Further, that new code, elegantly printed and widely circulated, would be virtually ignored-- except when the public relations department needed it for window dressing.

The fact is that most codes of ethics have no intellectual or moral heft to them. And that leads to the second problem, which is a complete paradox: most people today have never studied either moral philosophy or, for that matter, practical ethics. Thus, they fail to appreciate the difficulties involved: ethics is one of the most demanding of all disciplines. It has a vast historic literature, but, nowadays, few people are required to read it. It is not really their fault, for modern educational systems almost never require the study of ethics, whether in kindergarten or the university. Furthermore, it is no longer considered necessary to require a lot of reading: students do not like it, and too many teachers have found easier, "alternative," and supposedly therapeutic ways to deal with their classes.

Thus, the authors of most codes of ethics do not dig deeply enough into the literature, and some of the most important problems are never touched upon. Is it any wonder, then, that codes of ethics are in trouble?

A code of ethics, whether domestic or international, can be one of the most powerful instruments available to the modern organization. But for it to be such, it requires well-read and well-prepared authors and practitioners. But if our collective educational backgrounds in ethics are lacking, must we wait for a new generation, educated differently? Certainly not: we haven't the time to wait for that new generation. That brings us to the crux of the matter: where do we begin?

Obviously, when different countries agree that specific economic and managerial behaviors are morally wrong, laws can be enacted to deal with them. But most of the seemingly intractable problems arise out of cultural differences, which are not amenable to resolution through law. Their resolution will require, as the necessary first step, *the articulation and acceptance of a few fundamental moral values, acceptable across cultures, that can serve as a partial base for an effective code of international business ethics.* This raises the question: are there any transcultural moral truths?

## I. Are There Any Transcultural Moral Truths?

The first question concerning any code of ethics is whether the individuals covered by it actually *believe* in it. This leads immediately to the more difficult question of whether they believe the code fairly represents their most intimate moral beliefs. And it is here that the real confusion begins, for most people are not very clear about those beliefs. As Hannah Arendt wrote, in a somewhat different context: "The sad truth of the matter is that most evil is done by people who never made up their mind to be either bad or good."[2] Very few people are really clear about their value system, and fewer still know exactly how to go about examining their basic moral values. This is just one of the prices our society pays for ignoring moral philosophy.

Yet, ironically, those unarticulated values are fundamental to everything we do. In 1939, John Dewey observed that:

> . . . all deliberate, all planned human conduct, personal and collective, seems to be influenced, if not controlled, by estimates of value or worth of ends to be attained. Good sense in practical affairs is generally identified with a sense of relative values.[3]

Limiting our discussion to business ethics, it is clear that moral belief is the necessary predicate for effective action based upon a code of ethics and, to be

225

effective, such a code must be based upon moral values that are central to their lives.[4]

This fact compels us to confront the most confusing, difficult, and important question that has always faced humanity: are there objective, cross-cultural, and trans-temporal moral values, meaningful to all people, that should serve as the basis for moral belief and moral action? Stated another way, are there moral truths common to humans qua humans, regardless of their culture, that are the *sine qua non* of human flourishing? If so, then such moral truths should be self-evident (in the technical sense of the term) to those who seek them.

Personally, I believe that objective moral truths exist; that they originate in our common, innate human nature; and that they are accessible to all individuals through study, introspection, and moral discourse.[5] But it is neither my purpose to argue that position, nor to impose those beliefs upon the essay. Instead, I contend that there are a few human needs (expressed as moral values) that are so powerful and so commonplace that they must be dealt with by every culture. Because they are so common and so essential, they can provide a *partial* basis for a code of international business ethics.

Two of them are very apparent: courage and fraternity. While this essay will concentrate upon the concept of fraternity as a moral value, in order to illustrate my point about the cross-cultural nature of these two values, I will comment briefly about courage.

Both history and anthropology clearly demonstrate that all cultures praise courage and condemn cowardice. Granted, our respective cultures may shape our perceptions of the appropriate ways to manifest courage. For instance, I find no redeeming virtue at all in bullfighting--but I cannot deny the courage of the matador. Conversely (and quite wrongly), some cultures would look upon mountain climbing as a ridiculous waste of time, money and lives--even though they would admire the courage of the climbers.

The point is that all societies have a fairly universal conception of what constitutes courage, and what constitutes cowardice--and they prize the former as they malign the latter. Thus, courage could reasonably serve as one of the bases for an international code of ethics, although its applicability is a bit obscure.

To return to the major subject of fraternity, in a similar fashion all cultures praise fraternity and decry isolation. Unlike courage, however, fraternity is much more significant for organizational theory and practice.[6] The word is used to describe an association of individuals, sharing common values, who are bound together by their love of one another, and are quite often working toward a common goal. Because of the emotional intensity of fraternity, it is quite a different thing from simple friendship, especially the "watery" friendship of Western modernity.

As a philosophic concept, fraternity (in one form or another) has been a central theme in the history of Western political philosophy. In more modern times, it reached a high point in the writings of some of the philosophers of the 18th Century Enlightenment.[7] But the excesses of the French Revolution, with its battle cry of "liberty, equality, fraternity," dimmed the enthusiasm of many, and fraternity proceeded to get lost somewhere in the smoke and clatter of the Industrial Revolution.[8] As a result, it has been foolishly neglected.

Because it has such promising potentials for organizational life, I believe the idea behind fraternity can become one of the most important features of a code of international ethics. In fact, it is perhaps the most urgent need of our contemporary global society. The need is clearly demonstrated every day on television and in the newspapers: nations, and subgroups within nations, rally around the chimera of the *Volksgeist*, racial groups proclaim ineradicable racial differences; some tell us that the gulf between genders is unbridgeable; and in the name of a murky multiculturalism, universities and governmental institutions are dangerously weakened.[9] Xenophobia, racial hatred, chauvinism, and gender hostility can only be overcome by a rebirth of the idea undergirding fraternity. This brings us to the specific thesis of this essay: *the greatest need for an ethics of international business is a deliberate effort to foster and maintain a sense of brotherhood and sisterhood within all organizations.* And therein lies one of the most difficult challenges for this ideal: gender.

To illustrate the point, quoted below is, arguably, the most powerful statement of brotherhood in English literature:

> This story shall the good man teach his son;
> And Crispin Crispian shall ne'er go by,
> From this day to the ending of the world,
> But we in it shall be remembered;
> We few, we happy few, we band of brothers;
> For he to-day that sheds his blood with me
> Shall be my brother; be he ne'er so vile,
> This day shall gentle his condition:
> And gentlemen in England now a-bed
> Shall think themselves accursed they were not here,
> And hold their manhoods cheap whiles any speaks
> That fought with us upon Saint Crispin's day.[10]

If we *men* of the present had fought alongside King Henry that day, our differences would have been dissolved in the "fraternity of combat." No longer Englishmen or Scots, Muslims or Jews, Catholics or Protestants, Spaniards or Moors--we would all have become "We few, we happy few, we band of brothers."

But that brings us to the issue of gender. Suppose, on that Saint Crispin's Day, that King Henry's army had contained women as well as men, both under arms and engaged in the battle? How could he have expressed that sense of the fraternity of combat *in a language that contained no word for brotherhood and sisterhood together*?

Justice demands that we no longer pretend that the word fraternity includes women as well as men. Too much of the history of the word concerns men, and men alone. To make the point, reverse things. There is a perfectly adequate word for the profound friendships among women: the word sorority. It is a fine word, so why not simply expand the concept of sorority to include men? That will not do, for the same reasons we must reject fraternity.

That is why the epigraph by Anne Phillips is so apt. Given the increasing numbers of women who are working alongside men as equals--from business to the military-- we need another word to describe that profound sense of friendship King Henry described. Fraternity describes a human condition that is so precious that it constitutes one of the essential aspects of full human flourishing. But the word is so value-laden that it would be impossible to shake off the accumulated meanings. We need a new word to designate an increasingly important human association.

It is argued that "sodality" meets the need for a word that can identify brotherhood and sisterhood together, and as such, it should become a central concept in organizational theory and practice, in both domestic and international organizations.

## II. Sodality

In accomplishing that task, wisdom dictates that we should build upon the foundations laid down by moral and political philosophers through the ages. This calls for the recovery of the classical literature on the subject. The greatest problem in achieving this new condition is *gender*, and, specifically, the increasing equalization of the organizational roles of men and women. The problem does not arise from the issues of who is the boss and who is the subordinate. It certainly does not arise because of any significant differences in abilities. It arises from the fact that there are very few precedents of men and women, working together as equals in non-segregated environments, achieving sodality.

To repeat the argument stated at the outset, this is not a problem of men achieving fraternity (an excellent thing in all-male environments), nor of women achieving sorority (an excellent thing in all female environments). Fraternity and sorority are valuable, but they still separate men and women. As we try to develop is the concept of intergender friendships, we find that there are virtually no historical examples to guide us, nor is there a tradition of moral discourse about the subject.

We must, then, begin from the metaphoric "square one," which means we must begin with language. When this problem first occurred to me, I immediately browsed through my *Oxford English Dictionary* and was unable to find a word to describe the relationship under discussion. Of course, there may be a word in those many volumes, but there is no word in common usage.

While I most assuredly do not claim any expertise in modern languages, I thought this problem might be unique to English. However, when I browsed through my French and German dictionaries, I found the same problem.[11] I then called some faculty who teach various modern languages and explained the problem under discussion here. They were not aware of any specific word in their areas.

In my search for a word that would conflate the intense and affectionate feelings of brotherhood and sisterhood into one, I consulted a friend who teaches Greek and Latin. He quickly dismissed my suggestion of "gentility," and recommended "sodalitas," which is defined as "companionship, fellowship; society, club, association; secret society."[12] The word originally referred to Roman burial associations but, through time, it has come to refer to any voluntary associations of likeminded individuals who care for one another and try to promote their mutual welfare.

The English rendering of sodalitas is "sodality," which the *OED* defines as an "Association or confederation *with* others; brotherhood, companionship, fellowship." Also: "In the Roman Catholic Church, a religious guild or brotherhood established for the purposes of devotion or mutual help or action; the body of persons forming such a society." A sodality is, then, much more than just an association of individuals out to accomplish a goal: in a sodality, the participants must also care deeply about each other, a caring which may be the purpose of the organization, or which may be a characteristic of an organization formed for another purpose.[13]

Dictionary definitions are sparse, at best, and we need to fill out the definition. Borrowing from McWilliams' seven-part definition of fraternity,[14] sodality can be further defined as "a bond based on intense interpersonal affection . . . ," which affection is founded upon "shared values or goals"--in this case, the virtues. The acquisition of those virtues by an individual is reflected in his or her good character. Thus we may say that a sodality consists of a group of individuals linked together in interlocking and overlapping character-friendships. The presence of sodality makes endurable the necessary, mundane, obligations of organizational life, a given to the members of the sodality an elan that reflects on their work and their working relationships.

Thus, sodality can be adapted to fits our needs for a word that refers to fraternity and sorority together. First, it is not so value-laden as to render it useless: it can cut across gender boundaries. Second, it refers to an association of individuals who have come together because they wish for "good things" for one another. Third, from such a foundation, it is reasonable to argue that the defining characteristic of each individual is good character, and each appreciates the good character of all others. Finally, it is reasonable to argue that, as good character reinforces good character, the individuals will come to love one another.

In order to get a better fix on the word, we will look at the development of the concept of friendship.

## III. The Sodality of Good Character: Transcending Fraternity and Sorority

In order to develop the concept of sodality, we will begin with its most fundamental aspect, friendship. The best place to begin is with Aristotle, because if practical ethics had a "founder," it was him. His *Nichomachean Ethics* became the model for books about that subject, and the starting place for most future discussions of ethics.[15] In particular, Aristotle gave considerable emphasis to friendship, or *philia*, in the development of his ethical system.[16]

However, in his age, friendship had a more profound meaning than it does in contemporary English usage. In fact, it is difficult to find an English term that captures the full meaning of friendship, as Aristotle understood it. Nancy Sherman's definition is a good place to begin:

> Friendship (*philia*), Aristotle stipulates, is the mutually acknowledged and reciprocal exchange of goodwill and affection that exists among individuals who share an interest in each other on the basis of virtue, pleasure, or utility.[17]

True friendship must begin with a conscious selflessness, in the sense of a non-instrumental concern for the happiness of the others. That will seem hopelessly unrealistic to individuals, conditioned since childhood to believe the primary fact of human nature is the imperative to personal utility-maximization, yet there is sufficient evidence to support a defense of selflessness in friendship.

Aristotle emphasized that selflessness, but based it upon a hierarchy of friendship:

> We may describe friendly feeling towards any one as wishing for him what you believe to be good things, not for your own sake but for his, and being inclined, so far as you can, to bring these things about.[18]

The most important "good things" concern the *virtues*, from which can be developed a good moral character.[19] One can also wish for lesser goods, such as good health or prosperity, but the primary goods must always be the things of good character.

Terence Irwin made Aristotle's hierarchy clear, when he wrote: "In the best kind of friendship one virtuous person admires the other's objective merits, his virtuous [character]."[20] Since the highest form of human happiness comes from the actualization of virtue in the world, obviously the apex of friendship is to be found in the *mutual appreciation* of good character.

John Cooper terms this form of friendship "character-friendship," which is not only the highest form of friendship, it is the only one that can be "complete" or sufficient unto itself. Thus:

> The central and basic kind of friendship, then, is friendship of character. Such friendships exist when two persons, having spent enough time together to know one another's character and to trust one another . . . come to love one another because of their good human qualities . . . .[21]

It requires the presence of good character in oneself to fully appreciate the good character of another. It is not unlike the experience of going to an opera, performed by a stellar cast, with Beverly Sills and Placido Domingo: their mutual appreciation of the opera would be transcendent because they had sung opera. Furthermore, if they shared the experience with you, your own appreciation of the event would infinitely greater, but it could never be equal to theirs.

Since everyone, however, can achieve good character, character-friendship is available to all. And a shared appreciation of good character in each of the parties in a friendship produces a form of friendship superior to all others. In fact, Cooper argues that the parties in a character-friendship come to love one another, which certainly changes the nature of friendship as defined by the conventional wisdom. Nancy Sherman gets at the reasons for these heightened affections, when she wrote:

On Aristotle's view, the specific ends in a life are sustained and given their finest expression through friendship. Ends that are valued become more highly prized as a result of being shared; actions that are fine become finer when friends are the beneficiaries.[22]

Following Cooper, Irwin, and Sherman, we can amplify the notion of sodality: it must always be a *sodality of good character*.[23] Good character is the essential ingredient of sodality.

Cooper goes on to distinguished character-friendship from the instrumental friendships of pleasure and advantage. One can be friends with another because it is pleasurable (pleasure-friendship), or because the friendship is advantageous to oneself (advantage-friendship). But, by their very nature, such instrumental friendships are transient, because they end when the pleasure or the advantage ceases. But character-friendships -- and the sodality of good character -- are permanent: "Hence these people's friendship lasts as long as they are good; and virtue is enduring."[24]

There is a subsidiary question that must be answered: can individual A, in a pleasure-friendship or an advantage-friendship, wish for the good of partner B solely for its own sake -- as would seem to be suggested in the quotation from Aristotle's *Rhetoric*? Or, does A wish good for B simply because it will increase or insure A's pleasure or advantage? If the latter motive obtains, then the friendship can only be instrumental and cannot partake of the higher happiness of character-friendship.

But if the former motive obtains, then A demonstrates the quality of good character known as gratitude, and the friendship can partake somewhat of the nature of a character-friendship. The point to be made is that the ideal for friendship is that individuals should be prized in and of themselves, for their good character. Thus, our ideal must begin with character-friendship, which is attainable by all people who are willing to make the effort to be virtuous.

To take the argument another step forward, Aristotle made it clear that full human flourishing requires character-friendship. As Cooper wrote:

> For it is only [in character-friendship] that he directly expresses himself on the nature, and importance to a flourishing human life, of taking an interest in other persons, merely as such and for their own sake. In fact, Aristotle holds not only that active friendships of a close and intimate kind are a necessary constituent of the flourishing human life but also that "civic friendship" itself is an essential human good.[25]

# THE SODALITY OF GOOD CHARACTER

Here, the association is made between character-friendship and civic friendship, which refers to the good regard and decent respect citizens in a well-ordered polity must have for one another. As such, character-friendship " . . . is generally held to be the chief good of states, because it is the best safeguard against the danger of civil dissensions."[26]

But more is involved in modernity. For Aristotle, the polity was the dominant association through which individuals could actualize their full human potentials. But the modern state is too large for that to take place. If we go to the basic premise behind character-friendship, we see that it is essential to the good life, because it evokes in its participants a higher sense of purpose (a commitment to virtue), a more profound loyalty (the love of virtue), and a freeing of their creativities (the liberation of virtue). Character-friendship is justifiable in and of itself, but there are secondary benefits to the host-organization that are enormous.

I contend, then, that *any organization can foster the sodality of good character*, provided it makes possible the actualization of virtuous character. The question is: why should they? After all, isn't the sole measure of organizational effectiveness a good bottom-line? To believe that is to miss the essence of the sodality of good character.

To illustrate, nothing is more terrible than war, and few organizations seem so restrictive to the individual than an army. Yet even within the horrors of war, men -- often of different races, religions, and national origins -- can achieve such sodality. In the northern years of his life, the great citizen-soldier, Joshua Lawrence Chamberlain, reflected back upon his experiences in the American Civil War. While decrying the death and destruction, he concluded that "we may say war is for the participants a test of character; it makes bad men worse and good men better."[27] Such men proved themselves trustworthy to one another, and found a "fraternity of combat" that affected them all of their lives.

Again, the citizen soldiers of that war passionately hated combat, but, paradoxically, some of them found within it a transcendent sodality. Representative is the comment of a young Indiana infantryman: "None of us were fond of war . . . but there had grown up between the boys an attachment for each other they never had nor ever will have for any other body of men."[28] Whenever soldiers achieved that attitude, their effectiveness as soldiers was superior almost beyond imagination.

Hannah Arendt found the same feelings among members of the French Resistance in World War II. Discussing the feelings of the poet, Rene Char, she wrote:

> What Char had foreseen, clearly anticipated, while the real fight was still on--"If I survive, I know that I shall have to break with the aroma of these

essential years, silently reject (not repress) my treasure"--had happened. They had lost their treasure.[29]

Arendt was fascinated by the transcendent emotions evoked by sodality, even though she had ambivalent feelings about the usefulness of sodality for the polity.[30]

There is ample evidence, then, for the fact and the power of sodality. When we are a part of such a group, the feelings of affection are profound and the sense of heightened friendship is the distinctive characteristic of the organization. We move beyond friendship to love. As the morale climbs, so does the productiveness of the employees -- and even of the leaders. When we must leave such organizations, the memory of what we had there colors all that we do from then on.

Some contemporary management scholars and practitioners understand that and have made sodality (although they do not use that word) the *sine qua non* of successful management. To use three examples, it is central to the management philosophies of Abraham H. Maslow, W. Edwards Deming (of TQM fame), and Ricardo Semler. There are innumerable and similar examples from contemporary business, government, politics, athletics--in fact, in almost any organized human endeavor. To begin, nearly everyone has experienced sodality at some time in their lives, whether in politics, at work, in the military, or in athletics. Thus, we can point to a variety of groups and organizations that have achieved sodality: sometimes in high-morale work organizations (such as, in the 1970s, at Milestone Petroleum in Denver, or Physiocontrol, in the Seattle area; or, in the 1990s, at Northwest Hospital, Seattle, and Semco, Inc., in Brazil); sometimes in good political campaigns (such as the Barry Goldwater campaign of 1964, or the Robert Kennedy campaign of 1968); sometimes in a sport (such as an extraordinary ascent of Mt. McKinley, in the early 1980s, by four climbers: two women and two men); or sometimes in a military unit (such as the 173rd Airborne Brigade, Vietnam, 1966). There are countless other examples in countless other areas. Suffice it to say, sodality is an attainable ideal.

And the results are very nearly always the same: the establishment, among the honorable, of the sodality of good character which benefits the individuals and the organizations of which they are a part. The sodality of good character is an unequivocal good. For that reason, it is a primary responsibility of all leaders, public or private, to create, encourage, and maintain the conditions for character-friendships.

From what we know of sodality, it will enhance the creativity and productivity of the people within the host organization. But it must be emphasized that the reason we try to achieve sodality is not to achieve organizational ends more effectively. Rather, sodality is good in and of itself because it is the actualization of a necessary aspect of our human nature: we not only need to be loved, we need

234

to love.[31] As Adam Smith wrote: "Man naturally desires, not only to be loved, but to be lovely . . . ."[32] Sodality is the cake; increased organizational effectiveness is the frosting upon the cake.

To conclude, the attainment of sodality transcends the gender-limitations of fraternity and sorority. The love of one another within the sodality is both asexual and free from traditional roles. If I am a member of a sodality, then every woman is my sister and every man my brother -- and I am brother to them. The feelings of sodality are one of the highest manifestations of human flourishing and are good in and of themselves--always provided that it is a sodality of good character. The organizational benefit is secondary, but important: an enhanced creativity and productivity.

But the most important aspect of the sodality of good character is that it requires all parties within the friendship to be men and women of good character. Thus, in addition to the superior quality of the friendship, none of the friends is predisposed to commit any unvirtuous act, nor hold any unvirtuous thoughts. Right there you have a nearly complete foundation for an ethics of international business.

## IV. Some Problems Concerning the Sodality of Good Character

If we are to achieve the sodality of good character, we must look candidly at the problems that might arise as we attempt to bring it into being. The lesser problem involves intergender friendships. The greater problems are: the problem of evil, the problem of homogeneity, and the problem of exclusiveness.

To begin, such sodality--the profound feelings of brotherhood and sisterhood-- is much more emotionally intense than contemporary versions of friendship. For that reason, it will bring with it at least two unique and difficult problems: a traditional philosophic discourse that limited a woman's role to motherhood and the household;[33] and the problem of intergender attraction.

First, and with a few exceptions, most of the traditional moral and political discourse about the relationship of men and women has concerned the woman's role within the family, as wife, mother, and manager of the household. That relationship was usually described as hierarchical: being a husband presumed male superordination, while being a wife presumed female subordination. A woman's first, if not sole, loyalty was usually to her husband, and then to her family. Finally, as the primary nurturing parent, the woman-as-mother was effectively confined to the home and her concerns were only to be those of the household--and not for political and social affairs beyond the family.

But the feminine revolution of this century, and particularly in the last quarter of a century, has turned all of that upon its head. Thus, many thoughtful and articulate feminists have carefully and intelligently articulated the rights and roles of women in our organizational society. But the issue of the woman-as-mother has not been as fully discussed as its importance warrants. Nonetheless, if we grant the importance of the sodality of good character, and limit it only to organizational members, a significant number of women will be left out. I have no easy answer for the problem: just the statement that it is an area in which a considerable amount of work needs to be done.

Second, and within the organizational setting, there is the very difficult fact of possible intergender physical attraction, heightened by the intensity of the character-friendships within a sodality. At the risk of sounding Victorian, when men and women are in such an intense and close proximity to each other, some of them will be physically or even romantically attracted to others, which will occasionally lead to liaisons. In and of itself, this is not the problem.

There are at least two problem areas. First, many members of the sodality will be married, and the intense relationships will undoubtedly place strains upon those marriages -- even if innocence prevails. Second, even if the attachment is between two single members of the sodality, it still creates a problem, because the passion of romantic love leads to a sense of exclusivity that is antithetical to wide-ranging character-friendships.[34]

The solution lies in the reemphasis upon the good character of men and women of virtue. Again, I have no easy answer but, as before, just the admonition that it is a problem that deserves serious study and discussion.

The really serious problems, however, will require intense scrutiny and constant attention. The first is the problem of evil.

Even a casual reading of history reveals that organizations of evil ideology and intention can command the intense loyalty of their members, especially when led by a charismatic leader. The classic example is that of Nazi Germany and, particularly, of the "brotherhood" of Hitler's bodyguard, the SS legions. As Koehl wrote of them:

> Since the academic soothsayers had created an elaborate modern justification for what so many men in different times and ages have craved, a messiah, Adolf Hitler could gradually *evolve himself* into a magical, quasi-religious *Fuhrer*, the chief of a holy band of crusaders . . . . To be his bodyguard was to partake of his charisma, *to be important to him*. This sense of a special relationship to god-on-earth was a gift of

grace Hitler knew very well how to foster among his alienated . . . followers . . . .[35]

That sense of being "chosen," reinforced by the ideology of Aryan chiliasm that required racial cleansing and political domination, gave the SS the moral permission for murder, theft, and war. All these bestial acts contributed to the sense of brotherhood within the SS.

Because a perverted sodality has that potential, enormous care must be taken to insure that the participants are not only men and women of good moral character, but that they actively work to improve that morality. Further, it means that they must always be conscious of the virtues that define their good character. The moral worth of ends to be attained must always be considered, because the allure of being "a holy band of crusaders" is so powerful that even good men and women may be deceived by it. Good character must never be taken for granted.

Second, sodality can never entail a forced, or even unintentional, homogeneity. To the contrary, a sodality of good character must be built upon an appreciation of the uniqueness of each individual. Each must be alike in his or her love of virtue, but different in their manifestations of their unique excellences. David Norton's extraordinary ethical individualism rests upon "the complementarity of excellences [which] affirms that every genuine excellence benefits by every other genuine excellence. It means that the best within every person calls upon and requires the best within every other person."[36]

Finally, a sodality of good character must never be exclusive: all men and women of good character are potential participants. Since that sodality emerges from the best in the human character, it can never be the instrument of unjustly hurting another. Thus, to try to make the sodality into an "exclusive" group, excluding others of good character, for whatever reason, destroys the sodality.

Having touched upon some of the dangers, we must now address the contention that sodality not only creates intraorganizational harmony, but that it is also an essential perquisite for interorganizational harmony.

## V. Adam Smith and the Sodality of Good Character

There are two immediate questions that must be addressed. First, how does the sodality of good character enhance interorganizational harmony? Even if one grants the importance of sodality for intraorganizational harmony, how does its attainment in Organization A contribute to a harmonious relationship with

Organization B, which has also achieved sodality? Second, since competition is essential to capitalism, how can there be effective competition among firms that have friendly feelings one for another?

I will answer those questions by reference to Adam Smith, who anticipated them. But first, it is necessary to refer again to Aristotle's argument that the highest form of friendship is character-friendship. In the matter of good character, like appreciates like. In other words, only a virtuous individual can *fully* appreciate the virtue of another: just as it takes a courageous soldier to fully appreciate the courage of another soldier; or a talented musician in one culture to fully appreciate the talented musician in another culture; or a brilliant mathematician to appreciate her counterpart in another culture. More and more, we are beginning to appreciate the cross-cultural and transtemporal appreciation of such constants as virtue, courage, aesthetics, and science.[37] Such appreciation leads to considering the other as a competitor, not an enemy--and that immediately eliminates some of the most intolerant feelings that plague international associations.

This brings us to the second question: if the members of discrete businesses come to care for one another, how will they be able to compete with one another? That question was well answered, in the 18th Century, by Adam Smith: in his ideal, the conduct of business will be governed by the mutual sense of fair play among virtuous competitors.

Too many business scholars argue that Adam Smith based his ideal for free enterprise upon the primacy of self-interest, and they inappropriately cite selected passages from *The Wealth of Nations* (1776) to demonstrate their contention. But, as has been convincingly demonstrated, the key to understanding the economic system advocated by Smith is found in his moral philosophy, explicated in his first book, *The Theory of Moral Sentiments*.[38]

Without going into detail, Smith based his moral philosophy upon the concept of "sympathy," or the capacity of, and need for, individuals to care for one another, in a non-instrumental manner. From this, he developed his ideas about the importance of friendship for the conduct of all human affairs, from business through government. And, for him, the apex of friendship is found among men and women of virtue -- in other words, character-friendship. Thus:

> But of all attachments to an individual, that which is founded altogether upon the esteem and approbation of his good conduct and behaviour, confirmed by much experience and long acquaintance, is, by far, the most respectable. Such friendships . . . can exist only among men of virtue . . . . . Vice is always capricious: virtue only is regular and orderly. The attachment which is founded upon the love of virtue, as it is certainly, of

all attachments, the most virtuous; so it is likewise the happiest, as well as the most permanent and secure.[39]

Therefore, it is unthinkable that such individuals would ever conduct their business upon any other principle than virtue.

Obviously, character-friendship within an organization is very beneficial. To state the obvious, no intelligent business leader wants competition-to-the-death within his or her organization -- it would rip it apart and make it less than competitive in the marketplace. Let us, therefore, accept *intraorganizational* sodality as a good thing. The big concern is *interorganizational* sodality. What would "virtuous competition" look like, and would it provide the requisite benefits to the economic system? Why would any organization that had achieved the sodality of good character even wish to compete?

The answer lies in Smith's favorite metaphor of the game: we love to compete, when the rules of the game are fair. To put it simply, competition is fun. But let us begin with Smith's detestation of unvirtuous conduct.

In *The Wealth of Nations* (1776), wherein he supposedly laid down the principles of acquisitive capitalism, Adam Smith condemned certain sleazy, but accepted, business practices, referring to them as: "The sneaking arts of underling tradesmen [which] are thus erected into political maxims for the conduct of a great empire . . . ." I am not concerned with the specific practices he condemns, but rather with the lines that follow the condemnation:

> By such maxims as these, however, nations have been taught that their interest consisted in beggaring all their neighbours. Each nation has been made to look with an invidious eye upon the prosperity of all the nations with which it trades, and to consider their gain as its own loss. *Commerce, which ought naturally to be, among nations, as among individuals, a bond of union and friendship*, has become the most fertile source of discord and animosity.[40]

This theme--that international trade should bring "union and friendship"--is constant throughout the writings of Adam Smith, but almost no one takes that argument seriously. But that is exactly what he meant, as he explains in great detail, in both books. In the terms of this essay, he called for the creation and maintenance of the sodality of good character among business men and women, not for efficiency, but because it was morally right and that it was also one of the greatest rewards that comes from conducting free enterprise correctly.

But what about competition? Obviously, Adam Smith praised it: it pushed poor products out of the market; it provided the incentive for the creation of better products; and so on.  But Smith never advocated cutthroat competition between firms -- national or international: all competition was *always* to be guided by the principles of fair play.  Again using his preferred metaphor of the game, he wrote:

> In the race for wealth, and honours, and preferments, he may run as hard as he can, and strain every nerve and every muscle, in order to outstrip all his competitors.  But if he should justle, or throw down any of them, the indulgence of the spectators is entirely at an end.  It is a violation of fair play, which they cannot admit of.[41]

All very well and good, for the winners.  But what about the losers?  In a society reared upon the primacy of winning, the idea of losing does not sit well.  Would not the competitive effectiveness of sodality cause competitors to employ dishonorable means to prevent the loss?  Adam Smith dealt with that problem also.

One of the greatest benefits of fair competition was its effect upon the virtue of all participants: the knowledge that they had always played the game fairly.  Certainly losing hurt, but it had to be put into its proper perspective.  Referring back to the Stoics, whose writings were so influential for him, he noted that they considered life to be a game of great skill.  They understood the vagaries of fortune, but believed the great purpose in playing the game was to play it with honor.  And so:

> If notwithstanding all his skill, however, the good player should, by the influence of chance, happen to lose, the *loss ought to be a matter, rather of merriment, than of serious sorrow.*  He has made no false stroke; he has done nothing which he ought to be ashamed of; he has enjoyed completely the whole pleasure of the game.  If, on the contrary, the bad player, notwithstanding all his blunders, should, in the same manner, happen to win, his success can give him but little satisfaction.[42]

In other words, the purpose of the game is the game played fairly.  Out of such competition comes not only better play, but a quality of human life.  Smith concludes:

> Human life, with all the advantages which can possibly attend it, ought, according to the Stoics, to be regarded but as a mere two-penny stake; a matter by far too insignificant to merit any anxious concern.  Our only anxious concern ought to be, not about the stake, but about the proper method of playing.[43]

# THE SODALITY OF GOOD CHARACTER

Certainly the economic endeavor is more important than a "two-penny stake," because it provides the wherewithal for human life. But the game must *always* be fairly played, and the constant excuses offered by the cheaters are specious. Paraphrasing Cicero, Smith wrote:

> One individual must never prefer himself so much even to any other individual, as to hurt or injure that other, in order to benefit himself, though the benefit to the one should be much greater than the hurt or injury to the other . . . . [F]or one man to deprive another unjustly of any thing, or unjustly to promote his own advantage by the loss or disadvantage of another, is more contrary to nature, than death, than poverty, than pain, than all the misfortunes which can affect him, either in his body, or in his external circumstances.[44]

The greatest guarantee of virtuous behavior, Smith argued, was the self-approbation that comes from virtuous conduct. But, alone, we are apt to make mistakes or deceive ourselves. Thus, it is of the utmost importance that we have around us genuine friends, who can--through moral warnings and moral conversations--turn us away from our occasional moral blindness, and back onto the path of virtue.

The great guarantor of a virtuous society, then, is the creation and maintenance of the sodality of good character in every organization and association in that society.[45] Thus, *the intentional creation and maintenance of the sodality of good character should be the first responsibility of organizational leadership, regardless of the culture*. This is so because it is morally right and because it can serve as the basis of an international business ethics based upon our common human nature.

## VI. Conclusion

The purpose of this essay has been to present an argument for the adoption of a form of heightened organizational friendship that is inclusive, transcending race, ethnicity, and, especially, gender. The term used to signify that condition of being is the sodality of good character, which conflates fraternity and sorority into one thing. Certainly that is idealistic, but it is an ideal that can be, and has often been,

241

achieved. Its greatest possibility, however, lies in the fact that the need for the sodality of good character originates in our common human nature.

This form of sodality can be easily defended in many ways, but two reasons summarize the arguments. The first is that it is the actualization of an innate human necessity for brotherhood and sisterhood. It is one of the greatest rewards of human association, an essential aspect of human flourishing. The second reason is that the sodality of good character removes significant barriers to the expression of individual and collective human excellences, in all areas of human endeavor, which redounds to the benefit of society.

It is not possible to discuss the specific details of the sodality of good character: what is required to create and maintain it. That will have to be done in future publications. Suffice it to say that my defense of this form of sodality rests upon a hope that was expressed by de Tocqueville:

> It would seem as if the rulers of our time sought only to use men in order to make things great; I wish that they would try a little more to make great men; that they would set less value on the work and more upon the workman; that they would never forget that a nation cannot long remain strong when every man belonging to it is individually weak; and that no form or combination of social polity has yet been devised to make an energetic people out of a community of pusillanimous and enfeebled citizens.[46]

As Smith wrote: "Kindness is the parent of kindness; and if to be beloved by our brethren be the great object of our ambition, the surest way of obtaining it is, by our conduct to show that we really love them."[47]

**Endnotes**

1    ANNE PHILLIPS: *Democracy and Difference*, University Park (Pennsylvania State University Press) 1993) p. 25, as quoted in Shin Chiba, "Hannah Arendt on Love and the Political: Love, Friendship, and Citizenship", *Review of Politics*, 57 (Summer 1995) p. 513n.

# THE SODALITY OF GOOD CHARACTER

2   HANNAH ARENDT: "Thinking and Moral Considerations", *Social Research*, 38 (Autumn 1971) p. 438.

3   JOHN DEWEY: *Theory of Valuation*, Chicago (University of Chicago Press) 1939, p. 2.

4   There is another important question here: it is possible that people cling to values that are patently destructive (such as racism or sexism) and must be replaced if the individuals are to live good lives. Thus, there must be a set of alternative values that can be used to convert people away from the destructive values. This will not be discussed in this essay, but it does lead directly to the question of the reality of objective, transcultural moral truths.

5   I would base my defense of this claim upon the following: character ethics (virtue theory); the moral philosophy of ethical individualism, as presented by David L. Norton; the moral psychology of Abraham H. Maslow; and the organizational ethics of civic humanism. Among many others, the following books have been influential: J. BUDZISZEWSKI: *The Resurrection of Nature: Political Theory and the Human Character*, Ithaca, NY (Cornell University Press) 1986; DAVID L. NORTON: *Personal Destinies: A Philosophy of Ethical Individualism*, Princeton (Princeton University Press) 1976; ABRAHAM H. MASLOW: *Motivation and Personality*, New York (Harper & Row) 2nd ed., 1970; and J. G. A. POCOCK: The *Machiavellian Moment: Florentine Political Thought and the Atlantic Republican Tradition*, Princeton (Princeton University Press) 1975.

6   For a discussion of fraternity as a fundamental human need, see WILSON CAREY MCWILLIAMS: *The Ideal of Fraternity in America*, Berkeley (University of California Press) 1973, especially the first three chapters.

7   Some useful surveys of the Enlightenment that touch on fraternity are: JULES MICHELET: *History of the French Revolution*, trans. by C. Cocks, Chicago (University of Chicago Press) [1853] 1967; ERNST CASSIRER: *The Philosophy of the Enlightenment*, trans. by F.C.A. Koelln and J.P. Pettegrove, Princeton (Princeton University Press) 1951; and PETER GAY: *The Enlightenment*, New York (Norton) 1966, 1969, in two volumes.

8   Note, however, JAMES FITZJAMES STEPHEN: *Liberty, Equality, Fraternity*, Indianapolis (Liberty Classics) [1873] 1993.

9   For a stimulating assault on these ideologies, see ALAIN FINKIELKRAUT: *The Defeat of the Mind*, trans. by J. Friedlander, New York (Columbia University Press) 1995.

10  WILLIAM SHAKESPEARE: "King Henry V", *The Annotated Shakespeare*, ed. by A.L. Rowse New York (Clarkson N. Potter, Inc.) Vol. II, Act IV, Scene III, 1978, p. 580.

11  To illustrate, neither *The Concise Oxford French Dictionary* (1957) nor the *Harper Collins German Dictionary* (1990) have an entry for "sorority"--although both of them have entries for "fraternity". The French and German equivalents of the *Oxford English Dictionary* probably have some sort of an entry--but the word is not in popular usage.

12  JOHN C. TRAUPMAN: *The New College Latin & English Dictionary*, New York (AMSCO School Publications) 1966, p. 290.

13  While the word is not much used nowadays, it is interesting to note that it has been picked up by some feminist groups and some religious groups.

# DAVID KIRKWOOD HART

14 McWILLIAMS: *op. cit.*, pp. 7-8.

15 There are numerous editions of the book: the most readable is *The Ethics of Aristotle*, trans. by H. Rackham, ed. by J.A.K. Thomson, Baltimore, MD (Penguin) 1953, while the most authoritative is ARISTOTLE: *Nichomachean Ethics*, trans. by T. Irwin, Indianapolis (Hackett) 1985.

16 An excellent overview of Aristotlean ethics is NANCY SHERMAN: *The Fabric of Character: Aristotle's Theory of Virtue*, Oxford (Clarendon Press) 1989, especially Chapter 4, "The Shared Life," pp. 118-156. See also: JOHN M. COOPER.: "Aristotle on Friendship," in AMELIE OKSENBERG RORTY (Ed.): *Essays on Aristotle's Ethics*, Berkeley (University of California Press) 1980, pp. 301-340.

17 SHERMAN, *op. cit.*, p. 124.

18 ARISTOTLE: *Rhetoric*, trans. by W.R. Roberts, in *Aristotle, "Rhetoric" and "Poetics"*, New York (Modern Library) Book II, Chapter 4, 1954, p. 100. Modern business scholars would be more inclined to agree with the egoism of La Rochefoucauld: "We give help to others so that they have to do the same for us on similar occasions, and these kindnesses we them are, to put it plainly, gifts we bestow ourselves in advance." LA ROCHEFOUCAULD, *Maxims*, trans. by L. Tancock, New York (Penguin Books) 1959, Maxim 264, p. 72.

19 There is not room to discuss virtue theory, which is enjoying a revival. The following books should be helpful: J. BUDZISZEWSKI: op. cit.; PETER A. FRENCH, THEODORE E. UEHLING, JR, and HOWARD K. WETTSTEIN (Eds.): *Ethical Theory: Character and Virtue*, Midwest Studies in Philosophy, Vol. XIII, Notre Dame (University of Notre Dame Press) 1988; JOHN W. CHAPMAN and WILLIAM A. GALSTON (Eds.): *Virtue*, Nomos XXXIV, New York (New York University Press) 1992; and EDMUND L. PINCOFFS, *Quandaries and Virtues*, Lawrence (University Press of Kansas) 1986.

20 ARISTOTLE: *Nichomachean Ethics*, trans. T. Irwin, Glossary, p. 403.

21 COOPER: *op. cit.*, p. 308.

22 SHERMAN: *op. cit.*, p. 118.

23 While I mean more than just character-friendship by the term sodality of good character, for stylistic purposes, I will use them as nearly synonymous.

24 ARISTOTLE: *Ethics, op. cit.*, Book 8, Chapter 3, p. 213.

25 COOPER: *op. cit.*, p. 303.

26 *The Politics of Aristotle*, trans. E. Barker, New York (Oxford University Press) 1958, Book II, Chapter IV, Section 4, p. 46.

27 JOSHUA LAWRENCE CHAMBERLAIN: *The Passing of the Armies*, New York (Bantam Books) [1915] 1993, p. 295. The value of such character-friendships is seen throughout ALICE RAINS TRULOCK: *In the Hands of Providence: Joshua L. Chamberlain and the American Civil War*, Chapel Hill (University of North Carolina Press) 1992.

28 SHELBY FOOTE: *The Civil War: A Narrative*, New York (Random House) 1974, Vol. III, p. 1041.

29 HANNAH ARENDT: *Between Past and Future*, New York (Viking) Revised edition, 1968, p. 4.

THE SODALITY OF GOOD CHARACTER

30 The issues she raises are extremely important, but not essential to the argument presented herein. See the superb essay by SHIN CHIBA: "Hannah Arendt on Love and the Political: Love, Friendship, and Citizenship", *Review of Politics*, 57 (Summer 1995), pp. 505-535.

31 MASLOW: *op. cit.*, pp. 98-99.

32 ADAM SMITH: *The Theory of Moral Sentiments*, D.D. Raphael and A.L. Macfie, (Eds.) Indianapolis ( Liberty Classics), [1759; 1790] 1982), p. 113.

33 For examples, see SUSAN MOLLER OKIN: *Women in Western Political Thought* Princeton (Princeton University Press) 1979.

34 See NORTON: *Personal Destinies*, pp. 303-308.

35 ROBERT LEWIS KOEHL: *The Black Corps: The Structure and Power Struggles of the Nazi SS*, Madison (University of Wisconsin Press) 1983, p. xxi.

36 NORTON: *op. cit.*, p. 10. See also pp. 303-309 in the same volume.

37 See, for an example, LEE H. YEARLEY: *Mencius and Aquinas: Theories of Virtue and Conceptions of Courage*, Albany (State University of New York Press) 1990.

38 ADAM SMITH: *The Theory of Moral Sentiments*, ed. by. D.D. Raphael and A.L. Macfie, Indianapolis (Liberty Classics) [1759; 1790] 1982. Among the books supporting this contention, see, A.L. MACFIE: *The Individual in Society*, London (George Allen & Unwin) 1967, especially Chapter 4, "Adam Smith's *Moral Sentiments* as Foundation for His *Wealth of Nations*", pp. 59-81; GLENN R. MORROW: *The Ethical and Economic Theories of Adam Smith*, Clifton, NJ (Augustus M. Kelley) [1923] 1973; and PATRICIA H. WERHANE: *Adam Smith and His Legacy for Modern Capitalism*, New York (Oxford University Press) 1991.

39 SMITH: *TMS, op. cit.*, pp. 224-225.

40 ADAM SMITH: *An Inquiry into the Nature and Causes of the Wealth of Nations*, ed. by R.H. Campbell and A.S. Skinner, Indianapolis (Liberty Classics) [1776] 1981, Vol. I, p. 493. Emphasis added.

41 ADAM SMITH: *The Theory of Moral Sentiments*, ed. by D.D. Raphael and A.L. Macfie, Indianapolis (Liberty Classics) [1759; 1790] 1982, p. 83.

42 SMITH: *TMS, op. cit.*, p. 279. Emphasis added.

43 SMITH: *TMS, op. cit.*, p. 279.

44 SMITH: *TMS, op. cit.*, p. 138.

45 If this was a book, the next chapter would link together the concepts of the sodality of good character and the *impartial spectator*.

46 ALEXIS DE TOCQUEVILLE: *Democracy in America*, ed. by P. Bradley, New York (Knopf) [1840] 1945, Vol. II, p. 329.

47 ADAM SMITH: *The Theory of Moral Sentiments*, ed. by D.D. Raphael and A.L. Macfie, Indianapolis (Liberty Classics) [1759; 1790], 1982, p. 235.

# List of Authors

F. NEIL BRADY, Professor of Public Management, Brigham Young University, Provo, Utah, USA

FREDERICK B. BIRD, Professor of Comparative Ethics, Concordia University, Montreal, Canada

MARK C. CASSON, Professor of Economics, University of Reading, Reading, England

PHILIP L. COCHRAN, Associate Professor of Business Administration, Penn State University, University Park, Pennsylvania, USA

RICHARD T. DE GEORGE, University Distinguished Professor of Philosophy, University of Kansas, Lawrence, Kansas, USA

DAVID KIRKWOOD HART, J. Fish Smith Professor of Free Enterprise Studies, Brigham Young University, Provo, Utah, USA

PETER KOSLOWSKI, Director, Forschungsinstitut fur Philosophie Hannover, Germany; and Professor of Philosophy and Political Economy, University of Witten/Herdecke, Germany

SHUI-CHUEN LEE, Lecturer, Chinese University of Hong Kong, People's Republic of China

KAREN PAUL, Professor of Business Environment, Florida International University, North Miami, Florida, USA

BERTRAM SCHEFOLD, Professor of Economics, Johann Wolfgang Goethe-University, Frankfurt, Germany

KOTARO SUZUMURA, Professor of Economic Systems Analysis, Hitotsubashi University, Tokyo, Japan

MANUEL G. VELASQUEZ, Charles J. Dirksen Professor of Business Ethics, Santa Clara University, Santa Clara, California, USA